DIRECT POINTING TO REAL WEALTH

THOMAS J. ELPEL'S FIELD GUIDE TO MONEY

5th Edition

Dedicated to Mom.
You taught me that no goal is beyond reach.

HOPS Press
Hollowtop Outdoor Primitive School, LLC
12 Quartz Street
Pony, Montana 59747
http://www.hollowtop.com

Direct Pointing to Real Wealth
Thomas J. Elpel's Field Guide to Money
5th Edition, May 2000 ISBN: 1-892784-08-4

First Published as:
Hollowtop Outdoor Primitive School Field Guide to Money. Copyright: March 1994
Revised & expanded and reprinted as:
Thomas J. Elpel's Field Guide to Money (2nd Edition) Copyright: May 1995
Revised & expanded and reprinted as:
Direct Pointing to Real Wealth: Thomas J. Elpel's Field Guide to Money.
Copyright October 1996 (3rd Edition), July 1997 (4th Edition), May 2000 (5th Edition)

Photos on the back cover were taken by Will Brewster, Western Way Photography.
All other photos were taken by the author and his family.
Illustrations were done by the author.

Publisher's Cataloging-in-Publication Data
Elpel, Thomas J. 1967-
    Direct Pointing to Real Wealth: Thomas J. Elpe'ls Field Guide to Money / Thomas J. Elpel. —5th ed.

    Includes bibiliographical references and index.
    ISBN: 1-892784-08-4 $19.95 Pbk. (alk. paper)
    1. Sustainable Development. 2. Economic Development—Environmental Aspects. 3. Economics—
United States. 4. Human Ecology. 5. Finance, personal—United States.
    I. Elpel, Thomas J. II. Title.
    HC 79.E5 E46   333.7   00-102575

HOPS Press
Hollowtop Outdoor Primitive School, LLC
12 Quartz Street
Pony, Montana 59747
http://www.hollowtop.com

Table of Contents

*$1.00 from every copy of this book sold
is being donated to the
Alternative Energy Resources Organization*

AERO is a Montana-based, nonprofit grassroots membership organization dedicated to sustainable resource use and rural community vitality. AERO promotes sustainable agriculture, "smart growth" planning and transportation alternatives, renewable energy and conservation, environmental quality, and community self-reliance.

*AERO
32 South Ewing, Suite 214
Helena, Montana 59601
(406) 443-7272
aero@aeromt.org*

"Though I do not believe that a plant will spring up where no seed has been, I have great faith in a seed. Convince me that you have a seed there, and I am prepared to expect wonders."

-Henry David Thoreau, The Dispersion of Seeds

Forward
Gardening the Ecosystem
-The Do-Nothing Method of Real Wealth-

A suburban lawn is an artificial, yet basically stable environment—typically a monoculture of grass with only a few lowly weeds like dandelions. But if you take a rototiller and plow up a section in the middle of the lawn, something new will happen. Within a year or two the exposed soil will be full of all kinds of new weeds.

Ordinarily we think that weeds are "bad" and that we have to kill them to be able to maintain the landscape we want. They seem to "invade" or "take over" the fields or the garden. They "choke out" the "good" plants. The usual response to weeds is to fight them, to pull them up, to spray them, to eliminate them. From the way we talk about and deal with weeds, it would almost seem that they have conscious, malicious intent to do what they do. But the weeds could not invade the lawn until the sod is plowed under. In this simplistic example we can perceive that the presence of the weeds is affected by the habitat.

Weeds can only do one thing. They grow in the type of habitat that is conducive to their growth. The weeds do not suddenly invade the freshly plowed field. The seeds were there all along, but they had no space to grow in the virgin sod. Only the creation of habitat allows them to flourish.

In Japan there is a farmer by the name of Masanobu Fukuoka[31, 32] who practices what he calls the "no-plowing, no-fertilizing, no-weeding, no-pesticides, do-nothing method of natural farming". To him the idea that people can grow crops is egocentric. Ultimately it is nature that grows crops. He sees modern agriculture as doing-this and doing-that to grow crops, but it is meaningless work. With his do-nothing method he is able to get yields in his rice fields that are equal to the highest yields attained with chemical, do-

Habitat in the ecosystem can be tilted in favor of the crops we want.

something agriculture. What he does do, in essence, is to manipulate the habitat of his farm to favor the crops he wants to grow. He works within the laws of ecology to tilt the ecosystem in favor of the plants he wants. Then his crops virtually invade and grow like weeds.

The economic ecosystem can be cultivated in a similar way. Individually we can each influence the local habitat to provide us with an abundant harvest. Collectively we can work together to tilt the whole economic ecosystem in favor of a crop of peace and prosperity for all. This could be called the Do-Nothing Method of Real Wealth.

Western culture is very goal-oriented, and we usually count our successes by how much we accomplish. Eastern cultures can be very goal-oriented as well, but often with a different approach. While a Westerner sits on his laurels at the end of the day and adds up what he did, an Easterner might sit on his laurels and add up what he eliminated having to do.

1

As a simple analogy, you might say that a western artist does sculpture with clay, assembling an entire work piece by piece, while an eastern artist does sculpture in stone, eliminating everything that is not part of the final goal. It is two fundamentally different approaches to a similar point. Yet, there is still more to this analogy than that. The western sculptor may shape clay all day long, but the eastern sculptor sits in front of his stone and meditates on it. Then, at the end of the day he picks up his chisel and hammer and makes one strategic hit, revealing all at once a whole portion of the art!

In Zen it has been said that, "Reverence is the elimination of all that is unnecessary." The farmer, Fukuoka, sought a method of farming in harmony and reverence with nature as his goal. He then proceeded to eliminate all that stood in the way of the goal. Through careful observation of nature he eliminated the need for plowing, fertilizing, weeding, and pest control.

As a young man, I too envisioned a life in cooperation with nature. It was my dream to find a means by which both myself and my culture would be able to live in a sustainable balance with the environment.

Like many environmentally-minded people I started with the perception that industry and money were inherently bad. I watched, listened and read a lot of news as a kid, and it always seemed that ecology and economy were diametrically opposed to each other. The media portrayed a world where we had to make a choice between sacrificing the environment to save jobs, or sacrificing jobs to save the environment. Given this narrow perspective it was easy to perceive money as the root of the world's problems. The logical course of action seemed to be to get rid of money by returning the world to a pre-industrial, hunter-gatherer or subsistence farming life-style. This ideology remains fairly common across the environmental community today. Of course few people are truly willing to walk away from all that our culture has created to go back to a more primitive life-style. And those that are already living that life-style in third-world countries today have no intention of staying that way. Thus the idea of un-evolving our culture is quaint but rather useless.

I realized as a teenager that if humanity were going to live in balance with nature then people would have to want to. There would have to be something about living with nature that people would perceive as being better than what they have now. In light of this, the newly logical solution seemed to be to create a life-style for myself in cooperation with nature, that other people would desire to emulate for themselves. This pathway ultimately brought me back to the need to find modern solutions.

My desire to help "save the earth" was not the only motive at work here. As a teenager rapidly approaching adulthood, there were some very real wants and needs I would have to face. Like anyone else, I wanted a nice house, a good car, a great computer and the other amenities of our culture. But as a young adult I had few marketable skills, and I really did not want a job anyway. In fact the idea of getting a job and working all my life just plain scared the hell out of me! I had the dream or goal of being prosperous and helping the earth in the process, but also the strong need to avoid regular employment. Eliminating the obstacles of a mortgage, bills, and regular employment became an obvious path forward.

Like Fukuoka, our own successes were not just what we did, but what we eliminated having to do. We eliminated the need to spend thousands of dollars and several years to get good job training. We eliminated having a house payment or high-energy bills, and we eliminated much of the rest of the expenses of daily living. We successfully eliminated enough of our expenses that we are now able to eliminate having to go to work every day of our lives.

This book is intended to serve as a guide to help you utilize the do-nothing approach to achieving your goals as well. It is Not about copying what we did, because our goals and situations are inherently different. We had our own dream, and we took steps to eliminate all that was in the way of our achieving that dream. The purpose of this guide is to help you eliminate all the obstacles in the way of your own dream, whatever that may be. You will learn to observe the economic ecosystem and to use a do-nothing approach towards tilting the ecosystem to favor abundant crops for you.

Thomas J. Elpel
Pony, Montana
October 1, 1996

". . . for this end the {seeds} have been perfecting themselfs all summer, snugly packed in this light chest, a perfect adaptation to this end—a prophecy not only of the fall, but of future springs. Who could believe in prophecies of Daniel or of Miller that the world would end this summer, while one milkweed with faith matured its seeds?"
-Henry David Thoreau, The Dispersion of Seeds

Introduction
The Economy as an Ecosystem
-Spontaneous Organization-

Our species has been tinkering with nature for millenia, developing the sciences of agriculture and forestry, experimenting with controls like fertilizers and pesticides. We are so used to managing and manipulating the ecosystem that it is difficult for many people to believe that nature can function without our help. Indeed, one European tourist in Yellowstone National Park asked my sister, who worked there as a guide, "Where do you put all the animals at night?" In the tourist's native country, the farm animals were led back to the barns every night. It was a very alien concept to think that these wild animals could survive on their own, without someone to bring them in at the end of each day!

It can be hard for people to accept that no one controls the ecosystem. How could anything so complex seemingly create itself from nothing, materializing and prospering on a chunk of wet rock hurtling through the cold vacuum of space? The fact that life started at all on this planet is certainly a miracle, yet it is equally miraculous that life has continued to survive over these last 3.6 billion years. The sun has increased it's heat output by 25% in the natural course of it's own life-span, yet the temperature on earth has remained comparatively constant. Without the presence of life on earth, the oceans should have either frozen or boiled by now, or the water molecules should have broken apart and the lightweight hydrogen atoms escaped into space, taking with them any possibility of water on this planet. Even without freezing or boiling, the oceans should have become too salty to support life by now, given the amount of salts that wash off the continents each year[51].

The sun has increased it's output by 25% but the climate on earth has remained favorable for life.

How could simple organisms, like algae and bacteria, trees, grass, fungus, insects, birds and mammals, manage to keep the atmosphere intact and hospitable in such a hostile universe? How does the natural world survive for even a season without some pest getting out of control, killing off most of the other plants or animals on the planet? This entire living system is guided by the simple concept of many independent organisms struggling for survival, collecting energy and modifying resources for the singular self-interest of staying alive!

It seems that life on earth is somehow cooperating to modify and maintain the biosphere in a condition that is favorable for life, almost as the earth itself were alive. Of course the earth is not alive, and the effect is completely spontaneous—the result of billions of individual plants and animals simply attending to their living needs, yet collectively creating something so much greater.

In the late 1960's two British scientists, James Lovelock and Lynn Margulis, put forth the Gaia theory to propose that separate organisms could unconsciously modify the environment in a way that is favorable for life.

The principle of the Gaia theory is simple. Life has modified and been modified by the biosphere, a process called coevolution. The organisms that survive and thrive on the planet are those that help maintain the biosphere in a way that is favorable for life.

An easy way to understand this concept is through an analogy that Lovelock calls "Daisy World". A hypothetical planet is colonized by black and white daisies. The black daisies absorb light as heat and warm the planet, while the white daisies reflect light and keep the planet cool. Too many black daisies cause the planet to overheat, making the world uncomfortable for them, but better for the white daisies. Too many white daisies cause the world to become too cold, thus favoring the black daisies that can absorb heat.

The real biosphere is much more complex, with billions of independent life forms functioning as a spontaneous check-and-balance system to maintain the biosphere in a way that is comfortable for life as a whole. Plants, for instance, have pumped carbon dioxide out of the atmosphere and buried the carbon in the form of calcium carbonate (limestone) on the ocean floors and in fossil fuels. This has reduced the greenhouse effect and kept the planet cool, even while the sun has become warmer. Likewise, moisture over the ocean forms around sulfur particles outgassed by marine algae, thus bringing much-needed sulfur to the land organisms while also controlling the amount of cloud cover over the planet.

Bacterial colonies along the sea shores coat salt crystals with a sort of varnish that inhibits the salt from dissolving back into the water. This helps to remove salt from the oceans, while the combined weight of the salt and limestone deposits on the continental shelves may even be responsible for triggering plate tectonics—the movement of the continents across the globe. There is no detectable entity managing the globe, but each of the independent life forms on earth seems to contribute to the stability and success of the whole[51].

Like the natural ecosystem, our economy created itself from nothing, evolving from the simple actions of our ancestors struggling for survival, collecting energy and modifying resources for the singular self-interest of staying alive. The economic ecosystem is diverse, highly complex, but still spontaneously organized. It is very efficient at bringing us products as complicated as cars and computers, manufactured from minerals mined around the globe, refined, shaped transported, assembled and shipped when and where they are needed. Without any one person or committee in charge you might expect that there would be resource shortages every day, yet our stores are virtually always filled with the items we want. We take it for granted here in America, but people from non-capitalist cultures are often quite amazed that our system works at all. Right up to the end of the Cold War the leaders of the Soviet Union were certain that there was some secret agency in America, working behind the scenes to decide how much of everything to produce and where to send it![72]

In nature there is harmony...

The economic ecosystem is an artificial entity that we have created, and yet it almost has a life of it's own. Each of us affects and is affected by this ecosystem. Our simplest decisions and purchases cause subtle changes in the economy. The economy likewise affects our decisions, bringing us certain goods and services at certain prices, all of which are variable based on the current economic "climate". We created this economy, yet no one is directly in control of it, and like a living entity without dimension, no one knows exactly how to control it! The economic ecosystem is the result of millions of individuals each making decisions which they perceive will bring the greatest personal benefit.

When we step into a meadow we are likely to perceive a scene of beauty. We see a diversity of flowers and plants, insects, birds, mole hills, and sometimes deer, squirrels, or other wildlife. More often than not, we see harmony. What we may not realize is that the harmony is built from the unceasing competition of individual life forms struggling to survive, store up energy and reproduce. Sure, many species cooperate with each other, like the bees that transport pollen from flower to flower, but they do not help each other out of compassion, rather they help each other by obeying their individual genetic greed for resources. The bees are collecting pollen for food. The flowers willingly provide that pollen because it is an extremely efficient way to target and cross-pollinate with other members of their species growing dozens of feet away. There is a great deal of competition within the meadow, mostly between the same or closely related species vying for similar ecological niches. Spread apart the dense growth and look close; you will see spindly, pale plants struggling to get to the light. Some will live, but the vast majority of the seeds that hit the ground never survive to maturity. Every living being in nature is in an eternal quest for energy and resources. The energy is used to transform the raw resources into living products, with each species struggling to recreate itself to live on in future generations.

There is little waste in nature. In the contest for life every plant and every animal must hone its life cycle to total efficiency. Any energy that is expended for something other than the ultimate goal of reproduction becomes a liability to survival. Even the smallest percent of difference in the efficiency between one species and another can mean the difference between success and extinction. Indeed, 99.99% of everything that ever lived is now extinct, outclassed by newer models.

The business world is similar. Energy and resources are converted into products and services. A few of these products and services find an ecological niche among consumers. As in nature, the economic ecosystem is based on both cooperation and competition. It is cooperation because in order to survive a business must produce something that people want, yet it is competition, because they must provide their product or service at a good price, or someone else will.

... but that harmony is built from the unceasing competition of individual life forms struggling to survive, store up energy and reproduce.

The companies that ultimately survive and thrive in the economic ecosystem are those that can produce useful products and services while consuming the least amount of energy and resources. Businesses become extinct when they fail to produce a product with a niche, or fail to produce that product efficiently. As in nature, these ecological niches are continually changing. Newly evolved products out-compete old products for their consumer niche. Companies must actively evolve to find newer and better ways to keep their product territory, or find new niches to move into.

In nature there are predators and prey, parasites, starvation, and genocide. Certainly there is harmony and balance, but killing and competing are the sculptors that shape that harmony. What is ironic is that the predatory forces that make nature work so well are the very same things that we tend to hate about economics. Perhaps it is because in nature we are at the top of the food-chain, while in economics we are closer to the middle!

Survival is hard to deal with when we are part of the process. When another company in a different state or country finds a way to use a wee little bit less effort to create just a little bit more product, it can drive a local business into extinction. People we care about can lose their jobs. Thus we often react by protecting our businesses, such as by lobbying Congress to subsidize our business or to levy tariffs against the competition. Yet by doing this we only interfere and slow down the processes of nature. The company that outclasses our own does so by producing more wealth at a lower cost, and we benefit in the long run. If this kind of change did not occur then we would still be scrubbing the laundry on a washboard and riding horses for transportation. The economic extinction of our company may hurt us individually, but it benefits us collectively.

Fortunately the death of a company is not the end of it's employees. Extinction in the business world only means that more people are free to make positive new contributions to society. We always hear the sad stories of people losing their jobs to the competition, but the reality is that most are reabsorbed into the work-force within a few months. We seldom hear that part of the story.

The science and study of economics was born at the dawn of the industrial revolution in England in the late 1700's and early 1800's. With fewer gains in food production and a burgeoning population base, Thomas Malthus and other early economists forecast a bleak future, plagued by a class struggle for limited resources and mass die-offs of the human population to stay in balance with the carrying capacity of the land. It seemed apparent that people could only become wealthy at the expense of others, by taking more than their share of the resource pie. Capitalism was viewed as inherently predatory, because it allowed a few people to become rich at the expense of everyone else. It is a stigma that still lingers to this day. The pursuit of profit is still a questionable ethic to much of the population. Communism and socialism were ideals created to divide the limited resources more fairly.

A contributing factor to this one-pie view, according to Michael Rothschild, author of *Bionomics: The Inevitability of Capitalism*[72], was the fact that the world appeared so static and unchanging to people of that era. It seemed that God had set the sun and moon and earth and life in motion, and that the cycles of all would remain eternally the same. Isaac Newton figured out the laws of motion as to how the planets orbited the sun, but he perceived it as a perpetual system. In fact, the whole way of life seemed virtually unchanged from one generation to the next. People did not know then that life was continually undergoing evolution, or that technology and economy could ever be different than how it was. Only the population was growing.

The study of economics was logically patterned after Newton's physics. The economic philosophers went in search of the "universal laws" of economics. They developed models to describe the phenomena of supply and demand and to predict the price of products. But these models were designed for a static, Newtonian-type economy. They were useless if any of the factors changed. Remarkably, these original economic theories remain the foundation of economic thought today. Economists are using essentially three-dimensional models to interpret a very dynamic four-dimensional world. It is no wonder that every economic advisor seems to have different forecast for the economy!

Today we know and expect change; we see the evolution of our culture and economy taking shape all around us at almost lighting speed. We know that even solar systems evolve. They are born from stellar gasses, mature, and either burn out or explode, recycling their gasses back into the universe to create new stars. We live in a culture of continuous evolution, where the only thing that is truly constant is change itself. It seems as though evolution has been kicked into high gear. It has.

Our culture and economy has followed a pattern of development strikingly similar to that of biological evolution. In both cases change is driven by the creation and exchange of information. It is a process that tends to accelerate as time goes by.

Consider this brief history of evolution on earth. Life started in the oceans an estimated 3.6 billion years ago as single-celled organisms without a nucleus. These included bacteria and blue-green algae which are still with us today. These organisms reproduce asexually, each of them splitting in half to form two exact replicas of the original. Blue-green algae used the sun's energy to convert resources into living tissue; they grew, copied themselves asexually and populated the surface of the oceans. Each algae divided into exact duplicates of itself, so mutations were few and far between. That was pretty much the sum of life on earth until about 1.5 billion years ago, when cells developed specialized parts.

ERA	PERIOD	MIL. YEARS	EVOLUTIONARY EVENT
Cenozoic	Quarternary	0-1.65	Modern humans
	Tert./Neogene	1.65-23	Human ancestors, asters, pinks
	Tert./Paleogene	23-65	Primates, grasses, lilies, roses, peas, grapes
Mesozoic	Cretaceous	65-143	Flowering plants, broad-leaf trees, palms
	Jurassic	143-213	first birds
	Triassic	213-248	Dinosaurs and mammals
Paleozoic	Permian	248-290	First modern insects
	Pennsylvanian	290-323	Coal age —cycads, ginkos, primitive conifers
	Mississippian	323-362	Coal age —cockroaches, reptiles
	Devonian	362-408	Ferns, horsetails, club mosses, amphibians
	Silurian	408-440	Vascular plants, abundance of fish
	Ordovician	440-510	Plant/fungus symbiosis begins on land.
	Cambrian	510-600	Marine life: invertebrates, shells, predators
PreCambrian	Proterozoic	600-900	Bisexual reproduction/multi-celled life
		900-1,500	Cells with nucleus
	Archean	1,500-3,600	Fungi, bacteria, blue-green algae
	Pre-Archean	3,600-4,500	Earth's Crust and Oceans Form. No Life.

It was possibly the result of several bacteria joining together that eventually led to specialization within a single cell. Cells developed separate organs or "organelles" for storing DNA, digesting nutrients, burning sugar to produce energy, and for copying the DNA into new proteins. These proteins are shipped wherever they are needed inside the cells for repairs. This new cell with specialized parts became the basis for all new life forms, including you and I. The major difference between plant and animal cells is that plants have an extra set of organelles called "chloroplasts". The chloroplasts harness energy from sunlight and use it to combine water and carbon dioxide into sugar molecules. This stored energy is passed on to the other organelles for the rest of the process. Our cells get by without chloroplasts because we eat the plants (or other animals that have eaten the plants) that do that step for us.

This innovation of specialized cell parts allowed genetic information to be copied more readily and sped up the process of evolution, but just barely. Another 600 million years passed before the advent of another new idea: bisexual reproduction.

Bisexual reproduction allowed slightly different versions of genetic knowledge to be combined into new, living products. This accelerated the evolutionary process and led to the development of multi-cellular organisms within another 300 million years, the beginning of the Cambrian Explosion. These first creatures were essentially fluid-filled blobs with no bones, eyes, mouths, or brains. They may have had chloroplasts to produce their own energy.

The fluid-filled ocean blobs only lasted 70 million years before being wiped out by another new idea: the predator, also part of the Cambrian Explosion. (In this context a "predator" is any animal eating either plants or other animals.) Exactly how the first predators came about is still a mystery, but they quickly wiped out the defenseless blobs. Evolution suddenly favored nature's mistakes and mutants. Whole oceans of habitat awaited any organisms that mutated a defensive ability against predators. This, in turn, encouraged the evolution of more advanced predators, into a sort of feed-back cycle that quickly filled the oceans with all kinds of life, such as jelly fish, sponges, worms, shelled animals, and arthropods. (Arthropods were the ancestors of insects, spiders, and crustaceans.)

Surprisingly, the predator effect may have been the force that started the rapid colonization of land a mere 60 million years later, starting in the Ordovician Period. Previously, life in the ocean was sustained by the external flow of nutrients. Simple plants in the ocean survived by absorbing nutrients from the water. These nutrients reached the plants through disturbances at sea. Upwellings brought minerals up from the bottom while ocean currents brought minerals out from shore. Plants survived in these paths of disturbance, and animals survived by eating the plants. Otherwise, the ocean was (and still is) largely a desert because the minerals are not equally distributed.

To make the transition to land, plants had to evolve from floating in the nutrient stream to carrying the nutrient stream inside. It is theorized that this evolutionary jump was accomplished by the plants forming a symbiotic relationship with fungus, according to paleontological researchers Mark and Dianna McMenamin[55].

Fungus is neither plant nor animal. It is a third type of life that produces enzymes capable of breaking down dead organic matter, living tissue, and even rock. In theory, the presence of plant-eating animals made the open ocean a more hostile environment, thus favoring any plant life that could survive along the turbulent shore-line. It is speculated that somewhere along the seashore a defective proto-fungi attacked a proto-plant, but failed to totally kill it. Instead the fungus inadvertently began feeding the plant with minerals from the soil, while simultaneously extracting carbohydrates back from the plant.

Today, ninety percent of all plants associate with fungus in the soil, and eighty percent could not survive without their fungal partners. In many cases the fungus lives in the core of the plant. Some simple plants like the club mosses lack a complete vascular system for circulating water and nutrients, but their fungal partners live inside the stems and provide that function.

The McMenamins researched the fossil record for signs of symbiosis between plants and fungus, and found evidence of a link among the earliest fossils. They

Ninety percent of all plants associate with fungus in the soil, and 80% could not survive without their fungal partners.

examined slices of cells from high quality fossils and found fungal hyphae inside the plant cells. The plant-fungus association internalized the nutrient stream and gave the proto-plant independence from the ocean currents to grow and evolve along the shore and ultimately on land. The force of evaporation served as a pump to move the nutrient stream up from the soil through the plants.

This internalized the nutrient stream and gave the proto-plant independence from the ocean currents, to grow and evolve along the shore and ultimately on land. The force of evaporation became a pump to move this nutrient stream up from the soil through the plants. This symbiosis between plants and fungi set the stage for another explosion of new life forms. Within a 100 million years life on land was already more diverse than in the oceans. In the remaining 350 million years since then, life on land seems to have evolved at an ever increasing speed. Today there are twice as many species on land as in the ocean, and although the surface of the planet is one third land and two thirds water, the land area produces a whopping fifty times as much biomass (organic matter) than the oceans.

Today we say we are in the midst of the Information Age, but according to Rothschild[72] every age is an information age. Information is the very fiber of both cultural and biological evolution. DNA, for instance, is a biological means of encoding information, consisting of a unique set of assembly and operations instructions for each and every life form on earth. In the economic ecosystem, our products are our information. Every product is built of information we have gathered.

The evolution of human culture and technology has followed a cycle of development remarkably similar to the story of biological evolution. Change came very slowly at first. Our earliest ancestors began by using crude stone, bone, and wooden tools. This body of knowledge was copied by example from one generation to the next for thousands of years, before mutating into any new ideas.

But each new idea that came eventually led to another. The advent of human knowledge was like a snowball rolling in slow motion, gaining size and increasing speed over many thousands of years. *Homo Sapiens* first appeared about 200,000 years ago and spent most of the time since just developing basic technologies. About 35,000 years ago our ancestors started engraving information onto bones. This developed into a full-fledged written language in Sumeria just 5,000 years ago.

Our species was already replicating it's wisdom from one generation to the next, but the advent of writing made this copying more effective. It was still slow, because each piece of work had to be copied by hand. For example, a scribe might only be able to make one or two copies of the Bible in a year. It was the invention of the printing press that really put technological evolution into high gear.

As James Burke has so eloquently demonstrated in the television series *Connections*, the printing press allowed the cross-fertilization of ideas. For the first time in history, millions of books were put into print and distributed. Like the advent of bisexual reproduction in living organisms, the cross-fertilization of ideas led to an explosion of new knowledge. The industrial revolution was the result.

Today the innovation of the computer and the internet has led to a new cross-fertilization of technological ideas, as we communicate instantly all over the globe. The ability to collaborate with nearly everyone

Genes and Memes

The "genetic" information of culture and industry has a name of its own, called "memes"[35]. The term was coined in 1976 by Richard Dawkins for any idea or pattern of information which is introduced into culture and spreads like a virus from one person to another, usually undergoing further evolutionary change as it spreads. Technologies are not memes, but they consist of memetic information, just as any species consists of genetic information. Any piece of information which is successfully replicated is considered a meme, although some memes survive and spread more than others. The word "meme" is a good example, because after Dawkins introduced it, the idea spread and infected millions of minds around the world. If the term is still new to you, then you are being infected with that idea right now—plus a all the other ideas in this book—with the author's hope that you might become contagious and pass them on!

at once is continually leading to the symbiosis of ideas into diverse new products, transforming the world almost before our eyes.

Biological life forms mate to exchange and combine genetic information. This sharing of information leads to newer, more effective ideas for surviving into future generations. Knowledge is likewise exchanged in the economic ecosystem, leading to new and generally better products. Companies actively seek out new genetic material to keep their products evolving ahead of everyone else. The company that can put useful information on the market with the least expenditure of energy is the company that survives the fiscal year to put forth a progeny of new ideas in future generations of products.

Some people point out the apparent weaknesses of our integrated modern economic system, that factories only have enough parts on hand to do one day's work, or that whole cities only have enough food to last about three days. Everything is connected and dependent on one power grid and one information grid, so if one thing failed all of modern civilization would immediately grind to a halt. It was this fear of imminent societal collapse that prompted the hype over the Y2K computer bug. Even without the Y2K fear, there is a certain percentage of the population that constantly lives in fear that the whole complicated system has to come crashing down at some point in time. They are as baffled by the principle of spontaneous organization as were the leaders of the former Soviet Union.

While there is definitely wisdom in having extra supplies on hand at all times, it is important to note that the modern economic ecosystem is inherently very stable because it is based on the same principles as natural ecosystems. An ecosystem is like a matrix of self-repairing chains, where each link in the chain has the motive to stay connected or to repair itself if damaged. If for any reason a link in the chain cannot repair itself, then the immediately adjacent links merge to replace it.

For example, Mount Saint Helens blew a significant hole in the natural ecosystem when it erupted in Washington state in 1980. Yet, within a year the wasteland was already being revegetated by seeds drifting in and filling the wide-open ecological niches. If there is an ecological niche to exploit, then something will find a way to exploit it. The web of life quickly repairs the damage to the ecosystem and life goes on.

Similarly, we know that disasters strike the economic ecosystem, such as the earthquakes that topple buildings, destroy roads and interrupt power and water systems, but the damaged areas are quickly restored through the process of spontaneous organization. Businesses move in and take advantage of the situation to earn money by putting the urban world back in order. Every link in the chain has something to gain by fixing the matrix in the shortest possible time. The difference is that recolonization in the natural ecosystem is random, as seeds are accidentally distributed into the damaged areas, while recolonization within the economic ecosystem is intentional, and therefore much faster. Basically, the economic ecosystem has a much faster metabolic rate than it's natural counterpart. It would be like giving seeds their own propulsion systems and datalinks to find out where the ecological damage is done, so they could go to the sites where the opportunities are greatest. Even if computer networks did crash during the Y2K bug, the flow of goods would have been quickly restored because there are hundreds of millions of self-repairing links in the system.

Unfortunately, the strength and metabolism of the economic system is also a problem, in that it is destroying its natural counterpart. The economy was born from the natural ecosystem, but it threatens to consume its parent with its fast and furious throughput of materials and energy. It is using the strength and stability of ecosystem design to assimilate the entire living planet. The natural ecosystem has survived for billions of years through astroid attacks, ice ages, a hotter sun, and mass extinctions, but can it survive this voracious economic ecosystem?

We keep mucking up the natural world only because we want to control it to better meet human needs. For example, a meadow of wildflowers may be beautiful and harmonious, but not necessarily edible. We tear into the fabric of nature, rip up what was there, and replace it with straight rows of a single species in order to produce more of something that is useful to us. We live off the accumulated wealth of nutrients until the land is desertified, then we move on to other fertile fields. In our efforts to manage nature, we've only succeeded in denuding the landscape.

Today we appropriate roughly 40% of the world's biomass to cover human needs[59], far more than any other species on the planet, yet billions of people still live in relative poverty, wanting far more than they have. The biological systems of the planet are already stumbling through the initial stages of collapse. Already we have put a hole in the ozone layer. We have pumped the earth's atmosphere full of greenhouse gasses and melted more than four feet of the polar ice cap. We have cleared tropical and old growth forests and destabilized watersheds, causing floods and droughts, while permanently wiping out thousands of plant and animal species. We have created deserts that are thousands of miles in size. Even our vast oceans are being depleted of life from overfishing, and yet the human population is expected to nearly double again before finally leveling off later this century. If trends continue, we can expect that at least 80% of the world's biomass will be diverted to meet human needs. If we try to give every person in the world the same life-style we have in the industrial world then there will not be a single plant or animal left on the planet that is not being raised for human use. Now, maybe you can understand why ecologists are concerned!

There are people who wish the societal matrix would collapse under some great catastrophe, believing that the natural world would be better off, but it is a fruitless wish. Only a disaster on the scale of the meteorites that wiped out the dinosaurs could do that much damage to the economy. But a disaster on that scale would do even more damage to the natural ecosystem. Humans live in every corner of the globe, so hundreds of millions would survive even the worst-case scenarios. The survivors would still rebuild the economic ecosystem and recolonize the entire planet faster than the natural ecosystem could do the same.

Like it or not, the economic ecosystem is here to stay, and every minute spent wishing for its collapse is opportunity lost that could be applied towards constructively making it more compatible with its natural counterpart. As you will see through the pages of this book, it is inevitable that we will ultimately create an

Forty percent of America's crop and rangelands have turned to desert reports <u>Newsweek</u> magazine[69]. In this photo sand dunes are shown forming at the edge of a plowed field near Mud Lake, Idaho.

ecologically sustainable economy. After all, there is relatively little of the natural world left to exploit! People and corporations are discovering for the first time that it is more profitable to steward our resources wisely. As it turns out, it is very worthwhile to mimic nature, to use resources as efficiently as possible, to "get more bang for the buck" so to speak.

Any place there is waste there is opportunity, and right now the opportunities are virtually unlimited! In our homes and in our businesses there is waste all around us—wasted time, wasted money, wasted resources, wasted energy, and wasted talent. No matter where we live or what we do, there are so many ways that we can learn from and mimic the natural ecosystem to increase our prosperity and make the world a better place for all. The faster we can make this transition to a truly sustainable economy the more we will profit and the more of the natural world we can save.

Part I
The Nature of Wealth

"Most men would feel insulted if it were proposed to employ them in throwing stones over a wall, and then in throwing them back, merely that they might earn their wages. But many are no more worthily employed now."
—Henry David Thoreau, *Life Without Principle*

1-1
Real Wealth
-Taking Stock of our Capital-

Wealth is something that nearly everyone seems to want, but what is it? Too many people get caught up in the illusion of money and think that money is wealth. But just imagine if money was all you had. You might be able to stuff paper dollars in your clothes for insulation from the cold, or crawl into a big pile of paper dollars for shelter, write your journal notes on it, use it for toilet paper, or burn it for warmth, but you could hardly call it "wealth". It is only when you give your money away in exchange for the things that you want in life that you have real wealth— or at least real material wealth.

Material wealth is the physical stuff we have in our lives—our homes, furniture, cars, clothes, books, music and computers. These things are important for supporting an enjoyable lifestyle, so we don't have to worry about stuffing our clothes with bits of paper for warmth from the cold. But material wealth is only one form of wealth.

Other forms of wealth include the health and happiness of our families and the quality of our community and environment. After all, material wealth or money doesn't mean much if you or the ones you love are ailing, unhappy, constantly fighting and too afraid to breathe the air, drink the water or walk down the street alone. If you can successfully surmount all of these obstacles so that you and your family can live happy, healthy and physically comfortable, then you have indeed achieved Real Wealth.

Unfortunately, in the quest for material goods many people neglect other forms of wealth and end up merely trading one form of wealth for another, or simply losing it all. I have heard too many stories of people who have made their millions only to lose their families along the way. Sometimes the reward for their efforts is divorce, depression and subsequently bankruptcy and even suicide.

Of course neither you nor I would be so foolish, or so we like to think. Yet collectively we are doing the same thing, trading the natural wealth of the planet in for material wealth to be bought and sold at the Mall of America.

In traditional economics material wealth is thought of as **capital**. Capital is the net assets of an individual or business, such as money, real estate and equipment. With the aid of human labor and knowledge, the capital assets may be utilized to produce an income. For example, a bow and arrow would be the capital of an ancient hunter, useful to produce an income of venison for the family.

The odd thing about this traditional view of economics is that while the bow and arrow has value, the deer does not until it is dead and removed from the ecosystem for human consumption. The same is true for all other natural resources, from trees to gold ore to oil. Nature has no intrinsic value until it is plundered for human use. Resources are considered "free" for the cost of extracting them from the ecosystem. The problem with this view of economics is that the consumption of natural resources registers only as a gain in our economic indicators and not as a loss. The economic indicators might look really good if a hunter took a thousand deer in one year, even though he left none to reproduce the following year. Many people would say that the industrial economy is in a similar situation, celebrating prosperity and abundance today while consuming resources we should have saved for tomorrow. It appears that we have reached the limits to growth, so there is nothing left for the future.

One of the objectives of the emerging field of **environmental economics** is to find ways to assign a value to the natural world, so that the consumption of natural resources registers as a loss against economic gains made by consuming them. Putting a price tag on nature is an ethical hot potato, because it seems hardly different from putting a price tag on your own mother or father. How much are they worth? How much is one species of frog worth or the swamp that it lives in? What is the value of a coral reef or a tropical forest?

Environmental economists contend that assigning some value to the natural world is better than letting it continue with no value at all. According to this view point, natural resources are considered assets, which may be called "**natural capital**".

The process of assigning value to natural capital is inherently humancentric. The methodology is to ask what it would cost in human labor and materials to replace the services of nature. For example, what would it cost to regulate gasses in the atmosphere, process wastes, and purify and store water? Estimates average $36 trillion dollars per year (1998 dollars) to replace just seventeen services that the ecosystem currently provides for free. For comparison, the World Gross Product in 1998 was $39 trillion dollars.

The world average land value for natural services was estimated at $466 per acre, with the highest score in wetlands at $7,924 per acre for flood control, water purification and water storage. The average value for services from marine systems is estimated at $234 per acre with the highest score in estuaries at $9,240 per acre for recycling nutrients washed out from the rivers.

Even at these prices—or at any price—there is considerable doubt as to whether or not the effort to replace nature's services would be successful. Environmental economists point to the Biosphere 2 project as an example. Researchers spent $200 million to develop the fully-enclosed 3.15 acre artificial ecosystem, but they were unable to maintain the necessary balance of oxygen in the atmosphere for the eight people living inside. Fresh air, provided free from "Biosphere 1" (earth) had to be let into the structure to sustain the occupants[39].

The point is that the natural world is real wealth and it has real value. Maybe I am just particularly greedy, but I like to think that we can have our cake and eat it too, that we can all enjoy the real wealth of personal prosperity and neighborly communities and still have a healthy, wealthy environment.

In the past the environmental movement focused solely on the task of protecting nature from economic development, to try and prevent our natural wealth from being liquidated and converted to material wealth. In all regions of the world environmentalists often met great resistance from other people who felt that their livelihoods were threatened. When it comes down to a choice between material wealth and natural wealth, most people choose the former. But in recent years there has been a shift in approach from many organizations which are now working to save nature by encouraging economic development rather than trying to kill it. Instead of protesting clear-cut logging in developing countries, for example, some organizations are working with local citizens to establish sustainable forestry practices, even putting environmental funds into building schools and hospitals.

On the other side of the same coin, there are humanitarian organizations embracing environmental and economic solutions as ways to help raise people's quality of life. For example, Scott Bernstein, director of the Center for Neighborhood Technology in Chicago, does not consider himself an environmentalist in any conventional sense, but he often employs environmental solutions to help rectify social and economic problems in the inner city. When sky-rocketing energy costs drove rents up and renters out of inner city neighborhoods, Bernstein helped form a coalition to retrofit more than 10,000 apartments, saving in excess of $1.5 million every year in avoided energy use. His goal was to make the inner city livable, but it also helped to close the loop on wasted energy[50].

Businesses are also starting to embrace environmental thought, using resources and energy much more efficiently to make a greater profit with fewer materials. For instance, in the highly competitive market for producing silicon chips for computers, one Singapore manufacturer cut its energy use per chip by 60% between 1991 and 1997, saving $5.8 million every year from just $.07 million in retrofitting costs[39].

These kinds of projects indicate that it is indeed possible to increase our material prosperity while helping to conserve or enhance community and natural wealth. But this is only the tip of the iceberg compared to the potential. Any individual, social or environmental organization or business that can keep all forms of wealth in mind will inevitably find more solutions than they could ever use to make the world a happier, greener and wealthier place.

"A complex society is not necessarily more advanced than a simple one; it has just adapted to conditions in a more complicated way."

—*Peter Farb, Man's Rise to Civilization*[28]

1-2
Calories
-The Currency of All Economies-

Most economists rely on computer printouts of numerical data for their financial planning. By comparing one series of digits with another they can find the immediate trends in the economy and take advantage of those trends. To most people that seems normal. To me it is artificial. I have always wanted to help both people and the environment, and I learned at an early age that knowledge of the economy could be one tool to reach that end. However, I wanted more than just the knowledge of how to generate a positive series of numbers. I was looking for something bigger. I was searching for universal truths. I wanted knowledge about the economy that was constant from year to year, from culture to culture. I wanted knowledge that would be useful to a poor person or a rich person, in our culture, or in any culture. The truths about economics that I found were not in the New York Stock Exchange, but in anthropology and nature.

Some things have hardly changed since the stone age. We still have the same needs, just new ways of meeting those needs.

Some things haven't changed since the stone-age. We still have the same basic needs today as in millennia past for such things as physical and mental well-being, shelter, fire, water, and food—it is only the way we meet those basic needs that has changed. As hunter-gatherers we met our needs largely on our own; each of us produced every aspect of our culture, from shelter to clothing to entertainment. Today we have the same needs, but we more often meet those needs through the network of society, trade, and money. Nevertheless, if we look beyond the illusion of money we will discover that our economy today—like the economies of all past cultures—is based not on dollars or Deutsche marks or yen, but on calories of energy.

The **calorie** is a unit of measuring energy. Specifically, it is the amount of heat required to raise the temperature of one gram of water one degree Celsius. The caloric value of food is measured by igniting the food to find out how much heat it releases. As human beings, you and I require approximately 2,500 calories of energy to fuel us through each day. The calories we consume came from the sun. Plants convert sunlight into food that we and other animals can eat. Petroleum and coal also contain calories of solar energy, but that energy was captured by plants millions of years ago. The calories from these and other sources are ultimately the basis of all economies.

The economies of our ancestors may have seemed different from ours, without the institutions of finance that we have, but there were still similarities, even before there was money, and even before the very first trade or barter ever took place. Our ancestors of long ago may not have had money, but they still had to make decisions that were economical. For example, there were many edible plants and animals in their environment which they could harvest and consume for calories, but not all of them were worth the effort expended. Sometimes more energy would be expended in the process than was gained in the end, resulting in a caloric deficit. For a food resource to be economical, the people had to be able to gain enough calories of energy from the food to replace those expended, plus enough extra to expend on other chores and activities such as making tools and shelter, sleeping, or singing and dancing. At first they harvested only food calories. Later they started harvesting additional calories, in the form of firewood, which I call fuel calories.

Money is simply a token we use today to represent calories of energy. Strictly speaking, we use it to represent human energy, or human productivity. Each of us produces goods or services to exchange to others for the goods and services we need. We put a great deal of energy into the goods and services we provide, as does everyone else. Money represents that energy and makes it easy for us to swap our energies. I can make a product and sell it, and I get paid for the energy I put into it. I can then take that money and buy a product from another person. I give them my money to compensate them for their energy. Ultimately I have exchanged my energy for theirs, and money is just something that makes the exchange process easier. For simplicity we can say that money is a token that represents **calories of human energy or labor**.

Money is a token we use to represent calories of food and fuel.

Money also represents **fuel calories**, but not directly. One person can spend a day (and a couple thousand food calories) harvesting tens of thousands, even millions of fuel calories. That fuel can be firewood, petroleum, uranium, or any other type of fuel. A relatively small amount of human labor can be expended to acquire a tremendous number of fuel calories. These fuel calories can then be put to work for us to increase our production. One person can only consume a couple thousand calories of food per day, and is therefore limited in the amount of work they can do per day. But a person can also burn hundreds of thousands of fuel calories to run machinery and increase output. Fuel calories are like cheap slave labor. On average, it gives each of us the calorie equivalent of having between 100 and 300 slaves working for us 24 hours a day[16, 40]. We expend a few food calories to harvest a lot of fuel calories, and we spend a combination of food and fuel calories to produce the products of our culture.

It could be said that money only represents calories of human labor, since it takes human labor to harvest the fuel calories. Yet each of us uses a combination of food and fuel calories to do our work, so it is convenient to say that money is a token that represents both food and fuel calories. The fuel calories are obviously worth less than food calories, since they are so easy to come by. We easily expend millions of times more fuel energy than food energy in our country, yet the fuel calories still only account for three to four percent of the cost of producing all the goods and services of our country. This means we have only about three to four percent of our culture expending labor to harvest all that fuel. The rest of the cost goes towards the people putting that fuel to work to create our products. The specific ratio of food to fuel calories does not really matter, as long as you understand that money is a token we use to represent both.

Today every product we pick up has been shaped by food and fuel calories. For example, a simple drinking glass is made from the resources of the earth mined and shaped with the food calories of human endeavor, combined with the fuel calories from one or another source. The people that produce those food and fuel calories provide the basis of our entire economy. Directly or indirectly, we produce goods and services for the people who produce the energy that fuels us through our tasks. In return they pay us in calories of food or fuel to cover the energy we expended, plus they give us extra calories which we can trade to other people for the services and goods we need. We might think we pay with money, but really we pay with calories. We earn calories at our jobs, then pass them on to others to support them in exchange for their goods and services. The stuff we call money is just a token representative of calories. Without money we would have to carry around bags of food and bottles of gas, or batteries with electricity. Money is simply a token which represents calories and makes life a lot more convenient.

The only problem with money is that people get caught up in the illusion that it is real wealth. They manipulate numbers in an effort to make money, but they fail to create any real wealth. You can hear people doing this every day in advertising, get-rich schemes and political speeches. Their proposals may seem sound according to the math, but if you think in terms of calories you will find that their plans seldom bring about real wealth. This book will help you to think about calories, rather than money, because the flow of calories points directly to real wealth.

Consider someone who makes a living "trading money". There are, believe it or not, quite a number of people who earn a living by buying and selling money. The value of the dollar, the pound, the ruble, and all other types of money are constantly changing in relationship to one another. Moment by moment there are little fluctuations in the value of one currency to another. Money traders make a living by exchanging their money back and forth between different currencies, hoping to buy one currency when it is cheap and sell it when it's relative value goes back up. They may make a million dollars one day and lose it the next, but on the whole, they make enough money to keep doing it.

At first, this little game seems harmless enough. After all, they could be bulldozing the rain forest, or conning the poor out of their money. In fact, the idea of trading money might seem attractive, because it is like free money; nobody has to give up their money, nobody suffers. In that sense it may seem like an ideal way to make a living. But money is just a token for calories, and all calories come from somewhere, even if it is impossible to trace them to one pocket. We might be delighted if a money trader walked into our business and spent several thousand dollars, but think again. In the context of calories, there may be many of us working to provide for their needs, but they produce nothing in return. We may not be able to trace the path back to the pocket where their money came from, but ultimately it was our own.

If you take the time to think it through, then you will discover that all aspects of our economy are tied to calories, including inflation, taxes, insurance, stocks and bonds and interest. For example, **insurance** in a primitive economy meant having neighbors who would share some of their calories with you if you had an accident, and you would do the same for them in their time of need. Insurance is similar today. We all pay calories into a common fund, and any person or family that is in need draws from the fund. For example, if a person's house is destroyed then that person withdraws enough calories from the fund to rebuild the house. Having built our own house, I can tell you that you expend a lot of calories building a house. So the person whose home is destroyed withdraws a large amount of calories form the common fund to fuel the carpenters as they rebuild the house, plus enough extra for the carpenters to exchange for the goods they need. There is only one main difference between insurance in our economy and insurance in past economies. In past economies every member produced calories and contributed them to the insurance pool. In our economy today the insurance agents do not produce for the pool. We sustain them with a share of the calories we produce, and they serve us in return by overseeing the pool of calories and by doling them out to those in need.

Similarly, **banks** are essentially places where people can store calories when they have a surplus, or where they can borrow them when they do not have enough. Primitive banking may have started when a farmer borrowed calories from a neighbor's surplus to fuel the family as they built their house. They may have borrowed a certain number of calories with the promise to repay them when they grew crops the following season. This year they would build their house. Next year they would raise crops and repay the loan, and they would give back additional calories, which we call interest, to pay for the service. Today bankers are able to sustain themselves without producing any calories of their own. They are able to sustain themselves by loaning us calories with the stipulation that we must eventually pay them back more than they lent us.

Besides borrowing calories from banks, most of us also store them in banks. Banks are usually a safe place to store our extra calories until we need them. Bankers have found that they can loan out our calories to other people as a means to earn calories for themselves, as long as they can give ours back when we come for them. If many people store their calories at the bank then it is unlikely everyone will come on the same day to withdraw their funds; therefore the bank can loan out most of the total they have in store.

Even **inflation** can be discussed in terms of calories. Inflation is simply a word we use to describe the changing relationship between calories and the tokens that represent calories. Inflation has occurred when a given amount of tokens (money) cannot be exchanged for as many calories as in the past. Inflation is usually caused by the source that makes tokens, typically a government, and can be additionally affected by banking institutions. This is the subject of the following chapter.

Stocks and bonds are also related to calories. When you invest in stocks you become a banker and a gambler. You loan a business the calories they need for sustenance while they build their business. You then get a share of the profits when their business is up and running, exchanging goods and services for the calories people bring in. If they do well then you get extra calories back as profit. If the investment fails to bring back a net gain, then the business fails and the calories you invested were expended as sweat and tears, but no gain.

All in all, very little has changed since the stone-age. Throughout the ages the calorie has remained the universal measure of economic wealth. Each of us is simply working to harvest more calories than we expend.

Whether you are an individual, a business, or a policy maker, it is important to think through your ideas in terms of calories. Some ideas that seem financially sound on paper do not actually generate any real wealth.

Consider a clerk at the cash register. At first it may seem that he provides a valuable service running our groceries over the scanner that reads the bar codes. In caloric terms, however, the only changes that occur are that the groceries are bagged and moved about six feet closer to the door. The cashier contributes virtually no caloric value to the products, except when considered in context of the efficiency of the entire system. For this act of moving the groceries six feet closer to the door, we pay the cashier many calories of energy to provide for their shelter, food, clothing, and all other needs. I am not claiming that we should get rid of cashiers, only that they do not individually provide a service that is measurable in calories. It is for that reason that innovators are working to make scanners that will automatically scan and bill whole carts full of groceries, to eliminate the need for a cashier at all.

Likewise, gambling casinos may seem like a good way to produce jobs, by mining minerals, manufacturing the equipment, building the casinos and operating them. Gambling may appear to generate a lot of wealth, but in truth it only consumes it. When we employ part of the population to do all that work then the rest of us have to work harder to provide their food, shelter, clothing, automobiles, and other goods. As much as half our work force is employed consuming wealth without producing any.

We might be delighted to hear that a million new jobs were created, but would we be so delighted if we knew those jobs were all accountants? An accountant consumes a lot of calories and pushes around a lot of numbers, but does not add caloric value to any products, except when considered in context of the entire system. In our culture only a few people do produce calories or add caloric value to products. Everyone else is employed in quasi-services which may initially seem useful, but don't physically produce anything.

Politicians complain about the high cost of special projects like the space program, where a single space shuttle costs a billion dollars to build, yet as you will see in Chapter 7-2 *Taxes*, we collectively waste enough money on projects like accounting for tax purposes to cover the cost of hundreds of space shuttles every year.

Just imagine what might happen if we used our calories more strategically, instead of merely disposing of them as we do now. In theory, we could maintain the same amount of prosperity while dividing the existing, tangible work in half, thus making a twenty-hour work week. Alternately, another way of looking at it, we could all continue working forty hour weeks, but our surplus calories could be expended doing something new. For example, in terms of calories, we can theoretically afford to have half our population working in the space industry, if we desired that.

Regardless of what happens in government, there is still so much you can do right now at home and in business to increase your prosperity and freedom by closing the loop on wasted calories.

"Competitive potlatching went wild, particularly so among the Kwakiutl, where an intricate system of credits to finance the feasts developed.... (with interest rates of 20 to 200% or more).... In one Kwakiutl village, the population of somewhat more than a hundred people possessed only about four hundred actual blankets. Yet, so pyramided had the system of debts, credits, and paper profits become that the total indebtedness of everyone in the village approached 75,000 blankets."

—Peter Farb, Peter, *Man's Rise to Civilization*[28]

1-3
Inflation
-The Changing Relationship Between Calories and Money-

To truly comprehend the nature of money in today's world we must include an understanding of the intimate relationship between money and the institution that prints, circulates, and manages it—our government.

Money, as described earlier, is a token we use to represent calories of energy. I like to discuss economics in the context of calories because calories are relatively tangible; this makes it easier to think about and to track the movement of real wealth. Money, on the other hand, is much less tangible. It is only a symbol or token. The symbol has whatever meaning we assign to it, and that meaning can change.

You have probably heard of stories from foreign countries where people have lost their entire life savings to a quick spurt of inflation. They hold onto the money itself, as they stuff their mattress or their bank account with cash for twenty years. Then, in a moment of crises, the government increases the amount of money in circulation by tenfold, and twenty years of savings are reduced to ten percent of their original value. This would not happen if we exchanged actual calories, and had "pocket calories", instead of pocket change. But we do not have "pocket calories", and the meaning, or value, of money is changing at this very moment right inside your own pocket.

The reason governments occasionally create these sudden increases in the money supply is because it is an easy way to pay bills. It is often easier to print money than to collect it through taxation. If you own the printing presses then you can print as much as you want. Printing additional money does not increase the number of calories in circulation; it merely changes the ratio of tokens to calories. One calorie may have been exchangeable for one token to begin with, but the value is cut in half when the government doubles the amount of tokens in circulation. Then you need to exchange two tokens for one calorie.

After World War I Germany canceled its internal debts through the technique of printing more money (lots more). The German government printed tons and tons of paper money and instantly paid off all its internal debts. The total money supply in the coun-

People usually learn about inflation at an early age.

try grew to 4 quintillion (4,000,000,000,000,000,000) reichsmarks[81], but of course there were no additional calories of work produced. The result was "**hyperinflation**". The caloric value of the money became so diluted in the years 1922-1923 that people had to take wheel barrow loads of it to the store just to purchase basic goods. The effects of all this money on the German economy were both positive and negative.

To bring this home to our own terms, imagine for a moment that you have an annual income of $30,000 and a home mortgage of $100,000. Let's say bread costs $1.00 a loaf. Suddenly, the government injects gobs and gobs of paper money into the economy. The value of it becomes so diluted through hyperinflation that when prices are adjusted for it, the value of a loaf of bread rises to $1,000. Of course the bread is not worth more, the paper money is just worth less. Wages soon adjust to hyperinflation as well. Like the price of a loaf of bread your income increases a thousand fold, from $30,000 a year to $30,000,000 per year. As a result of hyperinflation you would be able to pay off your entire home loan in about a day! (Ultimately everyone in our own country will be millionaires, but only because inflation is gradually, and sometimes rapidly, devaluing the worth of a million dollars.)

On the other hand, maybe you worked hard in the past and saved $10,000. This would have been a lot of money when it was a third of your annual income. But as a result of hyperinflation your hard-earned savings would only be worth ten loaves of bread!

Any strategy of **debt cancellation** is good for people who are debtors and bad for those who are creditors. For example, debt cancellation is good for landlords but does nothing for renters. Likewise, it does nothing for those of us who have already paid for our homes. It is impossible to implement a strategy for debt cancellation fairly and equitably to all citizens. It is a drastic measure applicable only to drastic times, such as for restructuring a collapsed economy.

It should be noted that Germany's method of debt reduction only worked with internal debts. To pay external debts the country had to trade its reichsmarks for foreign currencies, and of course the German marks were virtually worthless as a medium of exchange[81]. To effectively erase foreign debts, all countries have to agree to the arrangement, which of course, helps debtor nations at a loss to creditor nations.

The Soviet Union, in about the same time period as Germany's debt cancellation, did succeed in erasing all its foreign debts. This came about as a result of the Bolshevik revolution. The new government simply refused to assume and pay for the debts of the old government .

Erasing The Deficit
-Paradox in the Time-Money Continuum

Stop for a moment. Think about your home. Let's say you have a nice home. You borrowed money, you bought your place, and now you are making payments on the loan. Okay. Now think about the person who built your home. There is a good chance that they are living in a similar home. They may have borrowed money, bought their home, and now they are making payments on that loan. Okay. So now think about the banker who holds the loans on both houses. The banker probably has a house of her own, and she is probably making payments on it just like you are.

Now think about your car. Like many Americans, you may be making payments on it. How about the company that made it? They are likely making payments on a billion dollar loan for one or more of their factories, possibly including the factory where your car was made.

Now think about the federal deficit. It's big. The deficit is so big that some one-third of the taxes you and I pay go towards paying interest on it.

Okay. One more. Now think about the rain forests. Third-world countries are hacking their rain forests into oblivion to pay off their debts to foreign countries. Some environmentalists in our own country are trying to pay off those debts as a means to save the rain forests.

So what would happen if one day we picked up a pencil and erased all these debts and set all the account books back to $0.00?

Perhaps you have heard of the paradox in the space-time continuum. You travel back in time and meet yourself. Because of this encounter, the other you makes different choices in life and therefore changes your past. Suddenly you could have never traveled back in time to create the circumstance in the first place. It becomes a paradox. Now consider paradox in the time-money continuum.

First, think back to when you bought your house and your car. Perhaps you got off work one day and you drew your paycheck of $1,000. "Whoa." you said, "This isn't good enough." So you went down to the bank. The banker took you in a time capsule to the future, and you scooped up all your future paychecks and brought them back in time. Then you went out and bought an $80,000 house and a $10,000 car. Cute trick.

So that day past, and suddenly you begin to encounter your future. You draw your paycheck and bring it down to the bank to put it into your account. Whoosh! Most of your paycheck suddenly vanishes into the time vortex and goes back to your past. You are left with very little to spend.

You are a little frustrated, but then you have this great idea. Originally you went to the future and scooped up all your future paychecks from the bank, on the assumption that someday you would be depositing all your paychecks there. But in the future, which is now the present, you get smart. You decide not to bring your paycheck to the bank. Then you can spend the same money again. You have learned that time travel is possible into the future and back to the past, but you know that it is not possible in

In our country inflation is also augmented by the banking system, although the banks are not a direct cause of inflation. Banks cause inflation by lending calories that do not exist, which is somewhat tricky to understand. Let's say you deposit a thousand calories in the bank, worth a dollar each. Now the bank is required by the Federal Reserve to keep part of that on hand, let's say 10% or $100. But the other $900 they can loan out. So someone comes and borrows that $900 and spends it on a new sound system. The retailer deposits the $900 back in the bank, or any bank. Now the original 1000 calories are back in the banking system, but the borrower also owes $900, meaning that there is now $1,900 representing a thousand calories. The $900 that was deposited is treated as new revenue, so 10% is set aside as required and the other $810 is loaned out, etc., A deposit of $1,000 can theoretically amount to $9,000 worth of loans, with no increase in the number of calories. Thus the money is devalued and we have inflation[82].

It should be understood though, that there has to be a new input of $1,000 to set this cycle in motion. Therefore only the government is ultimately responsible for inflation. Also, some money leaks out of the cycle to pay taxes, or is held as cash, so the total number of loans in the real world is significantly less than in this theoretical example.

The Federal Reserve is the specific part of our government that manages the country's money supply. The Federal Reserve tries to stimulate the economy without causing excessive inflation. This is done by **tightening or loosening the money supply**; the reserve has a variety of tools to do this.

One is to simply change the **reserve requirements** for the banking system. The Federal Reserve can require banks to keep more money on hand. The money is still there, but it is not in circulation. This tightens the money supply. Conversely, the Fed can lower the reserve requirements, so the banks can loan out more of their funds and pump more money into the economy. Raising or lowering the reserve requirements has a temporary effect on the economy, but in the long run it does not change the total amount of currency in circulation.

Another way the Federal Reserve affects the money supply is by **raising or lowering the**

the other order, to travel to the past and then back to the future. You will not negate the past, where you borrowed money from your future and bought a house and car. Your banker cannot travel back in time and stop you from borrowing that money.

Unfortunately, however, in the time-money continuum that we consider normal, this scheme does not work. The banker may not be able to travel back to your past, but she can sure show up in your present.

"You think you own this house and car?" she says.
"Sure." you say, "This is my house and my car."
"No." she says," You only think it is your house and car"
Drats! You rush to the bank and deposit your check.

But what if the banker, along with the rest of the world, were in cahoots with you? What happens if we erase all the debts in the world and start from scratch?

The work is already done. The houses are built. The cars are built. The highways and bridges are built. We built it all in the past. We borrowed money from the future and used it in the past to build the wealth we have around us today. The funny thing is, however, that while we can borrow money from the future, we cannot borrow calories from the future. It takes a very specific number of calories to build a bridge or a house, or anything else. You cannot build anything with a caloric deficit. People die and machines quit when they run out of calories. The only way we could have built everything we now have is if we already had the calories to do it. In truth, we never borrowed anything from the future at all.

We, the human species, created the economy. But it is the economy that controls us. The economy is an imaginary entity we have created, which exists as a series of numbers darting back and forth over the electronic circuitry. If the numbers are positive then we are happy. If the numbers are negative then it is a national concern. The economy becomes an entity which we must feed to keep it happy so it does not turn on us. There is a saying somewhere, in some spiritual text or another, or perhaps in many of them, the we live amongst great abundance; we can be as wealthy as we want to be. So why do we choose to live in poverty?

The economy is an imaginary entity which we have created. We need to stop for a moment and let it become less real. If we created it once, then we can erase it and create it again. We live in a time when our debts are creating instability within the fabric of our society. People are stressed to the breaking point trying to pay too many bills. Is it really worth putting ourselves through hard times just to protect an imaginary entity. Is it worth sacrificing the rain forests? Is it worth losing thousands of species of exotic living plants and animals, irrevocably, for forever, just for numerical convenience?

So what would happen if we all mutually agreed to stop channeling our money to the past? It is hard to say. We know for certain that our houses, cars, and infrastructure would not disappear into a time vortex. The work is already done, and we would still have the fruits of our labors. The unknown is what would happen to money? If we create a paradox in the time-money continuum then money becomes meaningless until we find a way to use it again as a unit of measuring energy in the new economy we create.

prime interest rate. The prime interest rate is the rate at which the Federal Reserve loans money out to the banking system. The banks borrow the money from the Federal Reserve and in turn, loan it out to businesses and individuals. Where does the Fed get that money to begin with? Is it tax dollars? No. They print it. That is why you frequently hear on the news that the Federal Reserve is raising interest rates to prevent inflation. Raising the interest rates immediately reduces the number of people borrowing money, and thus reduces the amount of money the Fed is printing.

The meaning of money is constantly changing.

A third way the Federal Reserve manages the money supply is by buying and selling **US Government bonds**. When the Fed sells a bond and takes in money for it, that money ceases to exist. The money is removed from circulation, and the Federal Reserve can simply shred the money, or save it for future circulation. It has no value. Later, the Fed can buy back those bonds. They print more money and use it to purchase the bonds. This increases the amount of money in circulation and again leads to inflation. Of course the Fed can only buy back as many bonds as it has sold, so in the long run there is no increase or decrease of the total money supply, except that the Fed pays interest on those bonds, and this does increase the money supply.

You may notice that none of these tools enable the Federal Reserve to permanently remove money from the economy. From that standpoint, it would seem that **deflation** is impossible over the long run. But that is not entirely correct. There are a couple ways deflation can occur. One is to simply collect taxes and shred the money. That decreases the amount of money in circulation. Then, instead of having ten dollars floating around for every loaf of bread, there is only one dollar available. Money becomes "scarce" and prices go down.

Deflation can also occur even as the money supply is increased. If business borrow money and invest that in increased production, then the growth can match the pace of inflation. Instead of decreasing the number of dollars you increase the number of loaves of bread. You raise the caloric production up to meet the rising number of tokens.

The same thing happens just on account of having an expanding population. If more and more people are sharing the money supply, then money becomes scarce, and prices fall.

You hear about inflation and deflation, the prime interest rate and treasury bonds on the news just about every day. So it is helpful to have an understanding of what is being talked about. Just keep in mind that money is little more than a token we use to represent calories of energy. Inflation and deflation simply reflect the constantly changing ratio between the calories and the tokens. Real wealth is a matter of using calories of energy to directly create the products and services that improve our quality of life.

"If one farm household or co-op takes up a new process such as the waxing of mandarin oranges, because of the extra care and attention the profit is higher. The other agricultural co-ops take notice and soon they, too, adopt the new process... competition brings the prices down, and all that is left to the farmer is the burden of hard work and the added costs of supplies and equipment. Now he must apply the wax."

-*Masanobu Fukuoka, The One Straw Revolution*

1-4

Prices and the Natural Ecosystem
-Understanding Caloric Relationships-

There are an infinite number of possibilities and opportunities for building wealth while making the world a better place. There are trillions of dollars worth of opportunities right now, waiting for people like you and I to come along and participate in the harvest.

Your personal hopes and dreams may call for a big harvest or a small one, and in either case, it is helpful to more fully understand how products and services relate to the natural ecosystem. Understanding these relationships will aid you in seeing where some of the opportunities abound.

First of all, there is a relationship of sorts between the value of goods and services and their "closeness or distance" from the ecosystem. Some goods and services are very tangible in caloric terms, and hence, are close to the ecosystem, while other goods and services are constructed more of human creativity, and thus are not as easily measured in caloric terms. These goods and services are not as "close" to the ecosystem. Those products which can be measured in fairly strict caloric terms tend to have market prices that directly reflect the calories put into them. The opposite is true for goods and services which cannot be easily measured in caloric terms; the more they are removed from the ecosystem, the less their price reflects the value of the calories put into that product or service.

Consider the market values of commodities, which are closely linked with the ecosystem. The day-to-day prices of commodities fluctuates with supply and demand. If wheat farmers everywhere have an abundant harvest then the market is swamped with grain and the price goes down. But droughts or floods sometimes destroy crops, reducing the supply and causing prices to go up, so some farmers lose big for a season, while others do okay. More importantly for our purposes is that individual farmers have virtually no **market power** to determine the sale price of their product. One grain of wheat is a lot like any other grain of wheat, so farmers cannot raise their price even a fraction of a cent above the going market rate. In the lingo of economists they are called **price takers**[41].

The price of basic products, such as wheat, gold, or paper, may fluctuate momentarily according to the current demand, but most of the time the price we pay correlates very closely with the amount of calories required to produce those products. As these basic commodities are processed into more refined products, however, the price becomes more variable and the output ceases to be a direct reflection of the caloric input required to make them that way. Let me explain.

Precious metals are expensive not because they are rare, but because it takes many calories of food and fuel to extract them from the ecosystem. Berkley Pit. Butte, Montana.

We commonly say that gold is expensive because the supply is rare in comparison to demand. It is true that increased demand can dramatically effect the day-to-day price of gold, but over the long-term the price remains remarkably stable. The total supply of gold in the world actually dwarfs the demand.

There is plenty of gold out there, and yet few people are working to mine it. The reason for this is because the cost of gold is a direct reflection of the calories of food and fuel energy required to mine it. Gold is expensive because it requires many food and fuel calories to extract it from the ecosystem. Whole mountains must be torn down, ground into powder, and washed with cyanide to get out very small amounts of the precious metal. When we buy gold we trade tokens representing many calories of energy, which the mining industry uses to replace those expended in machinery and people. The price of gold may fluctuate dramatically at times, but that is only in the short-term. The long-term price of gold is a reflection of the average number of calories required to mine gold. An increase in the price of gold means mining companies get back many more calories than they expended extracting the gold. This causes more people to start mining, which increases the supply and brings the price back down. Conversely, a drop in demand causes the price of gold to drop, such that mining companies fail to return as many calories as they expend. This causes many of them to go out of business, which reduces supply and causes the price to level out again. Over the long-term, the price of gold stays fairly consistent with the average value of the calories involved in its production. Demand does not effect the long-term price; it only effects the number of people employed producing the supply.

Similarly, the price of wheat may fluctuate dramatically from one month or year to another, but through the long-term the price remains closely tied to the amount of energy expended to produce it. A drop in price means farmers do not receive as many calories as they put into the crop, and they either switch crops or go out of business, and vice versa when the price of wheat goes up. To break even the farmer has to recover from the market the calories expended growing the wheat. Farmers drop out of the business when the price dips below their break-even point, and they get back in when the price rises again. Thus, over the long-haul, the price of wheat remains pretty consistent with the average farmer's cost of producing it.

Prices become much more variable as commodities are refined into products, making them more "distant" from the ecosystem. A farmer cannot choose the price she gets paid per bushel of wheat, but the cereal company can, within reason, adjust the price of a box of cereal. So the farmer may consistently get only a few cents for the wheat that goes into the cereal, but the cereal company will adjust the price of its product up or down from say $2.00 to $3.00 or more, searching for the price that maximizes their profits.

Demand can be thought of as what we want, while the quantity demanded is how much of our wants that we will purchase at any given price. The quantity demanded drops each time the price goes up, and rises each time the price goes down. A business may find that they increase profits either by raising prices and selling fewer products, or by lowering prices and selling more. In 1996 the cereal industry discovered it had finally raised the price of cereals so high that too many people were finding substitutes, and industry profits were falling. The major cereal makers then dropped their prices by about 20% to recapture lost business. This process of finding the price that maximizes profits is called price searching.

The farther a product or service is removed from nature, the less its price is tied to the expended calories. The miner has no say over the price of gold, but the jeweler can, within reason, adjust the price of a gold ring. Likewise, a piece of paper is a pretty basic commodity made from wood pulp. One piece of paper is going to cost roughly the same as the next piece of paper, and yet, I can make up my own price, within reason, when I modify those pieces of paper into a book. It costs me from $2.00 to $6.00 to print a book, depending on how many copies I print. Distributors buy the books at a 55%+ discount off of the retail price. But I am the one who sets the retail price and determines the actual profit.

The farmer may consistently get only a few cents for the wheat that goes into a box of cereal, but the cereal company may adjust the price of its product up or down from say $2.00 to $3.00 or more.

This hypothetical **demand curve** shows that sales (quantity demanded) of cold cereals double each time the price per box drops by one dollar. For this example lets assume the cereal costs $2.00 per box to produce and market. The cereal company can maximize their profits ($18 million) by retailing at $3.50 per box. (Demand curves tend to be counter-intuitive because you would normally expect the curve to rise with additional sales.)

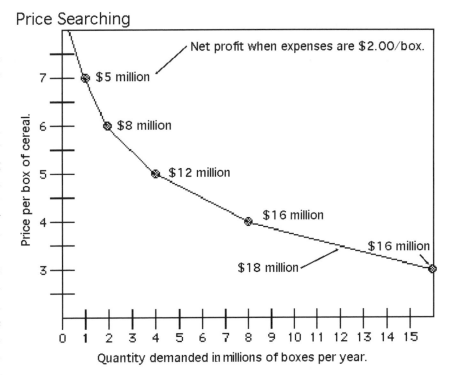

Price Searching

Net profit when expenses are $2.00/box.

Price per box of cereal.

Quantity demanded in millions of boxes per year.

Products and services that are less tangible and even farther removed from the ecosystem have prices that are even more variable. A carpet cleaning business is reasonably tangible because a certain amount of calories need to be expended to clean a carpet. Thus there is only a limited variability between the costs of hiring one carpet cleaner and the next. The services of a lawyer or a football player, however, are less tangible; neither produces, modifies, or services any kind of product. Both expend calories of effort, but neither converts those calories into products or services which we can physically measure. Therefore, the costs of their services tend to be much more variable. A lawyer might charge $50-$100 or more per hour, depending on the demand for their services. A good football player can negotiate for millions. Their jobs are based on unique personal skills so there is no tangible connection between the calories they expend and the incomes they take in.

It should be noted that demand raises prices. Tickets to a professional football game are expensive because we as a culture like the game and demand a lot of it. Our desire for a good game of football means the teams have to bid for the best players and pass the costs on to us. There is less demand for other sports, such as rugby or soccer, so tickets usually cost less, and the professionals are paid less.

Having read this you may think that the greatest opportunities lie in products and services that are far removed from nature. Especially, you might question, who would get into commodities if their value is always consistent with the cost of production? It seems that there is no profit in that. But take another look:

In basic products and services you may not have much control over the price, but you do have virtually guaranteed markets. You can be absolutely certain your wheat, gold, or paper will sell, just as you can be quite certain that someone will need to have their carpet cleaned. You do not need to control the market; you only need to control your expenses. You make your profit when you can produce your product with fewer calories expended than other people who are in the same business. When you deal in the basic services and commodities that everyone needs then you are in direct control over whether or not you make a profit. That is not the case with products and services that are further removed from the ecosystem.

Enterprises that are farther removed from nature may have the potential for fast money-making, but they also have a much greater risk factor. A writer can certainly produce a book, but there is no guarantee anyone will buy it. There are a few wealthy individuals who have made their fortunes with the pen, but statistically the average writer has a poverty-level income. Similarly, there are many rich football players, but not compared to the vast number of players who do not get paid at all. Enterprises that are removed from nature have all kinds of potential, but no guarantees.

All goods and services can be placed on a sort of continuum, based on their "closeness or distance" from nature. Some goods and services are closely linked to nature and can be measured directly in caloric terms. Success with those kinds of businesses lies in producing your products or services with fewer calories expended than what other people are doing. Other products and services are much more distant from nature, and success with those lies in making them desirable to people, so that they choose to spend their money at your offerings. Products and services that lay towards the middle of the continuum, as most do, require some of both. You need to provide goods and services which people want, and you need to keep your expenses, and hence your prices, down to levels that consumers consider reasonable.

"How many a poor immortal soul have I met well-nigh crushed and smothered under its load, creeping down the road of life, pushing before it a barn seventy-five feet by forty, its Augean stables never cleansed, and one hundred acres of land, tillage, mowing, pasture, and wood-lot!"

—*Henry David Thoreau, Walden*

1-5
Wealth & Work
-A Ten Thousand Year Old Pattern-

When we think back to our ancestry in the stone-age we sometimes pity them; we pity the poor people who had it so rough that they had to work their every living moment just to find enough food to keep them alive. But ironically, our ancestors typically worked much less than we do today. They had less work, less stress and less depression. Indeed, it is sometimes said that you could hear the laughter of a native village from two miles away!

Anthropologists have documented that cultural advancements usually result in people working more, not less. For example, studies in the 1960's of the !Kung people, a hunter-gatherer society in Africa, showed that they worked roughly half as much as people in industrialized societies. The !Kung worked only about twenty hours per week, or three hours per day, for their subsistence. Their other chores, such as building shelters, making tools and cooking, added up to another twenty-some hours per week for a total of 40+ hours per week. By contrast, those of us in industrial cultures work about 40 hours per week at a job and 40 hours more at home and after work (commuting, shopping, cooking, washing, cleaning, fixing), for a total of roughly 80 hours per week[49].

The Shoshone Indians, once a hunter-gatherer culture in the Great Basin Desert, had a life-style that was probably similar to that of the !Kung people. Observers from our own culture in the 1800's often called the Shoshone

A hunter-gatherer typically harvests only two or three calories of food for every calorie expended.

lazy because they never seemed to work. They were not lazy; they just did not need to work. They carried everything they owned right on their backs, and it did not take them long to manufacture such a small quantity of material goods. Their life-style simply did not require them to work all the time[28].

Understanding these relationships between material goods or "wealth" and the work it takes to produce it is crucial to the effort of gardening the economic ecosystem to produce a life of health and abundance, both for ourselves and for the planet.

Do not be mistaken into thinking that hunting and gathering is an efficient way to earn a living. I know from firsthand experience because I've spent a large part of my life learning and teaching stone-age living skills. A hunter-gatherer typically harvests only two or three calories of food for every calorie expended. By contrast a farmer with an ox and plow can grow and harvest about thirty-three calories for each calorie expended. A modern American farmer can produce 300+ calories of food for each calorie of body energy expended. This might be easiest to think of as plates of food. For every plate of food consumed, the hunter-gatherer harvests 2-3 new plates full, the ox and plow farmer harvests 33 plates full and the industrial farmer harvests 300 plates full[28]. Granted, industrial farming consumes vast quantities of fossil fuels to produce those 300 plates full of food, and that is an important subject we will return to. The purpose for now is to understand that with the aid of technology and energy we've been able to greatly increase the level of production per person.

Ultimately, the people of a hunter-gatherer society work less only because they produce less material wealth than people of other cultures. To understand this better, consider the wild animals. Think about deer, or birds, or coyotes, for instance. Have you ever seen or heard of an animal dying from hypertension, or getting ulcers from work stress? Probably not. You might see them forage intensively for a few hours, or they might nibble away all day, but rarely do you see them foraging frantically just to stay alive. They spend much of their time wandering, playing, or basically just "hanging around". There is a certain efficiency to a life-style where, for the most part, the only job you ever have to do is to eat. Life was probably pretty casual for our ancestors before they learned to make tools.

The evolution of tools made our species more efficient, but it also meant we had to work more. As animals, all we had to do was eat, but with the arrival of the stone-age we also had to make tools, shelters, clothing, jewelry, dishes and gather firewood. The evolution of tools meant that we could spend less time actually foraging, but it meant that we spend more time dealing with all the new chores. Still, on the whole, work was not too demanding. With the continuing evolution of culture, however, we found ever more and more work to do. The evolution of farming gave us a new level of prosperity, but it also gave us more work. When we started living in one place we began building fancier, more permanent shelters, complete with furnishings. We started living in bigger groups, and we found a need for some form of government, such as a spiritual leader, to maintain the stability of the community. That meant that those of us who farmed had to contribute a share of the food we harvested as a sort of tax to feed this non-farming person. Originally we only had to harvest enough food for ourselves, but with the advancement of culture we suddenly had to harvest additional calories of food for other people, from leadership, to toolmakers to artists.

Imagine being a tailor, one of several within a simple economy. You custom-cut and hand-stitch garments to exchange for your food, shelter, and other needs. Like other local tailors, it takes you a week to make an outfit for one customer, so your total annual production is 52 complete outfits per year. Therefore, those 52 outfits are equal in value to everything that you trade for and consume within the year. But then you get this idea, "What if I could make a device to assist with the sewing, so that I could produce more garments in less time. Then I could sell more garments and make more money, or I could take extra time off to hike in the woods."

So, after completing each day's tailoring work, you tinker with gadgets until at last you have built a simple sewing machine. Soon you are producing three outfits per week, or 156 garments per year, and your customers are still paying what they used to. For awhile you are the richest person in town. You spend a little less time working and more time playing and shopping. But then two things happen to burst your bubble.

First, with the extra garments on the market, not all the outfits are being sold. But it cost you less to produce them anyway, so you lower the price a little bit, knowing that you can still make a fantastic profit. However, the other tailors have meanwhile noticed both your spendthrift ways and your lower prices. In order to stay competitive they also invent sewing machines, so that each tailor is now producing 156 outfits per year. But with so many garments on the market, the value has to fall. In the end you are producing more clothing, but making less profit per unit. That's good news for your customers, who previously could afford to own only two outfits at a time. Now they can afford three outfits, so consumption increases.

However, even with increased consumption, there are still too many garments on the market. A price war ensues until none of the tailors are making a profit at all. Finally, one of your competitors drops out of the business completely and finds a new line of work. That reduces the number of garments in production, allowing prices to rise somewhat, although never as high as before. Ultimately you are making the same income that you were before inventing the sewing machine, but now you have to produce 156 garments per year instead of 52!

Producing those extra garments isn't any more work than before, just a bit more complicated. You used to sit out on the front porch stitching away all day long, but that isn't an option any more. With the increased throughput you need to stay focused on the sewing machine, operating and maintaining it, plus you need to order more material and make more space for it. If the sewing machine breaks or the wrong kind of material arrives then you've got added stress, because you have to keep production up to make a living.

Despite increasing production and making the same income as before, you are still much better off. Because while you were increasing your production capabilities, so was the butcher, the baker, and the candlestick maker. Each of their industries experienced the same ups and downs as yours so that production increased, prices plummeted, and some of the competitors were forced out-of-business to seek other forms of work. Given the lower prices you are able to buy more meat and bread and candlesticks for your family, so you are ultimately producing more wealth and getting more wealth in return, even while your income is unchanged. You even have a little extra money to donate to a neighbor who is struggling. The accompanying graph illustrates the increasing wealth and decreasing costs in primitive and increasingly advanced economies.

Increasing Wealth & Decreasing Costs

Advanced economies increase personal wealth and decrease the cost of basic goods, but the added wealth is spent on new cultural elements that did not exist in more primitive economies. Some new expenses are inevitable, such as higher taxes to maintain social order in a more complex society or the cost of paying for clean water or clean air, which the enviornment formerly provided for free. But there is still plenty of surplus wealth to spend on new frills like bigger houses, cars, telephones, junk food, or virtual reality entertainment centers, which were not a choice in more primitive economies. The irony is that despite more wealth, people in ad-

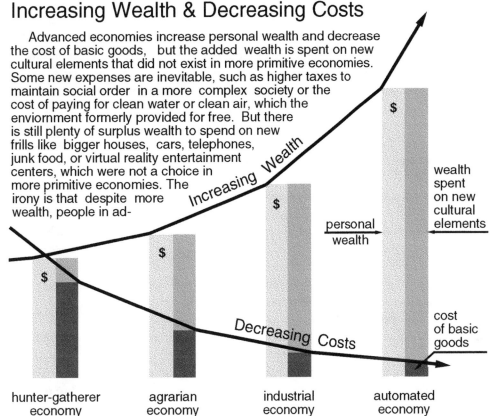

vanced economies often feel more impoverished. There is a larger gap between what you have and what you could have, and a larger gap between the rich and the poor. In the most primitive economies nobody has anything anyway, so there is nothing to miss! The most important point to keep in mind may be that in an advanced economy you have more wealth and more choice, and therefore, more control over your own destiny!

But what about all those workers who were forced out of tailoring, meat processing, baking, and candlestick making? They are not needed in any of the traditional roles, so they ultimately create new niches in the marketplace. One starts a laundry service to help clean all those extra garments, and one becomes a carpenter to build closets to hold the extra clothes. Another invents the oil lamp and sells both the lamps and the oil, so that you can stay up later into the evening, visiting in the parlor or reading a new book—written by someone who coincidentally used to be a candlestick maker.

The community could not have afforded such extravagance before, but now, with increased production and lower prices, everyone has a little extra wealth to spend in new ways. Soon there is a new standard, so that bigger houses, freshly laundered clothes, reading entertainment and oil lamps are no longer extravagances, but "necessities" everyone must work for.

On top of that, with the increased production and consumption, there are new waste problems to deal with as well. As a tailor, you once put any scraps of cloth on your garden for mulch between the rows. But now you produce more waste than you can use, so it has to be hauled away at an extra expense. A service that was once handled for free by the environment is now an expense. Besides, with the cost of produce falling like everything else, it makes more economic sense to sew more garments and trade for your veggies than to grow them yourself, so you let the garden go by the wayside.

Ultimately you are significantly wealthier than before, but you are also working harder too. Nobody said you had to pay for oil lamps and oil or books and freshly laundered clothes, but you would feel deprived if you didn't, so you work a little harder to give your family all the good things that life has to offer. And then one day you get this idea, "What if I could make a better sewing machine, so that I could produce many more garments in less time.

Then I could sell more garments and make more money, or I could take extra time off to hike in the woods."

As you may sense from this story of the tailor, the simple act of streamlining production efficiency has unintended consequences that reverberate throughout the economic ecosystem, ultimately changing an opportunity to make more money into a new standard for production and consumption that must be maintained just to stay even with middle-class society. Several points from this story deserve further emphasis, including that increased production 1) forces people out of old jobs to find new niches, but also makes us wealthier, 2) gives us more products and more freedom to choose, but also makes us work more, 3) results in a greater surplus to share with "non-producing" individuals such as government officials, nonprofit organizations, or the poor, 4) suggests that we will witness still more changes in the future, except 5) that increased production also seems to require increased throughput of materials and energy, and therefore causes greater ecological impact.

1) Increased production forces people out of old jobs to find new niches, but also makes us wealthier. At the beginning of the 20th century America was a nation of farmers, with most families producing enough food for their own consumption, plus a small surplus for trade. But industrialization of agriculture has allowed fewer and fewer farmers to produce more and more food. At the dawn of the 21st century only 1% of our population is still employed in farming, producing the food supply for the rest of us. (This figure is somewhat skewed, since millions of other people are still employed processing the food supply, but even the combined total employed in farming and food processing is a mere fraction of what it was in 1900.)

The transition from a nation of farmers to a nation of non-farmers was inherently painful. Evolution of the economic ecosystem led to many new advancements in production efficiency. Old niches in the ecosystem were wiped out and new ones created. Nearly every decade of the past century brought an exodus of people abandoning the family farms for jobs in the city, to produce completely new goods and services. The death of the family farm was agonizing and demoralizing for every Mom and Pop and their children forced to sell their holdings to start over in this unknown new world. Change is scary in any form, especially when you are not in control of it. But if we had not changed then we would be living in something like a third-world country today.

Consider that in a developing country a farmer's entire assets may amount to ten cows. His annual surplus may consist of only five or six half-grown cows each year. Now, would you really be willing to trade a year of your hard work and effort for a year of his?

In our own country a rancher may raise a thousand cattle and produce an annual surplus of several hundred animals. Every crash in the cattle market from overproduction and under-consumption leads to the tragic death of still more family farms and consolidation into ever larger farms and ranches. Individuals hang on precariously as long as they can, until a drought or some other natural disaster finishes off their operation. But this painful process also means that the remaining ranchers will produce a greater surplus for exchange. Your wages will buy more beef than ever, and the latest ranchers to lose their lands will become employed producing new goods and services. Industrialized farming may mean that 1% of the population has to produce enough food for themselves and the other 99% of the country, but it also means that 99% of the population is working to produce goods and services for farmers!

For example, videos did not exist before the 1970's, but today there are millions of people employed in the business to manufacture, distribute, lease, and sell VCR's, videos, and camcorders, and their next generation kin, the DVD's. What were all these millions of people doing before these technologies were invented? It is hard to say specifically, but many of them would have been farmers if it weren't for farm consolidations. Increasing farm production allowed videos and many other new goods and services to enter the marketplace, giving us all access to small luxuries that our ancestors never had.

2) Increased production gives us more products and more freedom to choose, but also makes us work more. Some people talk about reducing the work week from five days down to four. They look around at the technology that allows us to produce wealth so easily, and it seems as though we are near the point where we will be able to shorten the work week. But the reality is that we have more expenses and more possessions than ever before. We talk about working less, but the truth is that more and more Americans are working longer, taking on second or third jobs just to "survive".

For young adults it is especially difficult, because they want and expect everything they had in their parents house, and they want it now. They are thrilled to get a job and start making payments on a car, a stereo system, and rent for an apartment. Pretty soon they are spending more money than they earn, yet they have little to show for it except an endless stream of bills. The decision whether to work or not is free choice, but people like all the stuff our culture produces, and they willingly sell their souls to employment to pay for it. It is only after the bill arrives that they feel buyer's-remorse, caught in a trap of forever walking the treadmill of work. Mostly I think that people don't realize they have a choice, since they've never imagined anything else. For example, many people drink soda pop every day of their lives, although our ancestors certainly never had that luxury. The minimally "health conscious" might purchase diet sodas to avoid weight gain. Now, a diet soda is supposed to be a good buy because there is only one calorie per can. However, human beings need about 2,500 calories per day for sustenance. Therefore, at 50¢ per can it would cost $1,250 per day to live on diet sodas. Clearly there is no economic incentive to buy diet sodas, but people buy items like that every day and wonder why their broke!

One of the problems with increased production efficiency is that a smaller and smaller segment of the population is left providing for all the basic survival needs of the culture, such as food, water, clothing and shelter. When we indulge in a night of video rentals and soda pop we are in effect agreeing to work harder to provide for the people employed providing those goods and services. They are no longer providing their own food, water, clothing, and shelter, but we agree to do it for them in exchange for the luxury of a movie theater in our homes. The exciting thing is that there is no law that says we have to spend our hard-earned money that way. Each of us is completely in control over our decisions to spend or not to spend, to work or not to work. As you will see later in the book, there are many opportunities in life that you may have never considered.

3) Increased production results in a greater surplus to share with "non-producing" individuals such as government officials, nonprofit organizations, or the poor. Video rentals or soda pop are hardly essential goods and services, but increased production results in an income surplus to spend, so we do, thereby providing people in those occupations with all that they need. Similarly, think about how many people work for the city, county, state, or federal government. Each government employee may provide a valuable service to the public, but the rest of us have to work to cover their basic needs. Still, we are all a little richer with increases in production efficiency, so we can afford to pay higher taxes, some of which will be transferred to the poor, and we can afford to donate to environmental or social causes.

Greater production efficiency means there is more wealth to spread around, but it also means there is more demand for a share of the handouts. With every increase in efficiency there is a greater potential for some individuals to make much more income than other individuals, as opposed to more primitive economies where nobody has anything anyway. Giving money to the poor helps to close the gap a little bit, so that the poor are wealthy compared to our ancestors, even though they may be poor compared to mainstream society. Already we channel about 40% of our tax dollars directly from those who have money to those who do not, through programs like welfare, social security or medicaid. Individuals make additional contributions to social and environmental causes every day.

Nonprofit groups are gradually learning to capitalize on the available and abundant surplus to support their programs in big ways. For example, some non-profits have linked up with credit card companies to receive a small percentage of all sales when people use their card, or they have linked up with stores on the internet to get a percentage of sales for all the customers who pass through their gateway. With dramatic new increases in production efficiency just around the corner, we may soon see nonprofit social and environmental organizations with multibillion dollar budgets. Unfortunately, all that money won't be enough to close the growing gap between the have's and the have-not's.

4) Increased production suggests that we will witness still more changes in the future. As we move into the 21st century we are transitioning from an industrial economy where people use machines to produce material wealth to an automated economy where computers use machines to produce material wealth. Many people would say that the booming economy and soaring stock market which started in the 1990's was the result of free-trade and the subsequent corporate exploitation of low-cost labor in China and other parts of the world. While free-trade is certainly a contributing factor, I suspect that the primary cause of the economic surge is due to increased automation.

A large portion of our trade with China and other countries with low-paid workers involves trinkets for kids meals at fast food joints and other disposable toys. Most of these items are in the garbage can within a few days of purchase. That kind of trade does not increase our wealth, but only decreases it. The main cause of the economic surge is likely from increased production due to newer and better computers.

Computers were in use before 1990, but they were expensive and didn't do very much. New computers and computer networking, especially the internet, has led to many increases in production. An obvious example is Amazon, which offers customers many more books in one store. Customers do the work of placing orders via their own computers, while Amazon's computers do the work of automatically monitoring inventory, ordering books, paying bills and routing the customer orders to the right bins in the right warehouse. Amazon sells more books with less labor, so they are able to offer discount prices on many books that you would not get through traditional booksellers.

What we will see in the coming decades is increased automation in every sector of the economy. Already there are printing services that can keep an author's books in storage on a computer and print only as many copies as are ordered. If only one copy is sold today, then only one copy is printed. Soon we may see businesses like Amazon where paper and ink is delivered and put in place, but otherwise computers do everything from taking the order to printing, packing, and dropping it in a bin for the post office. There will also be many more electronic books where computers handle every part of the transaction without human involvement. What will these kind of technologies mean for the world we live in?

Just imagine if you were a tailor and you had a computerized factory where customers picked the styles they wanted via the internet, then typed in their measurements. Computers would custom cut, sew, pack, and mail every garment without human hands. Computers would handle all the billing and ordering—maybe even the returns. There would be work to maintain the equipment and put the rolls of fabric in place, but even those jobs have the potential for automation. Instead of hand-stitching 52 complete outfits in a year, you might push the "on" button and stitch 52,000 in a day. We are already millionaires compared to our ancestors, but in the decades to come we will be millionaires again, compared to where we are now. But can this cycle keep going forever? When do we have enough?

If trends continued into the future as they have in the past, then we would expect middle class families to own at least "one space shuttle per family" in future decades. With production costs falling and wealth therefore rising, it would be the affordable family sedan—even if it still cost 1,000 times the price of a car.

Many individuals are finally saying "enough" and deciding that it would be better to slow down productivity a little bit, for example, by sending more farmers back to the land to tend small, organically grown plots. People are also realizing that they have the freedom to do something besides work and spend, so they are making new choices.

Yet the vast majority is still enamored with increasing wealth and disposable life-styles. For example, with a booming economy more middle class Americans are buying gas-guzzling SUV's and even motor boats, which once belonged only to the "rich". But is this endless pursuit of growth and material goods sustainable?

5) Increased production also seems to require increased throughput of materials and energy, and therefore causes greater ecological impact. There are advantages and disadvantages to every type of economy, simple or advanced. The hunter-gatherer economy is the most simple economic structure. It doesn't produce much material wealth, but it doesn't require much work from the people either. The land provides food, water, and fuel free for the taking, so there isn't that much work to do, and waste management is a simple as moving to a new site when the old one is a mess. As long as the population remains within the carrying capacity of the land, then the system is completely sustainable.

An agrarian economy is a slightly more advanced economic system. It provides more food from the same land base to support a larger population. Production and specialization of labor increases, and those who are not needed for farming are available to provide new goods and services that were not practical in a hunter-gatherer economy. Some new goods and services are required, such as mining for iron and forging it into plowing implements, while others are new luxuries, such as larger musical instruments that hunter-gatherer peoples could not possibly carry with them. Overall, the agrarian economy increases wealth, but leads to new problems.

One problem is that increased production requires additional inputs of resources and energy and leads to more waste and pollution. The level of environmental disturbance is much greater than in a hunter-gatherer economy, and some of the goods and services that were formerly provided for free from the environment now require human labor to provide. For example, tilling the land to plant a crop displaces the wild foods that were formerly free for the taking. Surface water that was formerly drinkable may become polluted from people and animal waste, necessitating a well. Wastes that were formerly recycled where they lay now have to be hauled away.

An industrial economy leads to similar increases in production and personal wealth, but also requires a much greater throughput of resources and energy. Like the agrarian economy, the industrial economy requires more resources and higher-quality resources, such as more refined metals. The level of environmental disturbance increases greatly, and society has to take on additional roles that were once provided for free by nature. For example, an agrarian economy may disturb some land in logging and mining, but given enough time the environment recovers on its own. An industrial economy, however, disturbs so much land that reclamation work and tree planting is required, adding more work for people. Waste management, which was once a matter of dumping garbage in the nearest ravine, takes on new complications when dealing with toxic compounds that leach back into the food and water supply. Contaminated ground and surface waters require sophisticated treatment systems to clean the water both before and after use.

Given that advanced economies require so much throughput, it may seem that creating a sustainable modern economy is simply impossible, that the fate of the planet is sealed. However, there is more to it than that. In order to get a fresh perspective on how to make the world a better place, we must first come to terms with the industrial economy, that it is here to stay and it will continue to grow and consume. As strange as it seems it is possible to support an industrial economy without consuming the entire planet, as is laid out in the subsequent chapters.

In conclusion, there is no doubt that we are wealthier today than ever before. Life is relatively easy in the sense that we do not have to work very hard for anything. We only work harder because we are working for more than we ever did before—and that is a choice we have control over. The exciting part is that advanced economies provide more opportunities to choose how we spend our time and money, though few people realize it. In a hunter-gatherer society you have little choice to be anything but a hunter-gatherer. In more advanced, complex economies you have the freedom to choose what kind of work you want to do and even how much work you want to do. As you will see, it is even possible to have a prosperous life-style without damaging the world we love!

Part II
Principles of Economic Ecology

"The history of the woodlot is often, if not commonly, here a history of cross-purposes, of steady and consistent endeavor on the part of Nature, of interference and blundering with a glimmering of intelligence at the eleventh hour on the part of the proprietor. The latter often treats his woodlot as a certain Irishman I heard of drove a horse—that is, by standing before him and beating him in the face all the way across a field."

—Henry David Thoreau, *The Dispersion of Seeds*

2-1
Matter -& Energy
-Industrial Metabolism and the Laws of Thermodynamics-

Through the process of cellular metabolism all living organisms consume energy, modify resources from the environment and produce waste. That is an inescapable fact of life, and it is taking place in every cell of our bodies right now. Great quantities of energy and material resources from our food is consumed at the cellular level to build and maintain cells and to perform the tasks of muscle contraction, nerve conduction, and so forth. Carbon dioxide and other wastes from the metabolic process are eliminated via the lymph, vascular and digestive systems to be discharged into the environment.

Although metabolism is properly defined at the cellular level, for our purposes it may be addressed at the whole body level as well, since whole plants and whole animals also consume energy, modify resources and produce wastes. Plants harvest solar energy to split apart carbon dioxide and water, and the elements are recombined to make useful sugars. Oxygen and dead plant matter are waste products created and expelled in the process.

Humankind and all other animals consume plants (or other animals which have eaten plants) and split apart the sugars with the aid of oxygen to release useful energy. Carbon dioxide, manure, and the deceased are waste products from animals.

Given the elegance of the natural ecosystem, the wastes from one living being become useful resources to other living beings. Even dead plant and animal matter are useful resources, consumed by the microbes and ultimately discarded as the waste which becomes fertilizer for a new generation of plants.

As can be sensed here, matter is harvested, transformed and discarded in a never-ending cycle. This is the **Law of Conservation of Matter** at work, which states that matter is neither created nor destroyed, but can be converted in form. For instance, when you put a log on the fire, the wood may be completely consumed, but the matter is not. Energy is released from the wood as hydrocarbons are split apart in the presence of oxygen and recombined to form carbon dioxide and water vapor. The elements are still there, but they've been converted from a solid to a gaseous state. Other minerals are left behind in the form of ash. Ultimately, all will be re-assembled with the aid of new energy from the sun, by new plants to make new wood, which brings us to the **Law of Conservation of Energy**, also known as the **First Law of Thermodynamics**.

According to the First Law Of Thermodynamics energy can be converted in form, but is neither created nor destroyed. This means that the quantity of energy remains constant, but the quality can be altered. For example, plants harvest diffuse or low-grade energy (sunlight) and concentrate it into very dense or high-grade energy like wood, which may be further concentrated through heat and pressure to make oil fuels. Burning the wood or oil fuels transforms the concentrated energy back into a diffuse form, dispersing it as heat. The quantity is the same, but the quality has changed.

It is important to note, however, that while low-grade energy can be concentrated to make high-grade energy, it takes energy to make this transformation, which brings us to the **Second Law Of Thermodynamics**, also known as **entropy**.

The second law states that energy is always being degraded to less useful forms towards a state of equilibrium

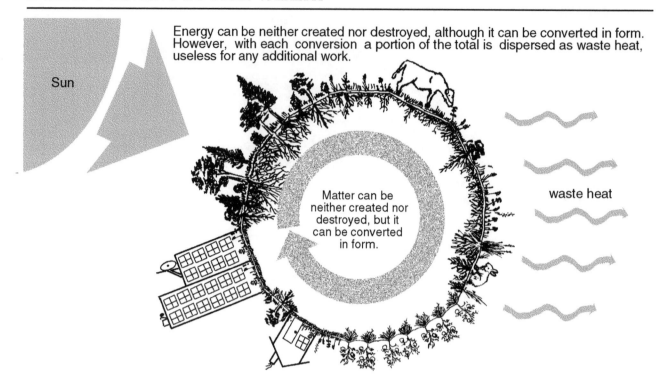

Energy can be neither created nor destroyed, although it can be converted in form. However, with each conversion a portion of the total is dispersed as waste heat, useless for any additional work.

Sun

Matter can be neither created nor destroyed, but it can be converted in form.

waste heat

The natural ecosystem functions as a closed-loop where all matter is recycled.

The sun's energy is captured by plants and used to metabolize raw matter into living tissues like algae, grasses, and trees. Animals eat the plants, metabolizing the stored energy and matter to make new living tissues like rabbits, cows, and people. All material waste is recycled again and again, so that the only true waste is diffuse heat, useless for any additional work. Our stone age ancestors lived exclusively within this natural cycle.

With the aid of technology our species learned to metabolize additional energy and resources, both living and non-living, into creative new forms, but at a rate much faster than the rest of the natural ecosystem can keep up. We are literally consuming the entire living planet.

where no further work can be accomplished. As energy is converted from one form to another a portion of the total is dispersed as useless heat. For example, energy in the form of coal can be burned to boil water to produce steam to generate higher-quality energy in the form of electricity. However, two-thirds of the energy potential is lost as waste heat in the process. That's why it is so expensive to heat your home with electricity. You burn three times as much coal by converting it first to electricity than you would if you burned the coal right in your home!

Life seems to buck the second law of thermodynamics by concentrating energy to create and maintain disequilibrium. Our living tissues are composed of complex molecules that should degrade into simpler forms, but we depend on food energy to maintain our complex forms. It is only when we die and stop using energy that we lose form and our bodies degrade towards equilibrium with the environment. The atmosphere of our planet is similarly an unlikely composition of highly reactive molecules that should break down into simpler forms. Without life on earth, the planet would become hot, waterless and would lose its oxygen atmosphere. Life never escapes the second law because it requires a constant influx of new energy from the sun to maintain the disequilibrium. Diffuse waste heat is steadily radiated back into cold space to keep the planet from overheating.

Environmental economics is a relatively new field of study which attempts to evaluate the true ecological costs of economic activities. Although the term "economic ecosystem" hasn't yet become part of the academic lingo, many similar ideas have, such as "industrial metabolism".

Industrial metabolism[59] simply acknowledges the basic facts of life, that all organisms, including man-made ones, consume energy, modify resources from the environment and create waste.

As illustrated here, producing the **final goods and services** we want as consumers involves the production of many **intermediate goods and services**. Each step in the metabolic process requires inputs of material goods and energy and results in outputs of material waste and low-grade heat, plus the goods or services that were the purpose of production.

For example, the process of pouring a concrete sidewalk in front of your house begins far away with big machines ripping limestone or chalk and clay or shale from the earth. Inputs of energy and material goods in the form of gasoline and equipment are used to extract the **natural resources** from the field. In the process the low-grade heat left over from the gasoline is discharged into the environment, along with material wastes such as low-grade rock, plastic oil jugs, exhaust (carbon dioxide, etc.) and worn-out equipment.

The next step in the process is to separate the **raw materials** into the pure materials calcium, alumina, silica and others, which requires new inputs of material goods and energy and results in new outputs of low-grade heat and material waste.

The **pure materials** are then mixed to make compound materials, especially tricalcium silicate, dicalcium silicate and tricalcium aluminate. The mixing process requires new inputs of material goods and energy and results in new outputs of low-grade heat and material waste.

Then the **compound materials** are formed into "parts", in this case by mixing the compounds in the right proportions to make cement powder. This requires more inputs and results in more waste.

At last the **parts** are assembled into products, in this case by mixing cement, lime, sand, gravel and water to make concrete which is poured in place and troweled smooth. New energy and material goods are used in the process, leading to the discharge of additional low-grade heat and material wastes, such as cement bags, exhaust from the cement truck, lumber from framing the sidewalk, etc.

Eventually you get to use the final **product**, in this case a sidewalk, at least until the elements crack it apart into useless **refuse**. In the end you will use further inputs of energy and material

Industrial Metabolism
(based on E. Ravenswaay)

Every step in the production process requires inputs of energy and material resources and results in outputs of low-grade heat and material waste.

goods to jackhammer the old sidewalk out and dispose of it to clear the space for a new one. The model of industrial metabolism applies to all other products too, from loaves of bread to automobiles, although simple products may shortcut some of the steps illustrated here.

The key difference between industrial metabolism and nature's version is that industry produces many complex wastes for which we have not yet found ways of recycling back into new and useful products. Living organisms have had hundreds of millions of years to adapt to each other, to occupy niches in the ecosystem, so that the waste of any one species becomes a valuable resource to another. In effect, the only true waste produced by the natural ecosystem is low-grade heat, too diffuse to use for any further work.

The classic case of industry mimicking the natural ecosystem, called "**industrial ecology**" is Kalundborg Park in Denmark[3]. It is considered an eco-industrial park because the wastes from some firms become the inputs to other firms. A series of materials and energy exchanges spontaneously developed over a twenty year period between neighboring industries, farm, and the local community. The exchanges were economically driven as each company sought ways to generate income from materials that were formerly considered "wastes". Recognition of the environmental benefits of these exchanges came later.

The industrial partnership includes a 1500 megawatt coal-fired power plant and an oil refinery, both of

DIRECT POINTING TO REAL WEALTH

which are the largest in Denmark, plus a major plasterboard (sheetrock) manufacturer, a biotechnology company, the city of Kalundborg, and many smaller businesses and homes.

The power plant operates at about 40% efficiency, so sixty percent of the fuel potential in the coal is waste heat. The waste heat was formerly discharged through the smokestack, but today it is piped as steam to nearby businesses and 3,500 homes as a heat source, displacing the polluting oil-fired burners that residents and businesses once depended on. The power plant uses salt water for some of its cooling needs, sparing the fresh water lake nearby. A portion of the hot salt water discharged from the plant is used in a series of 57 fish ponds in a commercial fish farm.

The power plant uses calcium carbonate in a reaction to pull sulfur dioxide out of the smoke stacks, thereby producing two-thirds of the calcium sulfate (gypsum) used at the plasterboard plant. The remaining desulfurized fly-ash from the power plant is used at a nearby cement plant.

The adjacent refinery burned a continuous flare of waste gases until the plasterboard company identified it as a potential source of low-cost fuel. Excess gas from the plant is now used at both the plasterboard company and as a substitute fuel to generate electricity at the power plant. Desulfurization of fuels at the refinery results in pure liquid sulfur, which is trucked to a sulfuric acid producer.

The biotechnology plant produces industrial enzymes and more than 40% of the world's supply of insulin. Sludge from the biotech plant and the fish farms is spread on local farm fields. Surplus yeast from insulin production goes to farmers as pig food.

The Kalundborg industrial park demonstrates the economic and environmental benefits of "closing the loop" so that the wastes of one enterprise become valuable inputs to another. The web of exchanges helps to conserve water, energy, and other material resources while reducing pollution and generating new revenues—or at least reducing the costs of waste management for those involved. Competition and the growing costs of waste disposal will require that more and more industries form these kind of partnerships to stay competitive.

Unfortunately, creating a complex and efficiently inter-linked ecosystem takes some time. The economic ecosystem has a long ways to go to match the elegance of the natural ecosystem. Industry still produces copious amounts of pollution, dumping into the environment all waste that isn't being properly used.

The economic ecosystem will reach maturity only when we close the loop on resource extraction and waste production so that all material wastes become useful to other enterprises or to the natural ecosystem, and the only waste ultimately produced is low-grade, useless heat. Low-grade heat is the only real waste produced by the natural ecosystem, and that is the model we must follow.

Since matter can be neither created nor destroyed according to the Law of Conservation of Matter, then we are limited to the resources available on this planet, plus what ever can be imported from off-world in the future—*but there is no limit to how many times we can reuse these resources*, at least in principle. Therefore, the true limitation is not a lack of resources, but the inability to "close the loop" to effectively recycle them.

Recycling **organic wastes** like lumber scraps requires returning the matter to the earth and waiting for the natural ecosystem to transform

"The economic ecosystem will reach maturity only when we close the loop on resource extraction and waste production so that all material wastes become useful to other enterprises or to the natural ecosystem, and the only waste ultimately produced is low-grade, useless heat. Low-grade heat is the only waste produced by the natural ecosystem, and that is the model we must follow."

it back into a harvestable resource. Unfortunately, the economic ecosystem has a much faster metabolism than nature, so the earth cannot renew organic resources at nearly the rate we are consuming them. Already we appropriate roughly 40% of the world's biomass to cover human needs[60], far more than any other species on the planet, yet billions of people still live in relative poverty, wanting far more than they have. The world population is expected to nearly double again before finally leveling off at around 10 or 11 billion people later this century. Therefore, if trends continue, we can expect that at least 80% of the world's biomass will be diverted to meet human needs. If we try to give every person in the world the same life-style we have in the industrial world then there will not be a single plant or animal left on the planet that is not being raised for human use. In other words, we are slicing up a pie of limited size.

On the other hand, recycling **inorganic wastes** such as aluminum or scrap iron requires little more than melting it down and reforming it. An aluminum can, for example, makes a complete life-cycle from the grocery store to the consumer, through the recycling sytem and back to the grocery story within a few months at most. A small amount of material is lost with contaminants each time around, but newer technologies keep improving the recovery rate. When nonpolluting energies like hydroelectric power are used in the process then aluminum and scrap-metal recycling very nearly fits the model of a perfect economy already, where the only waste produced is low-grade heat.

In essence, a sustainable economy can be defined as one that recycles all material wastes, either through the natural ecosystem or through the industrial ecosystem, so that the only true waste produced is low-grade heat, to diffuse for any additional work. Presumeably this economy would operate exclusively on renewable fuels, but fossil fuels might also be used—if the carbon and all other pollutants were removed or properly sequestered by the environment.

In other words, if we reduce the use of organic resources to levels the ecosystem can sustain and switch to inorganic resources for everything else—using nonpolluting fuels to process them—then we can recycle everything again and again without consuming the planet. That is the ultimate goal we must work towards.

> *"...if we reduce the use of organic resources to levels the ecosystem can sustain and switch to inorganic resources for everything else—using non-polluting fuels to process them—then we can recycle everything again and again without consuming the planet. That is the ultimate goal we must work towards."*

To understand this better, just imagine an colony on the moon or mars completely detached from the living ecosytem on earth. Without the natural ecosystem to recycle wastes, it must be done by industry. By necessity, the economy becomes a closed-loop system, where essentially material wastes are recycled and the only waste produced is low grade heat, too diffuse for any additional work. The economy on earth will probably always remain a hybrid, recycling some wastes through the organic ecosystem and all other wastes through the industrial ecosystem.

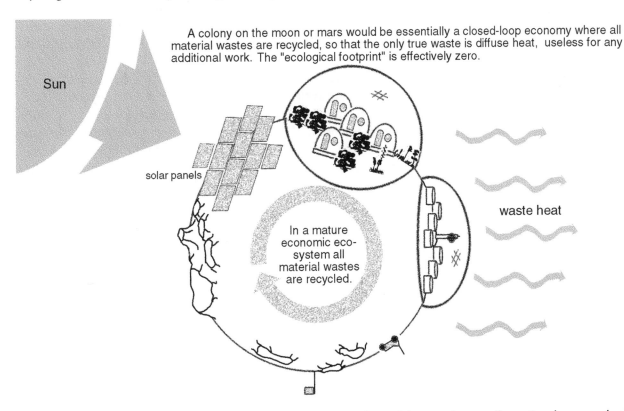

A colony on the moon or mars would be essentially a closed-loop economy where all material wastes are recycled, so that the only true waste is diffuse heat, useless for any additional work. The "ecological footprint" is effectively zero.

Sun

solar panels

In a mature economic eco-system all material wastes are recycled.

waste heat

A mature economic ecosystem functions as a closed-loop where all matter is recycled.

On planet earth we are developing a hybrid closed-loop economy, where some material wastes are recycled in nature and all other waste is recycled through industry. We are depending less and less on the natural ecosystem for waste management and more on the economic ecosystem.

The concept of a sustainable industrial economy is a simple one, but the much of the environmental movement hasn't yet been able to make the critical distinction between organic and inorganic resources. Yes it is true that we have already exceeded the maximum sustainable load of resource extraction and waste production that the environment can handle. Fisheries are crashing, forests are disappearing, soils are eroding, the climate is changing, and there is a hole in the ozone layer. The natural ecosystem processes are stressed to the point of failure, so it seems logical that we need to reduce consumption and live simpler lives. That is the basis for research projects like "ecological footprinting".

Ecological footprinting[60] is a way of assessing the arable land area that would be required to sustain a group of people such as a family, a city, or a country. Just imagine placing a glass dome over your home to create your own personal biosphere. How many acres of arable land would you need to provide all the food, paper, lumber and other organic resources you need to sustain your life-style, plus how much land would you need to grow all your own fuel, or at least to sequester the carbon from fossil fuels? Conservatively speaking, the average American has an ecological footprint of 25 acres—that's how much productive land each one of us would need to support our current life-styles.

With a global population of six billion we are already occupying virtually every acre of arable, productive land on the planet, roughly 20.5 billion acres. That works out to a fair share of 5.5 acres per person now, and half that by the time the world population stabilizes later this century. At present we maintain our affluent life-style only be expropriating resources from other parts of the globe, in effect stealing other peoples fair slice of the pie. People in India survive on an ecological footprint of only about 1.9 acres per person, but most would prefer to have a whole lot more.

These kinds of statistics have spawned movements such as the Global Living Project, with the noble purpose of proving that it is possible to live modest life-styles with ecological footprints at or below our fair share of 5.5 acres per person, mostly by returning to the past to live by homesteading—raising one's own shelter, food and fuel resources in harmony with the natural ecosystem. Although these projects are well-intended, they are simply not going to convince the rest of civilization to drop everything and live as homesteaders—nor do they have to.

Ecological footprinting ignores the critical distinctions between organic and inorganic resources. Yes, our organic resources are over-harvested, but there are always substitutes, such as e-mail in place of paper, steel or concrete construction in place of lumber, superinsulation in place of combustion heating, and solar electricity in place of fossil fuels. Ecological footprinting acknowledges the living surface of the land while ignoring most of the inorganic resources below ground which may be used over and over again indefinitely.

In the past we expanded the resource pie *horizontally* over the surface of the earth, by mining the living ecosystem and transporting resources from places that had them to those that didn't. New technologies enable us to expand the resource pie *vertically*, up towards the sun for energy, and down into the ground for mineral resources, effectively reducing the net area of our ecological footprint. As you will see, it is very possible—and ultimately inevitable—to create a sustainable industrial world economy that produces essentially no wastes except low-grade heat. To understand this more fully we must dive into the good and the bad of the Law of Substitutes in the next chapter.

"If a man walk in the woods for love of them half of each day, he is in danger of being regarded as a loafer; but if he spends his whole day as a speculator, shearing off those woods and making earth bald before her time, he is esteemed an industrious and enterprising citizen. As if a town had no interest in its forests but to cut them down!"
—*Henry David Thoreau, Life Without Principle*

2-2

Substitutes for Everything
-The Good and Bad of Expanding the Resource Pie-

In 1798 Thomas Malthus[72], one of the founding fathers of economic study, published *An Essay on the Principle of Population*. Malthus looked about his native England and saw an island of limited size inhabited by an exploding population of mostly destitute people attempting to produce more and more food from a non-expanding resource base. Although it was possible to make incremental or linear improvements in agricultural production (1, 2, 3, 4, 5....) by working every scrap of land more intensely, there was no way to keep up with the exponentially growing population base (1, 2, 4, 8, 16....). In other words, the world was like a pie, and people competed against each other for slices of the pie. An individual could only become prosperous by taking other's shares of the pie. Famine, disease and war, he wrote, were the only ways to keep the population in balance with the food supply. It was after reading Malthus' essay that writer Thomas Carlyle described economics as "the dismal science", an epithet that sticks to this day.

England was spared from Malthus' predictions—at least temporarily—by technological improvements that led to further increases in agricultural productivity, and by expanding the resource base through conquest, colonization, and subsequently importing goods back home to the Mother land. Similar episodes have occurred throughout history, both before and after Malthus' time, to spare exploding populations from the cruel fate of the mass die-off that are inevitable when any species exceeds the carrying capacity of its resource base.

Despite an even larger population today, England and the rest of the industrialized world prospers with material abundance, partly due to increasingly efficient extraction technologies, but also due to the political and economic clout to expropriate resources from the impoverished regions of the world.

As we enter the 21st century it seems that we have expanded the resource pie for the last time. We have exposed every hidden corner of the world and maximized resource extraction to feed our insatiable appetites for material wealth. Now we are faced with the question: Did we ever really expand the resource pie, or did we just find ways to consume it more quickly, through highly efficient extraction and transportation technologies? Have we run out of resources to exploit, so that the ultimate fate is finally upon us? Will we soon experience the mass-die offs that were so clearly inevitable more than two hundred years ago?

The answer is both "yes" and "no". Yes, we have already exceeded the carrying capacity of the world, and the biological systems of the planet are stumbling through the initial stages of collapse, but no, we have not run out of resources to exploit. As the world's organic resources become increasingly scarce over the coming decades, we will simply substitute in more and more inorganic resources. The good and the bad news is that like colonists on the moon or mars, we will have little real dependence on what exists outside of the artificial world we are creating. The economic ecosystem will thrive even if the natural ecosystem is completely dysfunctional. Understanding how and why this strange and alien vision of the future will materialize is critical to the goal of saving as much of the natural world as possible. Good or bad, the future revolves around the Law of Substitutes.

Both economic and environmental theory are based on the idea that **all resources are scarce**. This includes material resources such as land, water, or food, but it also includes human labor, a resource of time and effort.

Because resources are scarce, they must be rationed.

In the developed world we usually ration scarce goods according to the willingness to pay money. For example, crab meat is scarce and only available to those who want it enough to willingly give up their money for it. There are other ways to ration scarce resources, such as group consensus, central planning, or alternative inducements. Athletic awards, for instance, are rationed according to physical abilities.

Supply and demand is the process of allocating scarce resources in a monetary society. Demand can be thought of as what we want, while the quantity demanded is how much of our wants that we will purchase at any given price. The **law of demand** states that there is a negative relationship between the amount of anything that people will purchase and the price they must pay. This means that less will be purchased at higher prices. More will be purchased at lower prices. For instance, we may want to purchase dozens of different CD's from our favorite musicians, but the actual quantity we demand is dependent on cost. How many CD's would you buy at $100 a piece? How many would you purchase at $20? How about at 25 cents each?

Fortunately, for every scarce resource there are always substitutes. Consider the alternatives to buying CD's: you could buy records or tapes, or you could listen to the radio, sing to yourself, listen to the sounds of nature, or seek a completely different type of entertainment like rock-climbing. You will find more and more substitutes as the cost of a particular item rises. If CD's cost $100 a piece, then most of us would still favor the alternatives.

There are always substitutes.

Based on the **law of substitutes** we know that as organic resources become increasingly scarce and therefore more expensive, inorganic substitutes will become comparatively more economical choices. For example, wood houses are already on the decline proportionally as metal framing, concrete, and composite materials are chosen as substitutes. Wood itself is being replaced, or altered and enhanced, by resins, so that we are using less wood and more glue. This "manufactured wood" is an intermediate substitute that saves good lumber by reprocessing wood scrap into useable pieces. It is not practical for every human being in the world to have a wood frame house since resources are scarce, but it is possible for every human being to have a nice house, because there are good substitutes for traditional lumber.

Today we manufacture cars and most of our other gadgets with everything but living resources. A walk through any Walmart or Home Depot will reveal surprisingly few biologically derived products, but many composites of minerals, metals, and oil resins. We are becoming increasingly independent from the biological cycles of nature as we rely more on minerals to meet our living needs.

Extracting mineral resources still disrupts the natural ecosystem, but usually less so than extracting organic resources. A tree covered hill, for instance, may provide enough lumber to build a few hundred homes, but if the hill is composed of limestone then it can provide enough concrete to build thousands of homes. If we disregard the fossil fuel input for the moment, then the net ecological footprint of a concrete house is far smaller than the ecological footprint of a wood-frame house. With proper care in mining, the quarry can afterwards be reclaimed to become biologically productive once again. But what about all that fossil fuel input?

As fossil fuels become more expensive, either through scarcity, or more likely through environmental taxes, then clean energy resources like solar will become the least-cost choices. Note that the environmental movement was born in the '60's and '70's when it seemed imminent that we would exhaust our non-renewable energy resources before the turn of the millennium. According to expert forecasts back then, we should be nearly or completely out of both oil and natural gas by now. The obvious choice, and the rallying cry of the environmental movement since then is that we need to return to the land and grow our own food and fuel in tune with the cycles of nature.

Ironically the use of biofuels is hardly sustainable in many parts of the world. Many developing countries are stripping their lands for burnable fuels, both for firewood and animal dung. This organic matter is needed to build the structure of the soil, enhancing its fertility and water-holding capabilities. Burning every available bit of firewood and dung reduces these vital organic resources to inorganic ash. Excessive reliance on these biofuels short-circuits the cycles of nature, leading to depletion of the soils.

This environmental crisis is gradually being amended by substituting direct solar technologies for organic fuels For example, a number of efforts are being made to donate solar cookers to people in developing countries. The solar cookers are typically simple, often made with mere cardboard, aluminum foil, and glass. These and other solar technologies are typically lumped together with the organic biofuels as "renewables", but this combined categorization is misleading. Direct solar technologies harness the sun's energy independently from the organic ecosystem. This expands the resource pie beyond what the living fuels can provide and allows the organic resources to be recycled into the soil where they are really needed. Likewise, photovoltaic technology is enabling developing countries to expand their energy supplies beyond the limitations of the organic ecosystem. The cost of solar power is so low today that it is often the most economical source of power they can get. It is simply cheaper to put a solar panel on each roof than to construct a multi-million dollar power plant with transmission lines to every home.

Solar power would be cheaper for us too, if we did not already have the utility infrastructure in place. In any case, the energy crisis is already over. If we had to we could convert entirely to solar energies in only a few decades. If the price of oil started climbing then solar would become a comparatively economical substitute. As it is, however, new exploration and drilling technologies has put us into an oil and gas glut that will last for decades to come. Except for temporary fluxuations, oil prices are generally lower than ever when adjusted for inflation.

Besides the new oil finds there is also enough oil shale buried under this country to fuel the economy for several hundred years to come, but we will probably never mine it, at least not for fuel. Converting oil shale from a rock to a form useable in the gas tank is still more expensive than harvesting the remaining oil reserves, so there is not yet any economic incentive to exploit the resource. Given the growing concern over global warming, we can expect—and we should demand—much higher taxes on fossil fuels to make the clean alternatives more competitive. Either way it is inevitable that we will wean ourselves off of fossil fuels in favor of non-polluting alternatives. It is not a question of "if", but "when", and what will be left of the natural world when we finally do make the switch?

The worst-case scenario is that the falling costs of solar and other clean energies will not catch up with the falling costs of fossil fuels until we've burned up every last drop of oil and every mountain of coal and oil shale hundreds of years from now. Global warming coupled with on-going deforestation and ozone depletion would likely kill off most of the planet's forests and biodiversity and flood the coastal cities, but the natural world would still survive and the economy would still flourish. By then the greenhouse effect would be something that happened in the past, and it would be normal to live in a world where low-lying areas like New Orleans no longer exist above water. Sure, there would be a lot of chaos along the way, moving whole cities and millions of people to higher ground, but we have to build homes for hundreds of millions of new people anyway.

Despite falling birth rates, the U.S. Census bureau estimates that the U.S. population could potentially grow in excess of one billion people by the year 2100, mostly due to immigrants and their subsequent children. Moving the entire coastal population inland will be a big task, but it will be spread out over many decades. The job will be hardly a blip in a rapidly-expanding economy.

The problem with the law of substitutes is just that, that there are always substitutes. Already we have thinned the ozone layer across the globe and put gaping holes in it at the poles. But there are always substitutes, so people put on hats or sunscreen or stay indoors more. Already we have polluted the surface and ground water over vast regions of the planet, so people routinely use substitutes without even thinking about it. Cities build treatment facilities to clean the water supply, and home-owners install their own filters to remove any pollutants missed by the city. For lack of a proper filter they buy bottled water instead. Already you can buy bottled oxygen on the streets of Tokyo as a substitute for the polluted air. Already we are building tighter homes that are becoming like miniature biospheres with sophisticated atmospheric controls. Already we have kids looking at nature in dioramas, such as in the 200,000 square mile area irradiated by the Chernobyl nuclear disaster, where it is not safe for kids to play outdoors.

Many people, especially among younger generations, have woken up to the reality of our situation—that we are literally consuming the living earth. These are disenchanted youths who see what is happening and want the civilized world to pay for crimes against nature, for destroyed habitats and the thousands of species we have put to extinction. They wish, or at least they claim to wish, that civilization would fall apart at the seams, either collapsing from its own weight, or through a rebellion of natural disasters from Mother Earth. But any disaster, big or small, ultimately hurts the natural ecosystem more than our artificial one. The economic ecosystem is founded on the same principles of spontaneous order and stability as the natural ecosystem, but it has a much faster metabolic rate, so it always recovers faster than the natural world. In short the economic ecosystem is sustainable, but the real world is not! We can sustainably consume and destroy the entire natural world, because there are always substitutes.

Another problem is that like the law of gravity or other laws of physics, the law of substitutes lacks a compassionate clause. The law of gravity doesn't make exceptions for people who fall out of airplanes without parachutes, and neither does the law of substitutes make exceptions for species without habitat or people who are not part of the economic ecosystem. Remember, one of the substitutes for expensive CD's is to not listen to music at all. Likewise, a substitute for people or animals who have no food is to not eat.

Those of us who are plugged into the matrix of supply and demand have all our needs taken care of. We have all the food and fun we want and we are insulated from the collapse of the natural ecosystem around us. But a large portion of the world's population is not plugged into the matrix. They are stuck in the real world where pollution, climate change and starvation are genuine threats. We hardly notice now when a million people die of starvation. Will we notice when the numbers rise into the tens or hundreds of millions?

Even in the worst-case scenario the living ecosystem will survive and recover, just as it did after the asteroid impacts that wiped out the dinosaurs and most other species on the planet. The economic ecosystem will eventually assimilate all surviving pockets of the human population. We will no longer be dependent on the natural world for our physical needs.

Fortunately, we can expect to do somewhat better than the worst-case scenario. The conversion to a solar society is already underway, even if it is slow in getting started. As will be seen in a subsequent chapter, the transition will proceed exponentially in the coming decades. With the aid of tax incentives for clean energies and disincentives for fossil fuel use, we can speed up the change-over considerably and probably complete it before 2100 with most of our fossil fuels still in the ground. We might still lose New Orleans and parts of other coastal cities to rising sea levels, alter habitats all over the world, and wipe out half the world's species, but most people would hardly notice the difference. That is a brash thing to say, but chances are that you didn't notice how much we've altered the world ecology already. The world outside your window seems perfectly normal and it probably always will, no matter what we do to the it. I'll return to this topic in the next chapter.

In the best-case scenario, which is considerably less likely than the preceeding paragraph, we will complete the conversion to a virtually closed-loop, non-polluting society as early as mid-century and significantly reduce the world-wide ecological damage. Scientists have found that the average thickness of Arctic sea ice has already decreased by 4.3 feet over the last few decades[1], so it might be a good idea to accelerate the transition.

But what about food? After all, food is an organic resource, and we depend on a healthy and stable ecosystem to grow our crops. We are organic beings, and the need to eat other organic beings is an inescapable fact of life— and there are no substitutes for food!

Our journey apart from the natural ecosystem began many thousands of years ago. Our earliest ancestors lived an existence like any other creatures of nature. Throughout most of each year they had plenty of food, yet there was always a season of relative scarcity. The size of their population was determined by the amount of food available at the bleakest point in the year.

The development of stone-age technologies enabled our ancestors to begin breaking free of the cycles of the ecosystem. Food storage allowed them to sustain a much larger population through the seasons of need. Fire, clothing, and shelter enabled them to thrive in new habitats where they could not previously exist. In effect, they broke through the cycles of nature and greatly increased the size of their resource pie.

The development of primitive agriculture expanded the size of the pie again. Our ancestors did not at first embrace agriculture as a way to work less. In fact, it was more work to do all the planting, weeding, fertilizing, harvesting, and storing than to just wander and eat whatever was in season. But the land was at it's carrying capacity 9,000 years ago in the Middle East[72]. Farming was initially more work, but it provided a stable food supply and the carrying capacity of the land increased about a hundred times over. Over the last nine millennia we have continued to improve our resources extraction and transportation technologies support an ever expanding population.

Still, we will have to eat in the future, and food is an organic resource. The threat of massive starvation and die-offs seems imminent, due to the rapidly expanding world population and the ineptitudes of modern agriculture. Our farmers expend some 5 to 10 calories of fossil fuel energy, depending on the source cited, for every 1 calorie of

The Future of Food?
-From Fields to Factories-

In developing countries people routinely recycle every scrap of human or animal manure they can get. Manure is recycled through open fields and aquacultures, but algae cultures are also becoming popular. Raw wastes are composted or digested with microorganisms back to the basic nutrients, then used to fertilize vats of single-celled blue-green algae. The algae uses sunlight directly to photosynthesize it's own sugars. An algae culture can produce fifty tons of protein per hectare per year, compared to only two tons from corn[29]. Algae cultures are efficient because the organisms are so simple. Algae expends no energy building extraneous leaves, stems, or roots like other plants, nor the bones, brains and guts of the animals. The algae is pure food.

The endless quest to reduce expenses and maximize profits will soon lead to many of our common foods being grown in a similar way, much as scientists now grow tissue cultures in petri dishes every day. The difference is in scale.

Researchers have learned how to take tiny tomatoes off the vine and grow them to maturity with nutrient injections[11]. Before long we will skip even that step to culture whole vats of tomato cells for use in ketchup and other products where the soup of cells is a sufficient substitute for whole tomatoes. We will pipe in nutrients from treated sewage to culture vats of everything from wheat starch and milk to egg whites or yolks and meat.

Right now it is technologically easy to synthesize simple sugars directly from air and water. The reason we do not is because it is extremely energy intensive and living plants can produce sugars much more efficiently. We will never be able to produce sugar more efficiently than plants, but we do not need to either.

Consider, when we convert low-grade coal or oil fuels into high-grade electricity, we burn up three calories of the original fuel for each one calorie of electric output. We accept this loss only because the electricity is more versatile; it can power our computers, lights and robotics, while coal and oil cannot. Agriculture similarly converts calories of low-grade fuel energy into a higher-grade form at a net loss. Coal and oil is not directly edible, but through farming it can be converted to a form that is (well, kind of). As the next step in an evolving process, we may soon convert solar electricity directly into sugar at an even greater caloric loss.

The cost of producing all types of energy is continuing to fall in real dollars as we find ways to harvest more power with less labor. When the cost of energy falls low enough it will be more cost effective to synthetically produce sugar in a factory than to drive into a field and harvest it. At that point the total labor consumed in both harnessing the power and manufacturing the sugar would be less than the labor involved in growing a crop. Along with nutrients recycled from sewage, this synthetic sugar can be fed to vat cultures to grow whatever we want. Our food supply would be no longer be tied to the organic cycles of nature, and the resource pie would be expanded to the near infinite, meeting all our food needs on this planet and on any other planet

food produced. This is in addition to washing away thousands of tons of essential nutrients every year through erosion. These absurdities alone seem reason enough to return to some kind of sustainable farming, based on the organic ecosystem's ability to produce and renew. For the moment at least we actually have the ability to grow most, if not all, of our crops sustainably, at a net caloric gain, and at a profit, without sacrificing the soil. We can do it, and we should do it.

At the same time, however, we are gradually weaning ourselves from the need to grow crops in fields at all. Large sections of Mediterranean Europe are already covered with endless rows of plastic-covered greenhouses. Destabilization of the climate only increases the demand for crops grown under plastic, and plastic is made from fossil fuels—ironically the one thing we have plenty of. Other entrepreneurs are pioneering the art of hydroponics, growing plants in nutrient-rich water troughs in factory-like settings. But this is only the beginning. Since matter is neither created nor destroyed, we will one day close the loop on our food supply by piping treated sewage directly into these kinds of plant factories for recycling back into new food. Eventually we may even do away with the plants and animals too, and just raise all our crops as tissue cultures in vats (see sidebar: "The Future of Food?")

I am not suggesting that we should up and quit the use of the living ecosystem. It is possible to grow and harvest our organic resources sustainably, at a fixed level of use. But to sustain the human population that is here and coming, we must increasingly substitute resources from outside the living ecosystem, so life can continue the process of renewal. Sustainable use of organic resources can continue, but it will be only a fraction of the new economy.

Today conservationists are working hard to create nature preserves, to enact legislation to protect endangered species, and to penalize pollution so that it is more economical to use our wastes than to discharge them. Environmental and social organizations can expect much greater budgets to work with in the coming decades. The trends of wealth and work, as described in an earlier chapter, will almost inevitably make us all millionaires in a few decades, compared to what we have now. With a greater surplus than ever before people will channel tens of billions of dollars into social and environmental organizations. Groups like the *Nature Conservancy* will have multi-billion dollar budgets to buy and protect land. But will it be enough to save the natural ecosystem? Unfortunately not.

There are many ironies in the future, as you've probably sensed by reading these chapters. One of those ironies is that millions of acres of agricultural lands may fall out of production in the coming century, as we switch over to hydroponic and vat-grown food. The size of our ecological footprint will decrease as we no longer depend on our agricultural lands, and therefore we will have the opportunity to recreate the wild prairies and forests that graced the world long before civilization.

The only obstacle to creating such a world is that the wealth and work principle is also causing surging levels of personal wealth, igniting a land drive by individuals wanting to stake out their own personal fiefdoms. Farmlands used to be valued according to its production potential, but today the land is being sold for its recreational and aesthetic values. We are chopping the land base up into useless bits and pieces, and we have to act now to save as much as we can of what's left.

There is already discussion of Boston merging with Washington D.C. and all the cities in between to create one mega city. Doubling, tripling, or quadrupling the nation's population in the coming century (according to the U.S. Cenus Bureaus' range of estimates) will lead to growth from coast-to-coast that is difficult to fathom. The Denver-Boulder metropolitan area, which now consists of 2.5 million people, is already expected to grow by another million people just between 2000 and 2020. As personal wealth continues to rise and people commute to work via the internet, they will have little incentive to stay in the cities. The suburban sprawl will hit the countryside like a swarm of locusts consuming the landscape. Rural towns in scenic places like our nearby Gallatin Valley can reasonably expect to grow from fewer than 100,000 people to in excess of a million within our children's life times. This explosion of new homes and roads across the landscape is the greatest long-term threat to the natural ecosystem, and we must do everything we can to stop it.

I am not suggesting that we try to halt the influx of people. The land-base is a pie of limited size. It is self-evident and fair that the human population will ultimately redistribute towards a level of equilibrium. I am merely saying that we will all enjoy the future a whole lot more if we take the time to do some far-sighted land-use planning now. This strange vision of things to come may not fit your own romantic notions of about the future, but get over it; we've got work to do.

"Adaptation is not a conscious choice, and the people who make up a society do not quite understand what they are doing; they know only that a particular choice works, even though it may appear bizarre to an outsider."
—Peter Farb, *Man's Rise to Civilization*

2-3
The Human Equation
-The Evolution of Consciousness-

The world you see outside your window probably seems quite normal to you. Except for the new roads and houses it is the same world you've always known. But we have changed the world already, and almost nobody noticed. For example, when we think about Greece we typically imagine a mostly open, rocky landscape with a few small- to medium-sized trees. That's what the pictures show us of the old Greek ruins. We accept that as the normal landscape for Greece, yet it is a shadow of what the land once was. If you were to travel back in time before human intervention you would discover a very different land of deep, rich soils and thick, lush forests.

Human activity is similarly responsible for eliminating the forests that once covered much of the Middle East as well as wiping out the grasslands of northern Africa to create the Great Saharan Desert[46]. We accept these places as normal because that is the way they have always been in our lifetimes.

But the world is changing all around us right now, and you probably haven't noticed that either. For example, the Salt Lake City area was once described as having "grass belly high to a horse", yet that is not the landscape you see there today. The "natural" landscape doesn't seem grassy at all, but gray and brushy, because we've altered the landscape. The truth is that we are creating a new desert in America to rival the Saharan , but very few people can see a difference in their day-to-day lives. Probably less than 1 in 10,000 people is sufficiently trained in ecology to tell the difference between what was, what is, and what will be. To everyone else the world seems perfectly normal and it always will, no matter what we do to it.

Just think about the tumbleweeds you see blowing across western highways, or shown blowing across the fields in old western movies. They seem normal, but tumbleweeds are introduced weeds from other continents. They weren't even here during the old west days! While perusing a new wildflower guide recently I noticed that 25% of the flowers depicted were alien species, mostly adapted to desertifying conditions. These alien plants are some of the most abundant "wildflowers" you will find. Already 538 species of plants and animals native to the U.S. are missing or extinct, but hardly anybody noticed. Did you?

Did you miss the passenger pigeons today, which used to fly in such massive flocks with billions of birds that they would literally blacken the sky overhead? Did you ever stop to think about why you would have to buy a bottle of water at the store? Is there nothing odd about that?

Some people would like to say that wasting the environment is strictly a problem of modern civilization, and that our ancestors were too noble, too connected to their environments to do this kind of harm.

What you see outside your window probably seems perfectly normal, but the world is changing all around us. Already 538 species of our native plants and animals are missing or extinct. In this photo near Kooskia, Idaho all native plants have been replaced by weeds from other continents.

But as you can see from these examples of Greece, the Middle East, and the Sahara, these catastrophes date back thousands of years.

Others might point out that civilization of any kind is the problem, and that the only truly sustainable lifestyle is that of the hunter-gatherer, who intimately knew and cared about the land. Unfortunately, our ancestors who "lived with the land" didn't have a very good track record either. Paleontologists have documented that every time our ancestors migrated into new territory over the last 50,000 years there was a massive extinction of the large native mammals. For example, 73% of large North American mammals (counting by genus) disappeared with the of arrival of people on this continent, including the lions, cheetahs, horses, mammoths, mastodons, and giant ground sloths. In South America 80% of the large mammals were lost, and in Australia it was 86%[21]. Defenders of the idea of a noble primitive would argue that the extinctions also coincide with climate changes and that the weather may have been the problem more than people. Yes, it is true that climate change was often a factor in the extinctions, which may have reduced populations, but it was the arrival of people and technology that finished them off. In North America for example, many of the large mammals survived twenty-two previous ice ages, only to drop dead after the twenty-third, coinciding with the arrival of human hunters.

The best archaeological evidence exists for the most recent extinctions, such as in New Zealand, which was colonized by the Maori only a thousand years ago. As the Maori populated the island over the next five centuries, starting in the north and moving south, they wiped out all the easy prey in their path. The most well-known of their victims was a flightless bird, the moa. There were one to two dozen distinct species of moa, including some up to ten feet tall. The climate was stable when the birds went extinct, but archaeological evidence has revealed primitive ovens filled with the charred bones of thousands of the birds. The birds evolved in a land without predators, so they were not prepared for the arrival of people. The Maori found easy pickings when they arrived and feasted on every last bird. The bones were unearthed by the hundreds of thousands by the plows of British colonists in the 1800's. Several dozen other species of birds went extinct with the arrival of the Maori including large geese, ducks, swans and eagles[20].

We may exterminate half the world's species within this century.

Paleontologists have found the remains of recently extinct bird species on every oceanic island they have explored. By extrapolating to unexplored islands, it is estimated that roughly 2,000 species of birds fell victim to prehistoric exterminations. Just like people in the modern world, our ancestors probably never noticed what they were doing to their world. They exterminated huntable species left and right without realizing it. Of the remaining 9,000 bird species documented since 1600, an additional 1% have been declared extinct, although many more have not been seen in several decades.

What our ancestors started with a modest population and simple tools, we are finishing at an ever accelerating rate. Right now we are wiping out at least 100 *known* species of plants and animals per year. But there are several times as many *unknown* species in the world, which are being exterminated far faster than scientists can identify them. Biologists have named and described less than two million species of plants and animals, including insects, yet estimates suggest that there may be closer to 30 million species worldwide, most of them in tropical forests. If the estimate of 30 million species is correct, then we are now losing species at the rate of 17 per hour or 150,000 per year[21]. In some places there are scientists literally running in front of bulldozers in the jungle to document plants animals and insects before they are lost forever. We may exterminate half the world's species within this century.

But within this cloud of doom there is one bright spot: for the first time in history our species—at least a portion of the population—is aware of the destruction we are causing. The point of this chapter is to understand how this new awareness has evolved in human consciousness, and what it means for saving as much as we can of the remaining natural world.

Consider, the cougar doesn't stop to debate the environmental and ethical issues at stake when it chases and kills a jack rabbit. It doesn't wonder about how many jackrabbits are left, and how many it can sustainably harvest. It sees food and kills it, even if it is the last of its kind on the planet. There is no reason to expect that our ancestors acted any different.

Certainly our species has had the physical brain mass to consider ethical and environmental issues for hundreds of thousands of years, but the available evidence suggests that our ancestors utilized their brains in a very different way than we do today. In a nutshell, they relied on instinct and accumulated experience, rather than conscious thought.

For example, have you ever driven down the highway only to suddenly realize that you have no recollection of the last thirty miles of your trip? You executed a difficult and dangerous task—driving a car—sometimes to the point of moving in and out of traffic, and yet you were totally unaware of the experience.

Learning to drive initially requires a tremendous amount of conscious thought, but with accumulated experience your unconscious mind can automatically respond without you directly thinking about it. You function normally, yet you are literally in a hypnotic state, totally unaware of time or space. According to Dr. Julian Jaynes in his book *The Origin of Consciousness in the Breakdown of the Bicameral Mind*[47] this unconscious experience of the world is the normal mode of life for animals, and was the *only* existence our own species knew until about 3,000 years ago, when an increasingly complex society demanded active thinking to solve problems which could not be adequately handled from accumulated experiences of the past. The way our ancestors used their brains was neither better nor worse, than how we use our brains today, but definitely different.

Professional athletes often evaluate their performance consciously, using stop-motion photography and other tools of science to examine the finest details of their stride or swing so that they can improve the efficiency of every move. They learn new techniques and consciously work them into their routine until the moves are automatic. But at the moment of competition, good athletes know they have to disengage their conscious minds and allow their bodies to fly on instinct and accumulated experience alone. The same thing could be said about typing. I consciously, tediously learned how to type by thinking about each letter on the keyboard and practicing it until I knew it instinctively. Now I can type at the rate of nearly sixty words per minute, but I fumble immediately if I look at the keyboard and try to consciously direct my fingers.

Our ancestors lived in a much simpler world than we do today. They were able to learn skills completely without the need for conscious thought. For example, if you have ever raised children then you know they will mimic just about everything you do. Pick up a hammer and start pounding a nail, and they will copy your actions by finding any reasonable substitute and hammering on the furniture. Pick up a razor to shave and you will find two mirrors, the one you look into, and the smaller one that stands beside you mimicking your every move. As you feed the family, wash the dishes, and take care of the children, the kids "play house" doing all the same actions in pretend. Children will mimic everything you do, right down to the mannerisms and expressions you may have been unaware of until your children mimicked them back in exaggerated form. Talk about your neighbors or say something in adult conversation, and your kids will pick it up immediately and often start chanting it in meaningless repetition while they play. Like tape recorders, they record everything you do and play it back.

Monkeys learn the same way, by watching and mimicking as the adults use simple tools or specialized techniques to break nuts, harvest insects, or otherwise catch food. There is no conscious thought in the process at all.

I observed the apparent switch from subconscious to conscious learning in my own son, then two and a half, while teaching him sign language. I finger-spelled the alphabet to him and he mimicked each of the letters with his own hands. Mimicking was easy for him and he learned most of the letters faster than I did. But one time I reached over and tried to help him with a letter by putting his fingers in position for him. At that moment I sensed a change in his eyes as he looked at my hand and his and tried to consciously control his fingers. He struggled for a moment and said for the first time, "I can't".

Our ancestors accumulated vast knowledge and many new skills over the millennia, but only by accident. Consider that the archaeological record reveals that pottery was developed over a period of thousands of years.

Presumably, our ancestors first discovered pottery when a clay-coated basket was accidentally burned or perhaps intentionally disposed of in a fire. The basket was incinerated, but it left a piece of fired pottery behind. If this event had happened to any of us, being conscious thinkers, we would have immediately focused directly on the clay itself, engaging in systematic tests to discover the properties of this new material. But without the capability for conscious thought, our ancient ancestors labored very hard to make more baskets, which they subsequently coated with clay and incinerated. Biologically they had the same brains as we do now, yet it took thousands of years to make the simple leap in thought that separated pottery-making from basket-making. Subsequent pots were formed without using a basket form, but our ancestors still imprinted a basket-like texture on the pots for a very long time before developing pottery as its own medium.

If our ancestors used their brains the way that we do today, then we would have landed on the moon at least tens of thousands of years earlier than we did. In essence, conscious thinking is an acquired skill, part of our culture, which we pass on to our children. This process of cultural evolution is very similar to biological evolution.

Biologically our ancestors had the same brains as we do now, yet it took thousands of years to make the simple leap in thought that separated pottery-making from firing clay-covered baskets.

Biologically our species evolved through millions of years and tens of thousands of mutations. To the best of our scientific knowledge there was never any plan to make us what we are. Our evolutionary journey from amino acids to tool-using primates was, and continues to be, a journey of accidents which worked. Our ancestors did not have a goal to become *Homo Sapiens*, only to survive. Being here is the result of one mutation band-aided over another, and that over another many thousands of times. To our knowledge there was never any goal behind the process, only a desire to survive each moment, as individuals and as groups of individuals.

Likewise the evolution of culture and the economy has occurred without any plan beyond day-to-day survival. There was never any master goal behind the creation of the economy we have in the country and in the world today. Like biological evolution, cultural-economic evolution has been a haphazard process of "mutations and adaptations", or reactions to the problems and circumstances of each moment along the way. Our ancestors who traded meat for tools did not plan to evolve the New York Stock Exchange any more than their ancestors planned to evolve an opposable thumb or to stand up straight. Any mutations which proved to be "economical" or practical were retained as part of our cultural heritage.

Consider the differing food habits of cultures around the world. Many peoples eat rats and cockroaches while most Americans nearly retch at the thought. Similarly most Americans disdain the thought of eating dogs cats, or horses. Meanwhile most Hindu people think we are basically cannibals to eat beef, and the Moslems think we sin terribly when we eat pork. The basis behind these beliefs, argues Marvin Harris, author of *The Sacred Cow and the Abominable Pig*[36], is not in the quality of the food itself or in religion, but in practical economics.

For example, most of us in America may now dislike the idea of eating horses, but horse meat has gone through many surges of popularity and unpopularity, both in America and Europe, according to economic trends. Horse meat becomes popular when other meats are more expensive, and becomes unpopular when other sources of meat are more economical.

Similarly, Harris points out that while the Hindu people now abhor the idea of eating cows, that has not always been the case. The Indian people regularly consumed beef up until a few centuries BC at which time the rising population created more and more need for cropland, since crops can produce more calories and protein per acre than livestock. Stock needed to be kept for plowing fields, producing milk and producing dung for fuel. Over the centuries beef consumption dropped until only the wealthy priests consumed it. The disparity between rich and poor created an opportunity for the rise of the religion of cow protection among the peasant masses. Hinduism and cow protection became the dominate religion of the area because it reflected the economic reality of the area.

Likewise, Jewish and Moslem peoples today, who do not believe in eating pork, have ancestors who did domesticate and consume pork until economics made it impractical to raise pigs. That was at a time when the Middle East was largely forested and supported the rich foods and resources necessary for pork production. Deforestation, desertification, and competition with human crops made it impractical to raise pigs, and pork subsequently became "bad to eat" among religions of the area.

Harris goes on to suggest that we in America think mice, rats, and cockroaches are filthy not because of their habits, but rather because they are not economical sources of food in our culture. We could get protein by skinning and butchering mice, or by catching cockroaches, but it is not an economical source of protein compared to our other choices. Therefore, argues Harris, we scorn the uneconomical choices as being bad or filthy, even while people of some countries consider the same foods as delicacies.

As with our food habits, many other aspects of culture are largely tied to practical economics. Understanding the evolution of culture is important to an understanding of our economy, because although cultures make unconscious choices that seem to work, these choices are not necessarily the best choices possible.

We often look at other cultures and sneer at their beliefs, customs, and ways of thinking. We may laugh at them because their lifestyle seems different and backwards, compared to our own. We may joke about them for cutting and stretching their lips or ears for ornamentation, or we may sneer at them for eating dogs and cats. We may think it foolish if in a ritual they purposely burn all their worldly possessions which took uncountable calories of effort to produce.

Of course, the opposite is also true. Other cultures often look at our own as peculiar and nonsensical. They may shudder that we let confessed felons go free only because no one read them their Miranda rights. They may laugh at our concept of real estate, if they come from a culture where land is owned communally. They may think it is funny that we in our culture expend billions of hours of effort working to pay for land when the land was originally free and would still be here regardless of whether we worked all those hours to pay for it or not.

Throughout history, cultural practices have not been determined through effectiveness strategies or goals, but through the need to achieve and maintain stability within the social group.

Our food preferences about what is "good" and "bad" to eat are learned and passed on from generation to generation based on accumulated economic experience.

The purpose of a society and the government it creates has never been to lead people to the future or to achieve any particular goal, only to maintain the relative stability of the whole. When a level of stability is achieved it is typically as a reaction, rather than as a goal and plan. The collective group reacts to the problems at hand, and which ever reaction seems to keep the group intact becomes the "economical" choice. The reaction, no matter how extreme by our own values, becomes an economical means to hold the society together.

For example, many cultures all over the world have engaged in warfare with other cultures, not for the purpose of winning new land or resources, but as an "economical" means of maintaining internal stability. In what is now the northeastern United States, the Iroquois Indians and their neighbors, including the Huron and Algonkians, once fought incredible fierce battles amongst each other, but dominion was never a goal. They could have killed from a distance with bows and arrows, but instead they fought close in with clubs and tomahawks. One side would be defeated in a battle, and then the other side would be defeated, but no one group attempted to absolutely conquer the other. According to author Peter Farb in his book, *Man's Rise to Civilization*[28], the social-political structure of the tribe is frail in nature, and the Iroquois and their neighbors lacked the necessary institutions to maintain internal order. Similarly, they lacked the economic means necessary to wage an all out war, and they lacked the political structure to administer new territory. Living in a continual stalemate of battles with their neighbors gave the tribes an outlet for internal stress, thereby providing a measure of stability to each.

Some people have speculated that the modern stalemate between the Eastern and Western nations provided a similar stability for the countries of each side. The external threat from each other provided a degree of unity and cooperation within each. Some argue that the end of the Cold War has resulted in an increase in violence all over the world. In that sense, the Cold War was an "economical" means of maintaining stability[72].

At first we might think that these processes of biologic and economic evolution work quite well, since, after all, we are here. However, for each random mutation that survives there can be thousands that fail and die. In biological or economic evolution the odds of being a successful mutation are not very high. A mutation may survive and continue evolving into a new species, but may ultimately become extinct many mutations later. For example, there were once many other humanoid species, besides our direct ancestry; they branched off evolved were successful for awhile but eventually became extinct. Indeed, 99.9% of everything that ever lived is now extinct.

In economics capitalism and communism evolved from the same human stock, and both were successful for awhile, but we have witnessed the virtual extinction of one of those species in our time. The continued success and survival of the other species depends on whether it-our economy-continues to mutate and adapt successfully.

The right mutations of our economy and culture mean continued prosperity and peace for ourselves and our offspring. The wrong mutations mean the collapse of our economy, as happened in the former Soviet Union. But more so, the collapse of any economy brings with it the possibility of anarchy, just as potential anarchy now stalks the remains of the Soviet empire. Randomly reacting and evolving brings a possibility of continued success, and it brings at least an equal possibility of failure and collapse. Our species may have survived thus far by reacting to problems as they occur, but the path has been a bumpy one, much as we are now witnessing in the fallen Soviet state. The people there will ultimately evolve a new economy and a new stability, but it is hard to say what will happen along the way. How many lives will be lost and how much pain and hardship will be suffered? Reactionary evolution is inherently risky.

When we think back on human evolution we often think of the important thresholds our ancestors crossed that put us on the path to being what we are today. We might think about the evolution of the opposable thumb and the beginning of tools, or we might think about the evolution of consciousness, and how our ancestors began to ask questions and ponder the purpose or meaning of human existence. Now we stand at a new threshold in our evolution, a new development that is as significant as any from our past.

Throughout history our biological and cultural evolution has been an unconscious process. We lived our lives until we encountered problems; then we reacted and adapted to those problems or died. The reactions that worked helped to keep us alive and be-

For the first time in human history, our species is becoming aware of our impact on other species and the environment.

came part of our evolutionary course; thus we evolved forward without plans, only reactions. In terms of economic and cultural evolution, that may soon change. Our species is just now becoming conscious of cultural evolution, and this consciousness is leading to the conscious evolution of our future culture.

Our ancestors lost tremendous resources when they unwittingly hunted species to extinction. Flightless birds like the moa or auk were easy to catch because they evolved on islands free from predators. When the first peoples arrived they found meals so easy to catch that all they had to do was to walk up and club them in the head. Nature was a banquet and all anyone had to do was eat. Any other predator introduced to the ecosystem would have wiped them out too. But there is a price to pay for such disregard for other species. I know from my experience in practicing and teaching primitive skills. It is a lot more work to catch your next meal if it is runs and hides! Life would have been a lot easier in both the past and the present if people practiced better stewardship of the natural world long ago.

Today the world is a much more complicated place to live. Modern culture demands that we engage our conscious minds to solve new problems every day. As natural resources become increasingly scarce and we are haunted by the mistakes of our past, we are forced to look ahead at the future in a way we have never done before.

Consider the case of ozone depletion in the atmosphere. Chloroflorocarbons or CFCs were formerly used as a coolant in refrigerators and as a foaming agent in some types of insulation, until it was discovered that the chemicals were destroying the stratospheric ozone that protects the planet from the ultraviolet rays of the sun. Conscious exploration of the problem led to the conscious effort to end the world-wide production of CFCs to halt the damage. Granted, our reaction time was a little slow, and it is even slower to address the problem of global warming, but it is a start. Gradually we are learning to look farther and farther ahead, to forecast problems and avert them before they reach critical stages.

For the first time people are taking an interest in the tens of thousands of species that face imminent extinction, wondering what we might be losing through our ignorance. Researchers are searching the jungles for new medicines that have the potential to help our species. People are also realizing that all these species may have other values which lay beyond our ability to comprehend, and that we ought to protect them not for their utilitarian aspects, but just because they have the right to exist.

But the most important part is that more and more individuals, entrepreneurs and corporations are realizing that there is a profit to be made in consciously finding ways to live with the earth, rather than by unconsciously destroying it. The profit motive is critical, because it is the economic ecosystem that is consuming the natural world. We can only save the natural world when the economic ecosystem sees it as a profitable course of action.

For example, developers have been traditionally opposed to any kind of planning that limits their ability to put houses where ever they want. But a few developers have learned that good land use planning translates into higher property values and greater profits. Cluster housing with more open space and preservation of riparian areas can mean lower development costs and higher resale values. That which is good for the environment is also good for the pocketbook.

Likewise, companies that once generated vast amounts of waste are finding that it is more profitable to close the loop and utilize that waste, rather than to dump it into the environment. The businesses that are the most wasteful are starting to be beaten out by more eco-savvy competitors. The greatest obstacle to creating a cleaner, greener world is not the industrial economy, but the momentum of past uneconomic choices which people continue to make. At the consumer, business, and governmental levels, people persist in unconsciously mimicking the mistakes everyone else is making, rather than researching and forging newer and better paths. The fact that we have attained intermittent consciousness doesn't mean that we use it!

Fortunately, there are businesses like Atlanta's Interface Corporation[39], a carpet manufacturer, that are truly changing the way the world does business. Conventional nylon carpets are made from refined petroleum, using two pounds of fossil fuels to convert each pound of the black goo into a shiny new carpet. After ten years or so of wear and tear the carpet is ripped out and hauled away to the dump where it will last for about 20,000 years. Interface Corporation generated in excess of 5 billion pounds of the carpet that has since been buried in the ground before taking a fresh look at their operation.

Instead of incrementally improving their product line, Interface made the conscious decision to reinvent the carpet business from scratch, with the objectives to become both ecologically friendly and more profitable. Other carpet companies were developing processes to recycle waste nylon carpet back into new products like the foam backing for more carpets, but Interface invented a completely new polymeric material that could be continuously recycled back as new carpet. The carpet performs as well or better than nylon carpets, but all the materials can be separated into their components and remade into a fresh product. The process reduces the consumption of petroleum feedstocks and energy use, and therefore saves money while eliminating carpet waste.

More importantly, Interface has closed the loop on waste by leasing their carpets instead of selling them. Traditionally, businesses had to fork over a large investment to purchase carpet, remove all the furniture and install it. But Interface provides the service of a floor covering, where they install and maintain the flooring for a monthly service fee. The carpet is manufactured in square tiles, so that the most worn squares can be replaced as needed without moving all the furniture or replacing the entire carpet. The worn squares are returned to the factory and remanufactured into new carpet. Interface makes more money by providing a continuos service than by merely selling carpets, and yet they are using far fewer resources. The company is determined to completely wean itself off of fossil fuels in the coming years, through more efficient energy use and by switching to renewable energy sources. Each of these innovations makes Interface more competitive in the marketplace because they are generating more revenues while consuming fewer resources.

Ultimately the competition will be forced to follow their lead, or lose their niche in the economic ecosystem. Consciously creating these kinds of eco-friendly businesses is the key to saving the natural world, and it is the key to making a profit in the twenty-first century.

"The 1990 Clean Air Act... sets up a system whereby utilities can trade pollution credits back and forth. Companies that figure out how to reduce emissions fastest and cheapest will gain a competitive edge over their less ingenious competitors, and pollution can be cut more with a limited number of dollars."

—*Rocky Mountain Institute*[65]

2-4

Succession

Making Change in the Ecosystem

If you were to take a shovel and turn over a patch of sod and then leave it for a year, you would discover that the plants that colonized the disturbed soil were different from the ones that were there before. The site would first be covered by weedy, "pioneer plants" with carrot-like taproots, followed by a succession of new plants over the years. The tap-rooted weeds would eventually disappear, and the site would return to sod, with many small roots tightly holding the soil in place.

This is the process of **succession**, where bare surfaces are pioneered by certain species, then gradually replaced with waves of new species as the habitat becomes tighter and more stable. Given enough time and adequate moisture, bare ground will progress from weeds to rangeland to deciduous forest and will climax as an evergreen forest. Any of these vegetative states could be considered "natural", but certain states may be more desirable than others. The way we manage the landscape affects the successional process, tipping the balance one way or the other, towards higher or lower levels of succession. Manipulating succession changes the species that live there.

For example, a forest of pine trees favors specific plants and animals that thrive within the available niches. Burning the forest down alters the habitat, eliminating not just the pines, but also many of the plants and animals that were associated with them. The grass that invades and dominates the scorched landscape is a very different habitat that favors a new mix of plants and animals.

Another form of succession takes place over much longer periods of time, as certain species are replaced by others that evolve to fit a particular niche in the ecosystem. A new species can create its own niche by finding ways to utilize resources and energy more efficiently than the preexisting species. The new species takes over and the less efficient often become extinct. The new species does not just occupy habitat in the ecosystem, it helps define it too.

For example, a pine tree could be said to occupy a particular habitat in the ecosystem, but it also becomes the habitat, creating a niche for certain plants and animal species and eliminating it for others. A dominant species, such as a whole forest of pine trees, becomes the habitat that all other species adjust too. If there are available niches within that habitat then new species will evolve to occupy those niches.

In other words, succession in the ecosystem can be manipulated by introducing new species to alter habitats, OR by altering habitats to encourage new species. Succession in the economic ecosystem can be manipulated in a similar way. By studying how ecosystems work we can develop better strategies to make change in the economic system to create a better world for all.

Through the tools of government and popular opinion we can shift succession in the ecosystem to favor certain products and services over others. Conversely, with the aid of business and consumer choice we can introduce new and better products and services to out-compete inefficient old ones, ultimately creating a new standard or a new form of habitat that all competing businesses must adapt to.

Shifting Habitats to encourage New Products and Services

When we think about Greece we imagine an open, rocky landscape with a few small to medium-sized trees. But if you were to travel back in time before human intervention you would discover a very different land of deep, rich soils and thick, lush forests. Likewise, when we imagine the middle east we think of desert hills, sparsely covered with vegetation, yet it to was richly forested before people tried to improve upon it.

Human activity is similarly responsible for creating the Great Saharan Desert of northern Africa. The land once supported rich grasslands and flowing springs. The land was so rich that a person could walk the entire northern coastline of Africa in the shade of trees. Now it is a 3,000 mile strip of desert, sand and rock!

The pace of desertification continues today, including here in North America. According to *Newsweek*, 40% of North America's crop and rangelands have already turned to desert. But this is only the beginning. If we stay on the same course then we will create a desert on this continent to rival the Sahara[69].

When I look at the rocky, grassy hill behind my own home I can see it as it is now, or I can see it as it was more than a hundred years ago when it was less rocky and more grassy, with much deeper top soil. The hill has suffered from poor grazing practices, and worse at times, no grazing at all. I can also see this hill a hundred years in the future when it is mostly barren rock, assuming we fail to make a difference between now and then.

Halting this process of desertification and turning these barren, weedy places back into fertile, productive landscapes is relatively easy, but it requires playing by the rules of the ecosystem. If we listen and learn the ways of the ecosystem then we can restore the health of the land and still get the productivity we want.

Western rangelands can vary from a low level of succession with abundant weeds and bare ground to a high level of succession with dense grasses and forbs protecting the soil surface. Either level of succession is "sustainable" and "natural" but for obvious reasons we usually desire an advanced level of succession to protect the soil.

Cattle grazing in the arid west is a hot environmental topic in this country because people often believe the animals reverse the successional process, turning healthy grasslands into weedy wastelands. The animals are seen as destructive beasts that waste the land where ever they go, consuming the choicest greens, trampling vegetation, crumbling stream banks and fouling the water. Logically, cattle are perceived as a negative force that must be removed or greatly reduced for the landscape to recover to an advanced level of succession. Unfortunately, removing cattle from the landscape does not heal the land at all, but greatly accelerates its deterioration.

This cow track in freeze-thawed soils harbors dozens of new grass seedlings while the surrounding area is devoid of growth. Bennet Hills, Idaho.

Historically western rangelands were grazed and maintained by massive herds of buffalo. The important part was not the buffalo, but the sequence of grazing. Predators kept the buffalo clustered in tight herds. The stampeding animals left behind a swath of trampled vegetation and dung. Their hooves and urine killed the moss while desirable plant seeds were pounded into the soil to germinate. Old or dead vegetation was trampled into the ground where soil microbes could break it down. The organic litter helped retain moisture for plant growth. Gradually the debris rotted and returned the nutrients to the soil. The roaming bison left the prairie to recover without further interference, allowing for lush and unrestrained growth—a high level of succession.

Putting fences across the land and stocking it with cattle creates a new sequence of grazing, which logically has a different effect on the land. Without predators the cattle spread out and graze over wide areas—they no longer trample down the brush, so the brush spreads. Herds do not trample dead grasses, so the new grasses die at the base as light no longer reaches their growing points. Old vegetation stands for years, slowly decomposing through oxidation and weathering. Nutrients are locked up in the old growth—unavailable for living plants. With fences to keep the cattle contained, the young plants are eaten repeatedly as grazing animals return without allowing the vegetation to recover.

Without a protective covering of organic matter, raindrops strike the exposed ground, pulverizing and separating the soil, just like you might find under the drip line of a house. The fine particles of silt, sand, and clay dry to form a hard surface crust. Seeds cannot grow through the capped surface, and bare patches develop between the plants. Weeds and grasshoppers thrive in the open patches. New moisture is lost as runoff and may cause floods. Water bypasses the water table and old springs can dry up. Freezing and thawing, plus wetting and drying can also cause the top inch of the soil to become so porous and fluffy that seeds dry out before they germinate.

It may seem incredible that a mere change in the grazing sequence could have such a dramatic impact on the landscape, but it is the leading cause of desertification around the world. The cause of desertification is not the cattle, but a simple misunderstanding of the differences between brittle and nonbrittle environments.

In a nutshell, **nonbrittle environments** usually have sufficient moisture throughout the growing season to promote decay of old vegetation and the germination of new seedlings. **Brittle environments**, on the other hand, tend to dry out quickly, thus interrupting the processes of decay and seedling germination[74].

Capped soil in the front and freeze-thawed soil in the back surround a final stand of dead, oxidizing grass. Without organic matter on the soil to capture moisture, half or more of the rain that falls can wash away without soaking into the ground. Animal impact would enable new seedlings to germinate and recolonize this ground. Bennet Hills, Idaho.

The degree of brittleness in an environment is largely a factor of how predictable the rains are there. The Kalahari Desert in southern Africa is extremely brittle; the total amount of precipitation can vary as much as 500% from year to year[49]. Even when a region does receive its average annual precipitation, the moisture may be unevenly distributed across local geographic space. Some of the photos shown here were taken in Idaho in the Great Basin Desert, where precipitation is similarly unpredictable and may vary from as little as 3 inches in some years to nearly 20 inches in other years.

In a nonbrittle environment the regularity of precipitation allows bacteria to break down old vegetation and gives new seedlings a chance to grow, almost regardless of how the land is treated. A brittle environment, however, requires animal impact to trample organic matter into the soil to trap the necessary moisture to promote bacterial action and facilitate the growth of new seedlings. Half of the moisture that falls on the land can easily be lost if there is insufficient organic matter on the ground to capture it. That means that a region that receives twenty inches of precipitation in a year may get only ten inches of benefit!

Altering the sequence of grazing in extreme brittle environments leads to phenomenal changes. A lack of sufficient animal impact can quickly lead to a denuded landscape with a very low level of succession where falling precipitation simply washes away across the bare ground, causing floods downstream. Rain bypass the water table, causing age-old springs and streams to dry up and disappear. As incredulous as it seems, merely restoring or mimicking the historical sequence of grazing leads to a reversal of succession and a reversal of desertification—where dry springs and creeks come alive again and the denuded landscape comes back to life.

To effectively break down old vegetation in brittle environments requires concentrated animal impact, achieved by mimicking the density and movements of the original buffalo herds. Innovative ranchers like Don and Cleo Shaules, near Billings, Montana, restore the historical sequence of grazing by putting more animals in a smaller space for

The author used cattle to manipulate habitat on this brittle pasture in favor of more forage while halting desertification. Pony, Montana.

shorter periods of time. Additional impact may be achieved by herding the animals, or by putting feed or supplements in areas where impact is especially desired. The impact of the animals effectively breaks down old plants while also inoculating the landscape with bacteria in the form of manure. With heavy animal impact the Shaules have successfully trampled cactus and sagebrush into the dirt, while "rototilling" the soil to favor new seedlings. The rich, brown soil humus increased from 1/4 inch up to 1 1/2 inches in just ten years, and the Shaules have been able to more than double their livestock numbers[15]. In effect, they were able to manipulate or "tilt" the successional process in favor of a richer more abundant landscape able to support more cattle, not less.

The economic ecosystem can be manipulated in a similar way. By working with the ecosystem processes and the mechanisms of change, we can tilt succession in favor of a greener, more abundant world.

The problem is that when something isn't right then we tend to take the overly-simplistic approach of focusing directly at that one thing to force it back into order. It gets to be like modern farming, where we annihilate every weed and bug because they are "bad". If crime gets out of control then we try to clamp down on it. If inflation gets out of hand then we attempt setting price controls. If kids do not behave then we spank them. If the air gets polluted then we jump on the industry and penalize them for their actions.

Yet we know that these kinds of direct external controls do not work, at least not very well, on ecosystems. You can kill a thousand weeds, but there will always be a thousand more to take their places. Direct control of any complex organization, natural or human-made simply does not last. I am not saying that you cannot control such systems, but only that you cannot force them. It simply means that to get the desired results you need to play by the rules. You cannot take autocratic control over the economy, or people, or kids, or nature. The concept of natural farming is simply a way of tilting or nudging the ecosystem to favor the crops you want. Instead of trying to grow the crops yourself, it is a matter of gently manipulating the rules so that the ecosystem itself goes on to produce those crops for you. To get the outcomes we want in the economic ecosystem we must stop trying to control everything. We need to develop an ecosystems approach.

For example, over the years we have tried to regulate away every problem that afflicts the environment around us. Each year there is a constant push-pull, tug-of-war between environmentalists and industry. Millions of dollars and countless hours, days, weeks and months of human effort are wasted pushing and pulling each side of the issues. Environmentalists seek more control, while industries seek less. Through government bureaucracy, environmental organizations impose regulations that state specifically how much any company can pollute and even how that pollution must be controlled. The economic incentive for the industries in response to this external control is to buck the system. The longer a company can put off the installation of pollution controls the better its bottom line. The incentive is to lobby the government for lighter controls, or to sue the government on some fine legal points, or to otherwise stall the actual installation of pollution controls. There is no incentive to actually stop polluting.

Besides being largely ineffective, such laws are also unsustainable, as was discovered in 1994 and 1995 when legislators, both locally and nationally, suddenly trashed decades worth of environmental regulatory "progress". Environmentalists considered it a disaster, but it may be the best thing that could have happened for our environment. The regulatory approach is a painfully slow way to make any kind of environmental gains, and as we saw, it is not sustainable. If environmental organizations want to make any real and sustainable progress towards helping the planet, then they need to play by the ecosystem rules.

One way this has been done is by putting a value on pollution. The EPA successfully used this approach in the Los Angeles area, where smog has long been a chronic problem. In this particular case a cap was put on the total amount of pollution that could be put into the local atmosphere. New companies could still start up in the area and contribute to air pollution, but first they had to purchase "pollution credits" from preexisting companies. If another company was closing down, or otherwise limiting their pollution output then they could sell off their pollution credits to a new company. If a lot of companies should want to start up, then those credits would quickly become very valuable. Companies that hold onto those credits can, at any moment, weigh the value of their credits against the cost of installing cleaner energy technologies. As the credits become more valuable then there is an increased incentive to clean up their own smoke stacks so they can sell the credits to someone else. There is an equally great economic incentive for the new companies to start out with the most economical clean technologies available. In any case, it does not matter how many new industries start up, there is a cap on the total amount of pollution that can be put into the atmosphere.

In 1990 the EPA expanded the pollution credits program to help control emissions of sulfur dioxide from utilities across the nation[7]. Government economic models predicted the cost of the credits would be between $500 to $750 per ton of sulfur emitted. Above that price it would be more profitable to invest in the technology to reduce emissions, rather than to purchase the pollution credits. Industry models predicted the cost in the range of $1,000 to $1,500, a cost that might be passed on to utility consumers. However, implementing the free-market system created a habitat niche for innovators to find the cheapest possible ways to reduce emissions. The sulfur credits market opened at $250 per ton but dropped to $66 per ton by 1996, before rising back up to $207 by the end of the decade. Sulfur emissions dropped by 37% nationwide in just one decade, at a fraction of the projected cost[39].

A similar program is in the works to create an international system for reducing carbon emissions. The proposal would allot each country a certain number of carbon credits (less than what is currently emitted), which could be traded back and forth on the open market. Major corporations around the world are already putting the gears in motion

"Sulfur emissions dropped by 37% nationwide in just one decade, at a fraction of the projected cost."

to reduce their carbon emissions now, so that they can sell their pollution credits when the details are ironed out and the system takes effect. Dupont, for example, implemented a program to reduce its emissions to less than half of 1991 levels by the year 2000. The company will benefit twice from the investment, first in lower energy bills, and second in being able to sell it's carbon credits[39].

For conservationists, these programs immediately cap the total amount of pollution entering the atmosphere. Equally important, it provides a means to scale back pollution more and more. Since pollution credits can be bought and sold on the open market, even conservation groups or tax payers can buy the credits. Instead of using them, they might retire those credits to reduce emissions even more.

The worldwide transition to a truly sustainable economy is already underway, driven especially by resource scarcity. When businesses look at the cost of resource consumption on the bottom line, they look for new and innovative ways to do more with less.

For example, in 1976 most energy experts predicted the need for a rapidly expanding energy supply to keep pace with economic growth in the coming decades. Energy expert Amory Lovins, on th other hand, proposed that by extending resource productivity with energy efficiency technologies our economy could use less fuel, save money, and yet still greatly expand production. It was a proposal more than a prediction, but twenty years later the economy was much larger and energy consumption had barely changed. Today, with better technologies and more information, experts predict that the economy could increase resource productivity by another 75 to 90% within a single generation to maintain our existing standard of living with only a fraction of the materials and energy we currently use[39].

In the stiff competition of the global economy, businesses are starting to recognize the potential of wise resource use. Just imagine a factory that reduces its materials and energy costs by 75 to 90%, yet still maintains the same level of production. It would have a significant advantage over the competition. Ultimately all businesses will have to rise to a similar level of efficiency to stay competitive. The only reason our economy is still so inefficient today is a lack of the right information in the right places. People expect energy or resource efficiency to cost them more money. They simply don't know the opportunities they are missing.

The economy in the coming decades will be won by the businesses that can provide the most goods and services with the least throughput of materials and energy. The businesses that change the fastest will simply "make the mostest". Thus, succession is already tilting in favor of a cleaner, greener world. It is inevitable that the economy will mature as a closed-loop system, but there is still much that can be done to speed up the process.

Rocky Mountain Institute, an energy and resources "think tank" started by Amory and Hunter Lovins in Snowmass, Colorado is one organization that really knows how to use market forces as a tool to tilt industry in favor of a better world. Most environmental organizations work in vain to pass new laws, or they sue corporations and governments based on existing laws. But the people at Rocky Mountain Institute have merely worked to put the right information in the right hands, showing corporations and governments that resource conservation is good for business. In the past, for example, power companies sought to meet increased demand solely through increased power production. RMI gave the utilities a new accounting procedure, called "least-cost planning", which enables them to directly compare the cost of expanding output against the alternative of implementing efficient technologies to make the existing power supply meet the needs of more and more users. You may not have noticed the effects of their work, but they have changed the way virtually every power utility in the country does business. Since the early 1980's, RMI has probably made more change in the world, with fewer people and less money, than any other nonprofit organization.

One of Rocky Mountain Institutes major projects today is to bring fuel efficient cars to the market. Ultralight cars can be built of durable composite materials, with small gas engines generating electricity to power motors on each wheel. These ultralights have the potential to achieve up to 200 miles per gallon[39]. RMI encouraged a few start-up companies to begin designing these ultralights, then promoted the idea among competitors, showing them that they had better start researching ultralights as well, or risk losing out in the coming "revolution" of the auto industry. The result is that at least two dozen companies are now working to bring ultralights to market and early prototypes are already on the road. In 2000 Honda started mass-marketing its first gas-electric hybrid, the 70 mpg *Insight*. Before long it is likely that we will all be driving ultralights, the end result of RMI encouraging a little friendly competition in the markets.

Rocky Mountain Institute has worked behind the scenes, tinkering with economic succession in simple but dramatic ways to make big changes in the world. You too can help tilt succession in favor of a better world, and there are an infinite number of ways to do so, especially by jumping into the business world and showing the competition how to make more profit with less throughput. As you lead the way, others will follow.

Introducing New Products and Services to shift Habitats

In the *Origin of Species* Charles Darwin proposed that the whole gene pool of each species was continuously undergoing gradual change. However, there were problems with that idea. Specifically, it would be extremely difficult for any individual mutation to merge into the whole population. There would be a tendency for mutant genes to be diluted away in the gene pool. For example, the Huorani natives of Equador carry a recessive gene that gives many members of the tribe twelve fingers and toes. How does such a gene transition from recessive to dominant within a species? Naturalists were long bewildered by the absence of gradual change in the fossil record. There always seemed to be sudden, dramatic change from one fossil layer to the next.

The reason for this is because *new species evolve on the margin*[72]. Imagine a "valley" several hundred miles across and surrounded by mountains on all sides. Now suppose that only one type of grass seed is deposited into this valley. Coincidentally the whole expanse of the valley is the ideal habitat for this particular type of grass. The valley fills up and evolution virtually stalls. There are still mutations, but the grass is already optimized for the environment, and the mutations fail to survive. On the margins of the valley, however, there is a great diversity of habitats. Possibly it is wetter in the mountains on one side than on the other, or one area may be warmer or colder. There could be different chemistry in the soil. The valley grass may survive in each of these areas, but it wouldn't prosper. Over time there would be gradual mutations and a few of these abnormalities would be more optimized to the marginal environment, eventually creating a whole new species.

Then some sudden change comes to the valley. Let's say the earth's climate changes, causing this particular valley to become slightly warmer and wetter. The valley would become more favorable to one of the marginal grass species, resulting in an apparent "jump" in evolution from one species to another. The previously dominate species would be limited back to the margin or completely eliminated. Thus evolution proceeds both gradually and suddenly. Therefore, the recessive gene for twelve fingers and toes would not become a dominant gene unless something catastrophic happened to the rest of the human population.

Any time the environment changes it dislodges old species and creates new opportunities. Any optimized species living on the margin rushes in to fill the void. When there is no optimized species then evolution progresses at a rapid speed (relatively speaking), with many mutations surviving to fill each of the ecological niches. The process stalls when the habitat fills up. Because of this, some of the most favorable environments with the most fertile soils are the least diverse. Evolution fills the ecological niches and stops. But less-favorable environments may require more creative strategies from many different species to be able to economize on the use of resources.

The final step of our own physical evolution was apparently due to a cold snap some 2.5 million years ago. Some of our Australopithecine ancestry developed bigger bodies-(with less surface area per volume) as a means to conserve heat. This move towards larger bodies subsequently required a longer growth time to adulthood. And this in turn meant delaying reproductive maturity. To delay sexual maturity, the body retained more and more juvenile characteristics. Thus, our physical proportions today are more reminiscent of immature monkeys than adult monkeys. The most significant juvenile characteristic we retained was the large brain size to body mass. A newborn baby has a big head and a small body; but compared to our ancestry, we as adults also have big heads for our body size. Another juvenile characteristic we retained is our inquisitive behavior. We are like newborn animals exploring the world for the first time, but we never quite grow up. We keep playing around in our environment exploring like little kids. We just call it "science" to justify our behavior as adults.

Our own species began to diversify while living in isolated pockets all over the globe, evolving into many different races, or variations of human beings. Those differences are gradually diluting as we merge into one global community. Thousands of years from now there may be just one race of humans—an amalgamation of all of them. Any new species to evolve from us would develop in isolated pockets on the margin, such as in distant colonies on planets with higher or lower gravity or otherwise new habitats.

Like new species, new ideas and new technologies evolve on the margin, including ideas like photovoltaics. The first solar panels were extremely expensive to produce, costing $600 a watt. There is no way they could compete in a habitat with cheap oil. But oil was useless way out on the margin, on satellites in space. Solar panels were the most economical means of providing energy to the satellites. Evolution proceeded gradually, and by 1970 the price was down to $150 a watt. By 1980 solar panels were appearing on backwoods cabins, still on the margin, miles away from the power lines. It became more economical to install solar panels than to pay utilities thousands of dollars to bring in conventional power lines. The economics of solar technologies slowly crept closer and closer to conventional power sources. By 1990 the cost was down to $4.50 a watt, and it was estimated that photovoltaics were competitive to within 400 meters from the utility grid[63]. That means that if your home was 400 or more meters away from the nearest power pole then it was generally more economical to use solar energy (combined with energy-efficient appliances) than to extend the power lines. Each new technological mutation in photovoltaics has allowed them to invade more and more of the economic habitat of fossil fuels. Eventually—it really does not matter when—perhaps ten years, or fifty, but at some point in time, photovoltaics will become economically competitive right up to the utility grid. Solar cells will suddenly invade the economic niche of the fossil fuels, taking over the market habitat and dramatically altering the makeup of the economic ecosystem.

The illustration "Photovoltaic Economics" can be considered a graph. Just draw an imaginary line connecting from the satellite to the remote cabin, through the not-so-remote house, and extend that through the utility grid. At whatever point in time those lines cross, the transformation to a solar society will seem to occur virtually

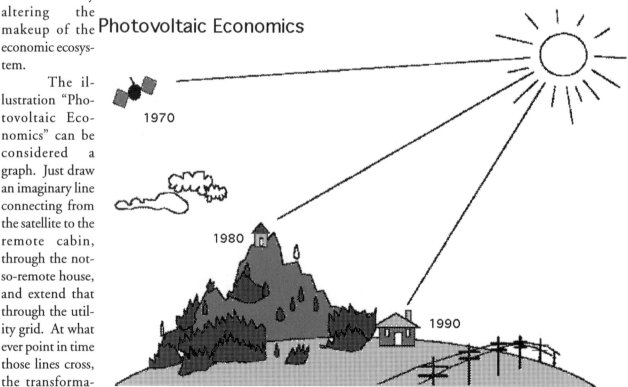

Photovoltaic Economics

1970

1980

1990

Photovoltaic technology has evolved on the margin, occupying niches in the economic system where fossil fuels cannot compete. Each year the technology becomes more competitive, slowly biting into former fossil fuel habitat. When photovoltaic electricity becomes cheaper than fossil fuel electricity, the technology will invade the economic niche, and the transition to a solar society will seem to happen almost overnight.

overnight. Indeed, just reaching the $3-per-watt threshold is expected by some analysts to cause a tenfold increase in sales. Some mass-production developments currently in the works are expected to meet that threshold and bring us ever closer to the point where solar becomes competitive with the grid.

Like photovoltaics, hundreds of other cleaner technologies are evolving on the margin, from electric or solar powered lawn mowers to high-efficiency automobiles, better batteries, and workable fuel cells. Entrepreneurs recognize the implicit demand for cleaner technologies to "close the loop" on pollution in the coming decades. These eco-pioneers are scrambling to be the first to occupy the new economic niches as they open up. Many of these new gadgets are being produced in test quantities already, to gather experiential data for next-generation improvements. Technological refinements, combined with further pollution restrictions, will increasingly tilt market forces in favor of these newer, better products, dramatically changing both our economy and its impact on the natural world in the decades ahead.

Some ideas, technological and otherwise, are so significant that they transform the entire economic/cultural landscape. Like introducing a carnivore onto an island that has evolved for millennia without any kind of predator, it changes everything. Animals that have evolved without defensive capabilities are quickly exterminated, and only those that can quickly evolve to fit the new environment will survive. The microchip is one such idea. It altered the entire economic landscape, driving old industries out of business and creating niches for thousands of new innovations. We are still feeling the effects of the change reverberating back and forth through our economy and we will for decades to come. Similarly, "New Age" memes like healthy diets, herbs, and acupuncture originated on the "fringe" of our culture, yet transformed mainstream culture in relatively little time. We don't hear the term "New Age" nearly as much now that it isn't so new or different from mainstream thought. Memes like these that transform the way we look at the world are often called "paradigms". Many newer paradigms and technologies will similarly merge into mainstream thought and use in the coming decades, transforming the world we know in the process.

With sufficient understanding of some of the new ideas and innovations that are coming, you can help accelerate transformation of the economic ecosystem. You can help make the world a better place and create a life of abundance and prosperity for yourself along the way.

Part III
Tools to
Work With

"To have done anything by which you earned money merely is to have been truly idle or worse. If the laborer gets no more than the wages which his employer pays him, he is cheated, he cheats himself."
—Henry David Thoreau, Life Without Principle

3-1

Creativity

-Eliminating the Obstacles to Your Dreams-

So far we have established that the economy is like an ecosystem, that it consumes energy and resources and produces waste. We know that to create a truly sustainable economy we need to "close the loop" so that all material wastes are properly recycled, either through industry or nature. We also know, in principle at least, that we can "tilt succession" in the economic ecosystem to achieve our personal Dreams while helping to make the world a better place. We can change the world through the purchases we make at home, the actions we take in business, and through popular opinion and legislation. That's nice in principle, but where do we start in the real world? The answer, in short, is "creativity".

Creativity is one of the key attributes that makes our species unique and different from the other creatures of nature. Our species has the ability to combine the resources of the world into completely new products. Innovation came slowly at first, in part because there was a limited variety of resources to create with—there is only so many new products you can make with sticks, rocks, and bones. But each innovation that came along provided new ideas, new tools, and sometimes whole new resources like clay, glass, or metals to work with. Today there are millions upon millions of resources to create with, and every day people innovate new ways to use these materials.

Creativity is by far the most powerful tool we have to work with towards changing the world and achieving our Dreams. The problem with creativity, however, is that we humans have a knack for making things more complicated, rather than less.

It constantly amazes me that we have access to so much knowledge, resources and tools, yet we use it all so poorly. For example, we have all the resources we need to economically build highly efficient houses that require neither heaters nor air conditioners for comfort. But instead we tack up poorly designed structures and use brute force to pump heat inside every day through the winters and to pump it back out through the summers. We have to scrape and repaint every few years; we replace the carpet, linoleum, and the water heater every fifteen to twenty years, and the roof every thirty to fifty. Through brute force alone we have managed to conquer nature and accumulate material wealth, but people have to work twice as hard for everything in life as they would with more thoughtful, more creative planning.

The first key to effective resource use is to creatively mimic nature in it's efficiency and synergism to close the loop on all kinds of wastes at home and in business, from wasted materials and energy to wasted time, money and labor. Just think about these kinds of wastes with everything you do—when you get in the car, when you spend money or pay the bills, when you flip on the light switch, while you are at work,

Creativity is the most powerful tool we have to work with for changing the world and achieving our dreams.

67

and while you are making dinner. That is the basic strategy Renee and I used to close the loop on mortgage payments, high energy bills, and the need for regular employment, so that we can have the house of our Dreams and the lifestyle we enjoy, without having to work all the time to pay for it. Closing the loop on waste works for consumers and it works in business.

The second key to effective resource use is to creatively find ways to "tilt succession" in your favor, so that the economic ecosystem produces the results you want, without you having to do all the work.

Synergism

The fiercest competition in the natural ecosystem is often amongst the closest kin[72]. When same or similar plants or animals compete for one ecological niche even the most incremental gains in resource efficiency can mean the difference between success and extinction. The result of this extreme competition is that species diversify and specialize in order to avoid competing. For example, cows and sheep share a similar niche as grazing animals, yet they have different dietary preferences. Cows prefer grasses, while sheep favor forbs and bushes. This minimizes the competition between them so they can share the same habitat with the least overlap.

By selling stone hot tubs we would not be competing through calories, but more through creativity.

Businesses also specialize to avoid competition. No single market can cater to the needs of everyone so there are many specialized economic niches, each with it's own clientele. For instance, there are many types and sizes of grocery stores from mini-marts, to co-ops, to supermarkets, to warehouse markets. They all sell groceries, yet they occupy slightly different niches in the economic ecosystem. The real competition is not between the big guy and the little guy, but between the most identical stores, such as where there is one mini-mart across the street from another. The moral is that the best way to beat the competition is often not at all.

Imagine starting a spa business in a town that already has several. You walk into any spa shop and all the hot tubs look remarkably the same. Each business in town is in direct competition with every other spa business because they are all selling similar products. There are certainly different brand names and different levels of quality but all the tubs still look about the same. To compete you would have to advertise how and why your spas are better than your competitors', while also keeping your prices comparatively low. Yet a new business usually has high overhead costs for the buildings, inventory, and staff. There are many expenses to pay before making

This hot tub has a waterfall built into the stone work above it that can be turned on and off.

the first sale. This beginning debt makes it difficult to compete with established businesses that have had years to pay off their own debts. They can lower their prices more because they have fewer expenses. Competition is based solely on calories, with each retailer trying to offer the public the most tub for the least calories. New businesses can be much more successful if they start out in an unoccupied niche along the habitat margin.

We once considered entering the spa market ourselves with our stone "HOPS Tubs". We would have still been in competition with other spa dealers, but not in exactly the same niche. The customer will only buy one spa, but stone spas are unique, and no one else offers them. Other spa dealers have to compete on the basis of calories—the most tub for the least tokens, but by selling stone hot tubs we would have been competing through creativity. We would not have to undercut other retailers prices because we would be offering such a different product. Having a unique product or service means you do not have to compete directly with other businesses. We chose not to enter the spa market because that occupation did not fit our goals. Basically I'd rather design the hot tubs in as part of a house or as part of a whole housing development.

An occupation that did fit our goals for awhile, which we intend to return to, is house construction. We built a stone house on "speculation", meaning that we sold it after we built it. Building the house was fun because people were so interested in it. All the other houses today are so much the same that people crave something unique. People stopped by our construction site nearly every day to ask about what we were doing. They looked at other new houses and they told us that those houses "lacked substance". We did not really need to advertise what we were doing because our product advertised itself. Furthermore, its uniqueness appraised to a higher price than similar-sized houses. We did not try to compete with mainstream contractors whose houses all look alike. We found our own niche.

Instead of competition, there is often a high level of symbiosis in the natural ecosystem, where living organisms exist together for mutual benefit. Lichens, for instance, are the "mossy" or scaly plants found attached to rocks, trees trunks, or any otherwise barren surfaces throughout the field and forest. Lichens are not true plants, but rather a symbiosis where certain types of fungi provide a protective structure encasing a colony of single-celled algae. Lichens do not have roots, but are nourished by the water and mineral nutrients that land directly on their surfaces. The fungi and algae are separate species that can survive apart from each other, but they are limited in the habitats they can colonize. It is only through symbiosis that they can utilize the harsh environments of barren rock and tree trunks.

The efficiency and elegance of the natural ecosystem is especially due to this kind of high level of integration between its component parts. There is a synergy between widely different species of plants, animals, and fungus as resources are used and recycled from one to another. Each organism produces "waste", but the waste is not "pollution", because the waste of any one species becomes the resource for another species. The only reason our industrial culture produces "waste" and "pollution" is because the economic ecosystem remains immature and businesses are just beginning to learn to utilize the resources that are currently being discarded into the environment.

In the past businesses tended to operate in a single resource mode, but the emerging trend is towards synergistic resource use. For example, a cement plant would have focused solely on cement production in the past, firing their kilns up to thousands of degrees, and then discharging unusable waste heat into the atmosphere. Today however, more and more industries are striving to utilize old wastes as new resources. For example, many factories are now generating electricity from waste heat, a process known as co-generation. Even low-grade heat can be captured and utilized through symbiotic relationships to warm other nearby businesses, homes, or greenhouses. This kind of synergy can save money for a business, as in lower utility bills, or can even bring in additional income, by selling the waste heat or even by growing and selling vegetables in a greenhouse.

Waste heat is not the only secondary resource being utilized by new companies. Rising disposal costs have caused more and more businesses to reexamine their waste in the hope of creating new and useful products to bring to the market, instead of to the landfill.

There are unlimited opportunities for productive synergism, and you do not need to own an industrial plant to do it. Consider Thoreau's quote at the beginning of this chapter, that an employee should always try to get more than just money out of their job. An occupation should be both educational and challenging. You will almost always be better off when you can find a paying job that also gives you new skills for achieving your dreams-even if you have to take a cut in pay to get that job. I personally have passed up more jobs opportunities in my life than I have taken, including many high-paying jobs, because I would rather be broke and enlightened than to give up my life to "earn a living". If a job does not help me advance towards my own dreams and goals, then I do not take it, period.

Creative synergism will help you be successful in every endeavor you undertake. Renee and I spent four years designing our house before we started construction because we worked hard to integrate many diverse parts into one efficient whole. Most buildings today are constructed without synergistic thought, where the architect creates a structure, then passes the design along to a mechanicals person to figure out what kind of heating and cooling equipment will be needed to maintain the environment inside.

Just imagine an automobile company trying to design a new car this way, where one department creates a body, the next creates a frame, and the next has to find space to install the engine and attach the wheels. A good car simply could not be built without intensive collaboration between all the departments, and the same is true in architecture. An integrated approach leads to a higher quality structure, and usually a lower cost.

Look around and you will notice opportunities for synergistic resource use wherever you go. Our local hot springs, for example, has enough extra hot water to run a significant greenhouse operation. I can't help but soak in the hot water and imagine a beautiful jungle-like atmosphere of ripening vegetables and a restaurant to use them in. A business like that could capture income from those who come to soak, and through the vegetables they grow, and through the people they feed. Certain types of fast-growing fish would do well in the warm water that is otherwise discharged into the creek, and the food scraps and greenhouse compost would raise quite a few hogs. I heard about one hot-springs in Idaho that even planned to raise alligators! All this and more could be produced from a hot water resource that is currently used only as a single hot pool with minimal facilities.

Synergism is a mode of thinking to help you imagine creative ways to achieve multiple goals with a single effort—kind of like hitting two home runs with a single swing of the bat! Consider that in business, most schemes for getting rich typically involve taking someone else's money. You might invent some widget and sell it to millions of people, or you might successfully market some service such as tree trimming. In any case, the consumer only has a finite number of dollars to spend, no matter where they actually spend it. But just imagine how successful a business might be if you could make people richer by taking their money?

The history of free enterprise has often been a story of exploitation at the expense of consumers and the environment, but it does not have to be that way. You can actually help make the world a better place for all through the businesses you start. One route is through the concept of selling savings. Essentially, it is a way of making money by helping others to save money. You can actually make your customers wealthier by taking their money. Indeed, their are hundreds of billions, perhaps even trillions of dollars, to be made by doing so, and the opportunities need to be exploited, for everyone's benefit.

In energy conservation alone, there are hundreds of billions of dollars worth of opportunities just waiting to be exploited, and yet there are few people taking advantage of those opportunities. For example, I often see newspaper ads by carpenters hoping to get miscellaneous work, but I have yet to see an ad from a carpenter proposing to make money for their clients. Many home owners might be delighted to save money through conservation retrofits, but that is not easy for most people to do. It may takes weeks or months for a home owner to become educated enough about the subject to make informed energy conservation decisions. Most people have jobs and families already; they do not have time to do the research. At the same time, there are millions of other people sitting around unemployed waiting for someone to call them to work. That is just not the way it happens.

As a carpenter you would have to wait a long time for home owners to become educated enough about energy conservation to tell you what they wanted done. Instead, you need to give them an energy audit and tell

Energy Retrofits
Save Energy . . . and Make Money!

-Free energy audit of your home-
-Free planning / designing assistance-
-Quality workmanship-
-Insulating / Weatherstripping-
-General Carpentry-
-Solar Installations-

Pay Nothing now . . .
. . .and even Less Later!*

*Payments can be made based on the amount we reduce your power bill. You keep all the savings for yourself after our work has been paid for.

them what they need done, then you can go to work.

Additionally, you may be able to sell your services to customers at "no cost to them". You save them energy, and in return they pay you their savings until your bill is paid off. Basically, they continue paying the amount of their original average power bill, only they pay less to the power company and more to you. Later, after your bill is paid, they collect the savings for themselves. It costs them nothing up front, and nothing later; they merely pay what they have been paying all along, until you are paid off. If your work is good and your prices are reasonable, then you may be able to connect with a bank that will carry the loans for your clients, so that you can be paid in full from the beginning.

There are vast fortunes to be made by helping other people to reduce their expenses. You can increase your own income by helping other people to increase theirs. You help them save money they are now losing, and you siphon off a portion of the savings. It can be a "win-win-win-win" deal. It is good for you; it is good for the customer you exploit, it is often good for the environment, and that together makes first class advertising material. You will have more customers than you want when you start advertising to make them money. Indeed, there are people making big bucks doing that already.

There are many financial services that make money by helping people to save on insurance policies, taxes, credit cards, and so forth. Such businesses do not produce anything tangible, but rather, they study the "fine print" of insurance and banking, and taxes, and sort out any information that can save people money in dealing with such things. They release that information for a price. One such business, called the Charles J. Givens Organization, charges people about $400 a year for membership. Members pay that sum for financial advice, and they usually save much more than they spend on membership. Even better, you can check out his books at the library and save an additional $400. (Note that the Givens Organization has been sued by individuals who claim they got faulty financial advice, so always read the material carefully and act according to your own conclusions.) Savings is a very lucrative product to sell, and there are hundreds of thousands of dues-paying members to the Givens Organization. That's big money.

Similar to the Givens Organization, but more home-spun are the many magazine and book publications, including the one you are reading now, that help people save the money they are now losing. If there is one type of publication that is relatively easy to sell, it is the one that makes money for the purchaser. For instance, in June of 1990 Amy Dacyczyn of Leeds, Maine started publishing the *Tightwad Gazette* to help people save money. The idea caught on and she was featured in *Parade Magazine* and on the "Donahue" show, which of course, brought her ample business. Later, in the issue of December 1992, Dacyczyn wrote that she was aware of 26 publications similar to hers—25 of which had started since she had her moment of fame![17] People want to buy savings, they are just waiting for the opportunities to do so. If you have a genuinely helpful product then you will have some genuinely interested customers.

The opportunities to market savings are as limitless as your imagination. You can make money by helping people to save money on just about anything they need. Let me give you one more example.

We are working our way into the construction business. I personally know that I would be delighted to make someone rich if they would sell me second-hand and recycled building materials at a savings over what we would pay for new materials. This customer is ready to spend money. All I need is for someone to exploit the opportunity and say they are open for business.

Tilting Succession Your Way

Masanobu Fukuoka[32] was schooled in conventional industrial farming but eventually became disillusioned with it. He recognized that agricultural scientists were always inventing something new for farming. First there was the plow, then fertilizer, then specialized seed, then herbicides, then pesticides-always something new that would "boost yields and increase profits". Fukuoka understood that each new cultural "advance" only caused the farmer to expend more money and more labor, or in our vocabulary, more food and fuel calories. He saw this as a snow-balling type effect; agricultural science continually marched onward, always creating something this or something that or something new for agriculture. Fukuoka took the opposite approach. Instead of finding new ways to add complexity to agriculture, Fukuoka researched ways to eliminate work. He studied diligently in his field for years to invent "something less" for agriculture. Through careful trial and error and observation in his rice and barley fields he learned how not to plow, how not to fertilize, how not to weed or use herbicides and pesticides. Basically he manipulates succession in the ecosystem to favor his crops so his crops can grow semi-wild. In effect he eliminated most of the cultural elements of farming beyond broadcasting seed and harvesting the grain. With his "do-nothing" approach Fukuoka succeeded in raising some of the highest yielding crops in Japan-with little effort expended in food or fuel calories.

The most productive use of time in my own life has been the days I spent wandering aimlessly in the mountains. It is at these moments that I took the time to reflect on my Dreams and to brainstorm the best routes towards achieving them.

Most people in our culture would feel too guilty to spend even a single day just walking. There is a strong work ethic in Western culture and people often feel like they should be working at something, regardless of whether or not their effort helps them to achieve any goals. But I can say from experience that wandering aimlessly can be immensely productive. A day spent walking alone, creatively brainstorming ways to eliminate work, can easily save a week of effort towards achieving your goals. Before you undertake any action towards achieving your goals you should ask yourself:

1) Is this action truly necessary to my Dream?
2) How can I simplify this project to eliminate extra work?

True laziness is a virtue. I do not mean the kind of laziness where you do not get around to pursuing your dreams, but the kind of laziness where you will do anything to avoid work along the path to success. A lazy person possessed with a Dream is a force to be reckoned with.

Among all tools for making the world a better place, this idea of creatively eliminating work is often the most difficult to grasp. The very idea of achieving a goal or dream implies action, a do-something approach. This is especially true in business, where the basis of success is production. Doing nothing to achieve your goals seems counter-intuitive.

In our western culture we are always trying new things, asking what happens if I do this? What happens if I do that? The do-nothing approach is to ask, "What happens if I do not do this or that?"

There was a time when gas stations sent a clerk out to pump the fuel, check the oil and wash the windows. But then someone asked "What would happen if we stopped offering full service, and gave people a discount to pump their own gas?" Once the question was asked, the new mode of business, called "self-service", quickly became the industry standard. More recently gas stations have been able to further reduce their personnel load by installing self-service electronic payment systems, so people can pay at the pump. Self-service payment saves time for customers who no longer need to stand in line to pay at the counter. More to the point in this example, self-service payment eliminates work, allowing gas stations to reduce their staff load and further cut prices for their customers. They do not have to serve their customers at all, a true do-nothing approach!

Tilting succession, or "do-nothing" farming is a mode of thought to help you imagine ways of letting the ecosystem work for you. For example, in the natural ecosystem there is no need to plant lots of seed, as long as the ecosystem is optimized for the plant you are trying to grow. Plants produce seed exponentially, so there is no need to spend time and money building the population of a new species. As Allan Savory writes in *Holistic Resource Management*, he would just yank a desirable clump of grass out of the ground in a place where it was abundant, and fling it out of the truck as he drove by a place he wanted it established—nature would take care of the rest.

Most **nonprofit** institutions operate on mere shoestring budgets, chronically under-funded and understaffed. Most non-profits beg continuously for money, competing against other non-profits for donations, while eating up much of their budgets in the quest for more handouts. But some innovative nonprofit groups are creating sustainable new sources of funding with an approach that author Bill Shore describes as "non-profits for profit" in his book, *Revolution of the Heart*[78]. For example, you've probably seen Paul Newman's salad dressings and other products at the store. Newman's Own, the company that produces the products, gives 100% of after-tax profits away to charitable organizations, totaling millions of dollars every year. The funds go to support worthwhile social and environmental causes around the world. Bill Shore founded the organization Share Our Strength and started the "Charge Against Hunger" campaign through American Express, raising millions of dollars for people in need.

Tilting succession can work for regular businesses as well, when the right ideas are introduced at the right place at the right time. One obvious example is "multilevel marketing". A good idea with a small beginning can quickly become a major company as each salesperson tries to sign other salespeople, making a small profit from each person's sales below them in the hierarchy.

Advertising is another good example. In any enterprise you undertake it is essential it is important to get the word out to let people know what you have to offer. The question is not "if" but "how" to advertise.

Short-term advertising.

Advertising is a gamble of sorts, where you expend some calories in the hopes of bringing in more calories. You do not generally produce any products or services for the advertising calories you expend, but you expend calories in an effort to get people interested in the products or services which you offer when you are not busy expending calories promoting them. Of course, any calories you expend through advertising have to be recouped out of your sales, and that means you need to either raise your prices or sell more of your product or service to balance out. Every time you advertise you are gambling that you will harvest more calories than you expended. The important part of advertising then, is not how many customers you get, but how many customers you get relative to how much it cost you to get them.

At times it may be more profitable to spend nothing on advertising and have perhaps only five customers, as opposed to spending a fortune and having a hundred customers. In some businesses, such as primitive skills, this can be especially true. For instance, in our first year of business we rented a booth at trade fair and thus reached the several thousand people who walked by our booth. People were very enthusiastic about what we were doing and said we had a great booth. For the three day affair we shelled out $350 for the booth and spent another $200 or so on printing costs for the brochures we handed out, plus we spent a week or so of our time preparing for and doing the show. Now, $550 is not a lot of money, but in our case, it represented ten to twenty percent of our potential total gross income for the year, if we maxed out all of our classes. As it was, we did not get even one participant as a result of the trade show.

We had a good booth at the show and a good product, and people told us so. In retrospect, I would say that we gained no business simply because no one had ever previously thought about taking primitive skills classes before. Primitive skills classes are the sort of thing that many people have to think about and dream about for quite a while, sometimes a couple years, before they are ready to invest both their limited financial resources and their limited vacation time in it. In this case, we found it was better to hang out and wait, rather than to expend a lot of effort attempting to force our school on the market. It cost us nothing when we had no customers, we just did other work for income instead. We relied principally on word-of-mouth advertising, and started growing.

Of course, all businesses are certainly different from each other and require individual advertising efforts. It is important, when advertising, to always weigh your choices with your advertising dollars. I do not just mean that you choose between one type of media or another, but that you choose between short-term and long-term advertising. **Short-term advertising** is where you expend time and money on television, radio, or newspaper ads, etc., plus the flashing neon lights and all the other hype, to get customers into your business immediately. **Long-term advertising** is where you invest that time and money into improv-

Long-term advertising.

ing your product and/or lowering your prices.

Short-term advertising has an instant effect, while long-term advertising has a sustained effect. Long-term advertising is the kind of advertising where you build up a reputation for quality products or services at low prices, while short-term advertising may just bring customers in once.

I almost always favor the long-term rather than short-term approach. For instance, I could spend an eight-hour day standing on the street corner demonstrating primitive skills and handing out brochures to attract a few customers. On the other hand, I could spend the same eight hours writing about primitive skills. Standing on the street corner may bring in a few immediate customers, but afterwards I may have to go stand on the corner again to bring in more customers. Writing about primitive skills on the other hand may bring in no customers today, but can eventually lead to having many customers, once my writing appears in book stores all over the country.

I believe that too many businesses rely excessively on short-term hype and not enough on long-term quality. For instance, no matter where you go in the country, one grocery store is an awful lot like the next; each typically is the aesthetic equivalent of a warehouse, and each prints and mails coupons to lure people in. All the stores are so alike that each has to fork over the advertising money just to keep from losing business to their competitors who are all doing the same thing. A grocery store could potentially be more prosperous by investing in long-term quality rather than short-term hype. Instead of investing in hyper-excitement, a store could invest in a more wholesome excitement, by making the store an interesting, comfortable, and inspiring environment to be in, a place where people feel good about coming to and look forward to coming back.

Short-term advertising often tends to be just purely obnoxious, and sometimes it seems that it becomes more that way all the time, as customers become numb to the previous levels of obnoxiousness. Long-term advertising can be more subtle, more interesting, and it can even be news. One of our own primary strategies is to make each of our businesses interesting enough that people will want to hear about us through the news. For example, I have published over fifty articles about primitive skills and economics between three newspapers and four magazines. Additionally, we have appeared four times on the local television news, and six times on local radio shows. We have had two newspaper features written about us, and at this point we are really just beginning. We have spent little money on advertising, yet we are always running into people who say, "Yes, I've heard of you. "

Thus, when we have a $100 and a couple days to spend on advertising we have to make a decision. We have to decide between short-term hype and long-term quality. Usually we choose to invest it in making our school that much better so that we can attract more news attention and thus, free advertising.

In promoting your own enterprises you will have to make the decisions as to where your investments will bring you the greatest advertising returns. You may find that a combination of both short-term hype and the long-term quality is the most effective strategy for you.

In nature resource efficiency is everything. The species that use energy and resources most economically are the ones that survive to put forth a new generation of progeny. In our homes and in our businesses we can be most successful if we creatively mimic nature to use resources as economically as possible to achieve our dreams. Using resources with synergism and a do-nothing approach may take a lot of creative brainstorming, but the results are worth the effort!

"{The scientist} pores over books night and day, straining his eyes and becoming nearsighted, and if you wonder what on earth he has been working on all that time it is to become the inventor of eyeglasses to correct nearsightedness."

—Masanobu Fukuoka, The One Straw Revolution[27]

3-2
Materials to Work With
-Open Niches in the Economic Ecosystem-

Living organisms extract resources from the environment and modify them into useful products. Material waste and low-grade heat are by-products of this metabolism, but the material wastes become resource inputs to other organisms, so the only true waste is low-grade heat. The natural ecosystem is a closed-loop system where all material wastes are recycled.

To create a truly sustainable economic ecosystem we must also form a closed-loop system so that all material wastes are recycled back into new and useful products, and the only waste discharged is low-grade heat. From this perspective the problem of sustainability seems as simple and as complex as figuring out what to do with our garbage. The logical route forward is to examine our wastes and find ways to put them to use. Or is there more to it than that?

It amazes me everywhere I go to see how many under-utilized resources of all kinds there are in the world. I drive along in the car and see woodlots that are overgrown and full of dead wood. I see old vehicles or tires parked and forgotten in backyards. There are piles of lumber and bricks and scrap metal out back. I see trees with fruit falling to the ground and yards that are not even planted! There are houses and buildings abandoned and falling apart. Hot steam is vented out industrial smokestacks into the atmosphere, and behind every business there seems to be a dumpster full of resources to haul away.

Whether you are building a home or starting a business, you will find many resources to work with in the world. Sometimes you will work with materials recycled out of the waste stream. Other times you will use virgin materials extracted directly from the ecosystem. Some resources you will gather yourself and others you will pay for. For personal use you might just need a one-time supply of materials, but for commercial enterprises you will probably need a continuous resource base.

It amazes me everywhere I go to see how many under-utilized resources there are in the world, from piles of lumber and bricks to abandoned cabinets, to factories venting steam and even unplanted yards.

This chapter is about far more than just finding ways to recycle existing wastes. It is about effectively utilizing all material resources—either raw or recycled—through your home and/or business. As you will see, you can even help to close the loop on waste while ignoring the waste stream and harvesting new virgin resources! Effective resource use can be accomplished in several ways, including: 1) recycling, 2) preventing waste before it happens, 3) choosing alternative resources, and 4) extending resource productivity. You will find many ways to profit as you help close the loop on waste and make the world a better place.

Recycling

In nature there is a scavenger class of critters such as vultures, crows, dung beetles, hyenas, and bacteria that recycle the wastes and decaying corpses of others in the natural ecosystem. These life forms are equal to any other living beings, but we humans attach a stigma to the occupation of scavenging. Nevertheless, in the economic ecosystem the wastes produced are so vast and so under-utilized that scavenging is really an easy niche to make a living in, with little need for conventional work.

I've been proud to be a member of the "scavenger-class" of the economic ecosystem for much of my life, salvaging second hand materials to build our home, shopping at thrift stores, recycling scrap metals, and digging in dumpsters for anything that might be useful. There is so much waste in our culture that a person can live off the waste stream with little need for a steady monetary income. Even food, which I always thought was carefully channeled into the food bank system for the needy, is thrown out right and left like you wouldn't believe. I never would have thought to look in a grocery store dumpster myself, but one of the interns that helped out at our school was a professional at it. He came from a family with plenty of money, but couldn't see spending money on food when there is always so much of it in the dumpsters going to waste. While staying with us he kept our larder stocked with gourmet breads, bags of perfectly good flour and sugar, and sometimes brought home blemished fruits and vegetables and dented cans of pop. I've since learned that an estimated 20% of America's food goes to waste![45] Ironically, about 20% of Americans still go hungry. Our trips to town were few and far between but it was evident that a person could feed an entire family for free just by driving around from dumpster to dumpster.

With the aid of tax laws increasingly bent to channel money from those who make it to those who don't, the scavenger class can be one of the least-work, least stress ways to prosper in the economic ecosystem. Indeed, it is because of such thriftiness in my family that we've had the extra money to afford decent computers and I've had the necessary freedom from work to hang out and build a writing career.

While it may be economically lucrative to live off the industrial waste stream, such a lifestyle does very little to close the loop on waste. There is only so much of the waste stream that can be utilized in this fashion. I know from digging in dumpsters. Most of it is garbage.

Even good materials from the waste stream can be uneconomical to work with in business. In order to maintain the flow of production it is essential to have an uninterrupted supply of raw materials. Few enterprises could afford to check every dumpster every day for the necessary materials to keep production up and running. That is a key reason why there is so much resource waste—it is simply easier to extract new materials from a known and reliable source, than to continuously search through the waste stream to find each additional batch of second-hand materials. It is much easier to close the loop on waste if you have a dependable source of waste to work with.

Closing the loop on waste is much easier when working with a reliable source of pure wastes, or relatively pure wastes, such as glass, aluminum, or plastics from recycling centers, old tires from tire centers, or industrial wastes like sawdust from a sawmill or left-over cleaning solvents. If you have a large quantity of a specific kind of waste then it is much easier to find ways to constructively put that waste to work.

For example, because there are so many billions of used tires left sitting around the country, more and more uses are being found for them. Innovative builders are stacking the tires like bricks and tamping earth inside them to make inexpensive, massive-walled houses called "earthships". On our place we have a sandbox made from a bulldozer-sized tire and horsy swing cut from a regular car tire. Door mats are also available from used tires. Several companies around the world are turning tires into high-quality sandals. I have my own designs for a hiking sandal that I intend to mass-produce.

Tire sandals (with moccasins) made by the author are just one of many ways to put waste tires to good use.

Highway departments are grinding old tires and adding them to asphalt to make more flexible roads. Tires can be even be melted in used motor oil to produce a lighter oil that can be refined into gasoline or diesel. The residue can be added to roads to slow the aging of the asphalt[57].

One of the best ways to close the loop on tire waste may be a system called pyrolisis which uses heat in the absence of oxygen to break the tires down into useful resources. One tire can produce the equivalent of 60 cubic feet of natural gas, the petroleum coke equivalent to seven pounds of medium BTU coal, a pound of steel scrap, and recoverable process heat which may be used to produce hot water, steam or electricity[76]. The upfront cost of the system is relatively low, but it loses something in efficiency, since it takes so much heat to drive the pyrolisis. Solar parabolic dishes focused on the tanks may make the systems more economical to operate. The point is that there are many uses for any large quantity of a relatively pure resource, and I bet you could think of many more good applications for used tires and other waste goods.

Dealing with mixed wastes is clearly the greatest challenge in creating a closed-loop economy. At some point in the future, possibly later this century, the problem of all wastes will be forever solved with the aid of molecular robotic disassemblers, which can take apart any piece of trash atom by atom and separate all the parts into separate piles. But we can hardly afford to wait for advanced new technologies when we are already swimming in trash. More effective waste recovery now can greatly help to reduce the impact of further resource extraction from the environment. Part of the solution is to manually separate wastes, so that there are more pure forms to work with. That is the realm of conventional recycling.

Personally, I like recycling. I see it as a challenge to reduce the amount of garbage we throw out as much as possible. It is also a good way to examine the waste stream for possible opportunities of profit. Of course we recycle the usual stuff like bottles, tin cans, aluminum cans, and cardboard. We don't subscribe to a newspaper as it is just a complete waste of materials and money. We compost all of our food scraps, and we use paper trash and wood scraps to light the fire. A few recyclables are worth money, such as brass, aluminum, copper, and scrap metal, so we recycle those too. We rarely haul anything to the dump other than mixed plastic wastes. Eventually we will find some means to recycle those too.

A particular advantage for us in waste management is that we still use an old-fashioned wood-fired cookstove. We have to start the fire every time we want to cook something, so we easily consume every scrap of paper and wood we can find. The cookstove also generates hot water. With the aid of ultra-clean fluidized bed technology there may be an opportunity to build and market a more modern version of the household trash burner. Scrap wood, tree trimmings, waste paper and possibly even plastic could be dropped in the hopper and chopped into little bits, then injected into the fluidized-bed combustion chamber to fuel a hot water heater or house-hold furnace. Hot temperatures, lots of air, and thorough burning makes it possible to eliminate most pollutants through this kind of incineration. The amount of paper and wood waste discarded in the U.S. every year is reportedly enough to heat a billion homes!

Another solution to this kind of waste may be a shredding composter, so that paper, plastic, and food scraps are all shredded and composted together. Most present-day plastics do not decompose, but they can add a small amount of loft and water-trapping capability to the soil. Many plastics are photo-degradable, so the shredded bits in the garden or flower bed will gradually disappear. Newer plastics are being designed to be biodegradable, so there may indeed be a good market for a shredding composter. I personally would love to purchase such a unit, because we would virtually eliminate the remaining trash we still haul to the dump.

It may seem more idealistic to completely close the loop on wastes, so that paper and plastic wastes are returned to the their original uses. However, even if this waste had a higher use, it would still take more energy and more resources to properly separate it and return it to a plant where it could be remanufactured. As in nature, it can be advantageous at times to allow waste to completely degrade and start over from scratch.

At the level of a single home or small business, there may not be too much potential profit in the waste stream, but in communities or larger businesses there are always more opportunities. In our very small community there are still enough aluminum cans being thrown in the dumpster to easily pay for a new and badly needed computer for the local school every year. In this community there is also enough wood waste being hauled off at an expense to the landfill to meet all energy needs of the local school or of a small industrial business. After the initial investment in generating capacity, the fuel supply is functionally free. These are opportunities that can be exploited to help close the loop on waste and improve the profitability of the community. The first step is to watch for these kinds of opportunities every day and every where you go. You will easily find more opportunities—more niches to fill in the economic ecosystem—than you can exploit in an entire lifetime.

It should be noted that some wastes like old appliances and television sets, require unique disposal solutions. Most municipalities now separate out water heaters, refrigerators, washers and dryers for scrap metal, usually charging more at the dumpster for the extra work of recycling. Other appliances with high plastic content like televisions or stereos are much less recyclable, so they end up in the landfill.

In many European countries there are new "take back" laws intended to help prevent all kinds of appliances, either metal or plastic, from ever entering the municipal waste stream. In essence, the company that manufactures a good and sells it to you is responsible for disposal of that good when you are done with it. You might purchase a refrigerator and use it for fifteen years, but the company that built it is still owns the job of disposal. An appliance like a television may contain up to 4,000 chemicals, many of them toxic, so it can greatly simplify waste disposal to prevent them from being mixed with other garbage[38]. Americans throw out 7.5 million television sets every year, enough to make a line stretching from New York to Denver. Take back laws will drive innovation towards products that are designed to be dismantled and recycled. Such laws will likely appear in the U.S. in the coming years.

Preventing Waste Before it Happens

While there are many good opportunities to recycle existing wastes, it is not always the best route to create a closed-loop economy. Sometimes it makes more sense to start from scratch and rethink the kinds of waste we generate in the first place.

Finding new and better ways to design products—to keep them out of the waste stream to begin with, can be a much better alternative than merely finding ways to recycle products after they have failed the first time. For example, if we can design new houses that do not need constant repairs and replacements, then we will be able to prevent many thousands of tons of valuable resources from ever entering the waste stream, a much better option than merely trying to recycle all that waste into something else.

Outside of every construction site there is a great big dumpster to hold all the scraps of boards, insulation, sheetrock, buckets of paint, etc. Yet, that big dumpster is a drop in the bucket compared to the wastes that will continue to be generated from the site through the lifetime of the house. There are certainly plenty of opportunities to put all these wastes to use in constructive and profitable ways, but more creative thought up front could eliminate much of the waste in the first place. Now wouldn't that be the better solution?

For example, just imagine a well-designed house that is cast in a mold with little or no waste, made from materials which require little or no maintenance work over a lifetime of many centuries. With proper design it is possible to make these houses as essentially closed-loop systems with no need for heating or cooling energy, no ties to the utility grid, no need for water or sewer hook-ups, and relatively little waste disposal. It is possible to build such structures, but it requires starting over from scratch in the design process, re-inventing the house in materials, form, and function. (For more details read *Living Homes: Thomas J. Elpel's Field Guide to Integrated Design and Construction*.) Building such houses may require many virgin resources from the earth, but it effectively closes the loop on waste by eliminating waste, both now and in the future.

You can find similar ways to eliminate waste up front by thinking about all the goods and services you use on a daily basis and searching for ways to meet those needs while generating less waste from the very beginning. In my own community there are many individuals working to make a profit while eliminating waste by producing local eggs and honey and garden fresh greens. Neighbors investing in a greenhouse today will soon provide fresh vegetables to the community all year long, thus eliminating the waste of packing and shipping food hundreds of miles to get here. What ideas do you have?

Choosing Alternative Resources

The focus through much of this chapter has been on utilizing waste or preventing it, but you do not need to get into any kind of manufacturing business to help close the loop on waste. After all, someone needs to sell all these next-generation products.

For example, consider something as mundane a lawnmower. Lawnmowers utilize inefficient 2-cycle engines, which cause much more pollution per gallon of gas than automobiles. We know it is imperative that we wean ourselves off of fossil fuel use and getting rid of gas lawnmowers is one good place to start. Now, the more environmentally conscientious would point out that the best alternative is to plant a diverse and wild landscape of flowers, bushes, trees, and even unmowed grass, which may be true, but also somewhat irrelevant since most people really like having at least a small area of neatly mowed lawn. It fits our cultured sense of order and makes a fun place to play too. Few people are going to be convinced to let their lawns grow completely wild, and those who do sometimes end up in the newspaper in violation of city ordinances. Instead of giving up their lawn mowers, it is much easier to give people a reasonable substitute, such as an electric lawn mower.

Granted, an electric lawnmower still depends on fossil fuels in the form of the coal burned to generate electricity, but it is still far cleaner than a 2-cycle gas-powered mower. More to the point, we know that the economy is transitioning—slowly—to solar and other clean energy sources. A person could invest in photovoltaics today, but solar is still too expensive and it won't run that gas-powered mower anyway. Therefore, doesn't it make more sense to purchase the electric mower first, to be properly equipped for the clean energy sources that are coming? You can only make change as fast as your income comes in, so start with what you can now, and the rest will come in good time.

The electric lawn mower greatly reduces carbon dioxide emissions compared to 2-cycle gas powered mowers.

Purchasing an electric versus a gas-powered mower makes only a very small change in the economic ecosystem. It tells the manufacturer to produce one more electric mower and one less gas mower. It tells the retailer to similarly purchase one more electric model and one less of the other. It also serves as a model to the neighbors who are going to wonder about this new and very quiet machine. The net result in tilting the ecosystem is very small, although cumulatively important as many other individuals make similar choices. It is important to note that the size of the change in the ecosystem depends on the size of the action.

Buying one electric mower for yourself is a small action, while retailing them through a local store and extolling the benefits to your customers is a bigger action. Manufacturing electric mowers and promoting them to retailers all over the country is a much bigger action, and being the inventor who makes the technology feasible is a greater action still. You can make as much of a difference as you want to, depending on where you want to jump into the game. We cannot make the change in a single day, but there are plenty of opportunities for us either as consumers or in business to facilitate the transition as fast as we can.

Extending Resource Productivity

Extending resource productivity means simply getting more mileage out of fewer resources, just as aluminum cans are made thinner now than in the past. That way more cans can be made with the same amount of resource. Likewise, energy consuming devices such as incandescent lightbulbs can be replaced with more efficient models like fluorescent bulbs, so that the same amount of energy provides three times as much light. Extending resource productivity helps reduce throughput in the economy, so that we have the same level of prosperity with less impact on the natural world. Extending resource productivity is often very profitable, since a business can make more sales with less material.

For example, the logging industry has run into shortages of materials in many regions by exhausting its resource base. Lumber mills are slowly being forced to make do with small scale, sustainable yield from fixed plots. Mills used to cut mountains of wood into boards, generating mountains of wasted sawdust and wood scraps, but more and more they are learning to use less raw materials while producing more salable products. Scrap material can be compressed to make chip board, and smaller lumber can be glue-laminated to make longer, more expensive beams. But some mills take over even more steps in the manufacturing process, taking in trees at one end and spitting out finished window frames or furniture at the other end.

These "**value-added**" industries allow a smaller resource base to employ more people and generate more income from fewer materials. In economic lingo this is also known as a "**vertical monopoly**"[41]. In essence you fill multiple niches in the economic chain from raw resources to finished products. You earn profit on jobs that would have otherwise been contracted out. The profit potential is there for so many of the investments you might make in either your home or business.

We made a lot of "profit" in the form of savings while building our own home because we used as many raw resources as we could and modified them all the way to a finished product, our house. We saved tens of thousands of dollars in construction costs that way and hundreds of thousands of dollars on the interest.

Similarly, I spent most of my childhood summers with my grandma in Virginia City, Montana, a small tourist town. I remember thinking it was so strange to have gift shops full of plastic trinkets labeled "Virginia City, Montana" on one side and "Made in Taiwan" on the other. The products were hoaky, and the gift shops were exporting a significant portion of their limited income dollars half-way around the world to Taiwan. As a summer tourist town, much of the Virginia City population was unemployed from Labor Day in September to Memorial Day weekend the following spring.

Most businesses only deal with a single step along the chain of converting raw resources into salable products. The gift shops in Virginia City, for instance, usually only sell products, rather than manufacture them. These businesses could make additional income by taking over other links in the chain. In Virginia City there is ample time and labor available between September and May to manufacture interesting local products which would greatly increase net incomes throughout the town, instead of sending that money to Taiwan.

One of the finest examples of a vertical monopoly I have ever seen is the *Wheat Montana Bakery* located only thirty miles from my home. Most wheat farmers sell their wheat straight off the field and barely make ends meet, but at *Wheat Montana* they grow their own wheat, do their own milling, and bake and distribute the final products. They even grow varieties of wheat that are especially suited to the breads they bake, so their breads taste good and have a long shelf-life without preservatives. They filled economic niches all along the chain from raw resources to salable products. Their unique approach has made the company news-worthy, so they have gotten free advertising as well, through newspaper and magazine articles, and even a spot in this book! It is no surprise that the company has been immensely successful.

Wheat Montana extends resource productivity by milling their own wheat and baking and distributing their own bread.

"Flood a field with water and stir it up with a plow and the ground will set becoming as hard as plaster. If the soil dries and hardens, then it must be plowed each year to soften it. All we are doing is creating the conditions that make a plow useful, then rejoicing at the utility of our tool."
—Masanobu Fukuoka, The Natural Way of Farming[28]

3-3
Technology
-Putting Calories to Work-

We have many tools at our disposal, from human creativity to labor and money, but usually, when we think of "tools" we think of technology. Technology includes everything from pen and paper to cars and computers. It is technology that has enabled our species to escape the cycles of nature, to harvest bigger crops, to thrive in cold climates, even to leave the biosphere for space. Technology enables us to express our creativity and accomplish great dreams.

A lever is a simple tool that enables us to move much greater objects than we could with just our bodies. A crane can move even greater weights. There is so much we can do with the aid of technology that we could not do by muscle power alone. It is no wonder then that we like our tools so much. Technology gives us power. But it is a dangerous power. Our technology can set us free, but it can also enslave us.

It is not like me to hate anything or anybody, but I hated being in the locker room in junior high. During hunting season the other boys would talk about how they took their guns out and blew away some coyote or deer or other animal. Their guns gave them a false sense of power over nature, and they abused it. It is easy to do.

As a species, we like our tools so much that we reach for them even before we have defined our goals. As author Allan Savory points out in his book *Holistic Resource Management*[74], people reach for quick technological fixes without looking at cause and effect in the ecosystem. We get a sense of power when we use a bulldozer, or chemical fertilizers and pesticides. We treat the symptoms of problems more often than the causes, like building dams to control deteriorating watersheds, instead of working with nature to restore the health of the land. Savory describes these "fixes" as non-goals.

Everyone of us is prone to misusing tools. Judiciously used, technology can enable us to achieve our greatest dreams, but we too often seem to take on projects only because they are "technologically feasible", as if the only reason we do them is because we can. Technology can save us time and labor, but too often we make more work for ourselves, just so we can use our tools.

It is amazing to me that we have so much knowledge and so many tools, yet we use it all so poorly. We pump heat into our homes every day through the winter and pump it out through the summer. We have to scrape and repaint our homes every few years; we replace the carpet, linoleum, and the water heater every fifteen to twenty years, and the roof every thirty to fifty. We use our technology to mass-produce all the materials we use, but we are only mass-producing more work for ourselves. It is no wonder that sustainability seems so implausible to so many people when we have to practically rebuild the entire infrastructure of our country several times each century! We have the knowledge to build houses that are comfortable without the need for heaters and air-conditioners. We have the knowledge to build houses and other products that last. But people reach too quickly for their tools and build without thinking and planning. Heaters, air-conditioners, and other maintenance expenses are technological fixes that do not address the real issues. They are non-goals.

Wise use of technology lies in planning and organization. You can profit when you choose the most appropriate technologies to close the loop, creating the most real wealth with the least possible waste.

Mass Produced Goods & Services

One of my first significant experiences with tools was while I was working with my brother Nick in the Seattle area, building railings for decks and stairs. I did not know much about carpentry at the time, but he bid on the job and had more work than he could do, so he invited me out there. He did the deck railings while I did the stair railings. We made a prototype stair railing to make sure it looked okay, then he set up a template for me to work off of. I had to take individual measurements on the length of each railing, but otherwise I just cut the pieces to fit the template and nailed them together on top of the pattern. I hauled each railing to the stairs and installed them. With the template I was able to work very quickly, and being paid per foot of railing, I averaged a hundred dollars a day for twenty days, which was pretty good considering I was young and had no real carpentry experience. I actually made higher wages per hour than many of the seasoned carpenters at the site, and I did better work than the previous carpenter who tried doing the same job. More than anything, however, I learned the importance of organizing work into repetitive, simple tasks. I learned how to achieve consistent quality and relative speed, the essence of mass-production.

Mass-production benefits us all by making products cheaper to produce and buy. Making interchangeable parts and streamlining the assembly process means fewer calories of effort can be expended to produce material goods. Consider that a new car would cost hundreds of thousands of dollars if the auto company brought all their tools to your house and assembled it in your driveway. A completely customized car could cost millions. Mass production dramatically brings down the cost per vehicle, so that cars are reasonably affordable.

The cost of housing could fall by a similar amount if houses were mass-produced the way automobiles are. The visionary architect and inventor Buckminster Fuller saw the advantages of mass-production in the 1920's and developed innovative house models over the next few decades that could be factory-made. Fuller advocated mass-production as a means to maintain quality control and bring down housing costs. His ideas were remarkably advanced for the time. He designed houses with their own power plants, moveable interior partitions, vacuum sealed double pane windows, gray water systems, and automatic doors. Fuller utilized engineering concepts to construct the most house with the greatest strength out of the least materials. The parts were so compact and lightweight that they could be transported in a cylinder and assembled on site by hand—and later disassembled and moved. Fuller's ideas were too revolutionary for his time, especially because the dome-shaped structures were so different from the conventional housing people were accustomed too. He had a initial bid from Beech Aircraft in the 1940's to produce his kit homes, but neither the company nor it's bankers would put forth the capital needed to tool up for production. (Like an automobile factory, it would have cost billions in today's dollars.) Fuller had to return 3,700 unsolicited orders to people who liked the idea enough to put up money in advance.

Trailer houses are the closest facsimile we have to Buckminster Fuller's concept houses, although he would probably be insulted by the comparison. Trailer houses are mass-produced and portable, built with lightweight aluminum, as were Fuller's houses, but they lack his thoughtful, integrated planning.

Today the housing market remains a wide open niche in the economic ecosystem. Most houses are still put together the old fashioned way, with every house plan different and every piece individually measured, cut and hammered in place. Modular homes are making a dent in the market by prefabricating house sections at one site, with all the same size materials and only a few designs. The problem with modular homes is the builders are still using the same inefficient materials and designs as traditional construction, so the new houses are hardly different from the old ones.

A house is typically a person's biggest investment in life, and also the most environmentally harmful, because there is such a large throughput of resources to build and maintain the structure. To achieve true sustainability, we need to close the loop on wastes. Mass-production offers the potential to produce houses that are far more efficient, less costly, and very profitable.

With the aid of mass-production it is possible to make low cost virtually self-sufficient or "closed loop" houses that require no inputs of energy for heating or cooling, no ties to the utility grid, and no need for water or sewer hookups. To achieve that level of efficiency there absolutely must be as few parts as possible, because at the junction of every part there is a potential for a loss in materials, time and energy. By casting these structures in large molds from lightweight insulating, but structurally sound materials, it would be possible to transport the modules to a site and assemble an entire home in a matter of a few days. (Read *Living Homes: Thomas J. Elpel's Field Guide to*

TOOLS TO WORK WITH

Integrated Design and Construction for more details.) This is an industry I wish to pioneer when I one day finish my writing projects—unless someone else grabs the opportunity first.

Closing the loop on housing wastes has the potential to truly transform the world we live in, but it is only one segment of our economy and there are so many more opportunities that desperately need to be exploited to make the world a better place.

Hand-crafted Goods & Services

While mass-production can help reduce wastes of time, energy and materials, it is not the answer for everything. There are some goods and services, such as handicrafts or haircuts, which are not readily mass-producible.

It simply isn't possible or desirable to streamline haircut efficiency to the point that a hair stylist can speed up from one hair cut every half hour to one every half minute. Some increases in efficiency are possible by sharing a workspace and advertising costs between several stylists, but it would be difficult and potentially disastrous to try increasing the rate of haircuts! Therefore, the price of a haircut and other similar services always remain comparatively high while other prices continue to fall.

The same could be said for handicrafts like natural wood furniture. In the age of mass-production there is considerable demand for completely unique, hand-built furniture like pole-frame beds. Ironically, mass-production is what makes hand-crafted furniture "affordable". Streamlining production throughout the economy has reduced the price of most of our goods and services so that people have more surplus wealth to spend on otherwise uneconomical choices like hand-crafted furniture. In other words, there are still many opportunities to make a living without mass-producing anything, but keep in mind that the income potential is much smaller too.

There are limits to how many hair cuts or how many rustic pole bed frames you can create per unit of your time, so it is difficult to increase your income beyond a certain point. On the other hand, there are fewer limitations to the broker who owns the salon you work at, or runs an internet store to sell hand-crafted furniture. They can increase the volume of haircuts or pole-frame beds sold, and merely contract out to more individuals to meet the demand. The income potential is greater, but the risks may be greater too.

Economies of Scale & Diseconomies of Scale

The term "economies of scale" goes hand-in-hand with the idea of mass-production. If you build a big, highly specialized factory to mass-produce a product, then you can dramatically reduce the cost to produce each item. As the size of the factory goes up the cost to produce each unit goes down. The automobile industry is a good example, with billion dollar factories turning out thousands of cars at a fraction of the cost to custom build them. Unfortunately, the bigger the factory, the more units that must be produced in order to break even. That is one of several "diseconomies of scale".

Farm foreclosures have been driven by economies of scale. With increased investments in materials and equipment, industrial agriculture allowed farmers to produce more food for their labor, but also required farmers to produce much more just to break even. The ease of production and the need to recover the investment led to such

great surpluses that the price of wheat hasn't gone up since the 1940's. With the profit per bushel falling to just a few cents, farmers have to produce more and more just to stay in the middle class. They are forced to either get big or get out.

Alternatively, many farmers have sidestepped the problem of scale by switching to small-scale specialty crops. Certainly a farmer cannot make a living from fifty acres of wheat when the price is so low, but there are always new niches to be found in the economic ecosystem. Farmers that have embraced change have been able to stay in business and prosper while growing new crops for new markets. Some continue to grow commodities like wheat, but they are switching to organic markets to fetch a higher return, or they are plant-

Farm foreclosures have been driven by economies of scale.

ing chic alternatives to conventional grains, like quinoa or amaranth. Wheat Montana Farms created their own specialty market by making and marketing their own breads from their own varieties of wheat.

Others farmers are switching to herbal crops for spices and health supplements. Some are finding new markets with the aid of greenhouses to produce seedlings or to provide vegetables all year long. Community Supported Agriculture is another alternative, where families pay a certain income each year for a share of a diverse crop of local vegetables from one farm. There are even farms where people pay to come pick their own vegetable or fruit crops. Any farm family with a flare for innovation can find a way to dodge the diseconomies of scale, so that they can stay in business with smaller acreages.

As you may see, economies of scale don't always work as one might expect. Centralized mass-production technology helps to decrease the cost of many goods and services from cars and airplanes to travel services (i.e.: internet ticket reservations), but there are many situations where it is not as economical or efficient as once thought.

Given the complicated nature of an automobile, it would be inefficient to produce them without centralized billion-dollar factories, but other products can often be produced more cheaply in many smaller, local factories than in one big factory. One problem is that a single, highly specialized factory must be custom built for its task, resulting in much higher costs.

For example, coal, oil, gas, or nuclear power plants are big plants designed to mass-produce electricity. But each plant is typically unique in design, making it expensive to build and maintain, one of the diseconomies of scale. Power plants would cost at least ten times less per kilowatt of generating capacity if we mass-produced many small plants instead of a few big ones, reports Amory Lovins in *Soft Energy Paths*. This still requires a big factory, like an automobile plant, but the factory mass-produces small power plants rather than building just a few big ones.

In fact, the nature of the energy industry will change radically in the coming decades as factories scale up to mass-production of photovoltaics and fuel cells. The diseconomies of scale behind operating and maintaining the national power grid has left a wide-open niche for small, localized power supplies to fill.

Falling costs are making it increasingly economical to put solar cells on the roof to replace or supplement power from the grid. Buildings equipped with photovoltaics can also produce hydrogen gas with an electric current by splitting water apart into hydrogen and oxygen.

Hydrogen gas is most useful as a substitute for poor battery technology. The gas can be stored and converted back to electricity as needed with fuel cells to power homes or automobiles. Early fuel cells are already in use in some civic bus systems.

Fuel cell technology also enables any building or automobile to produce its own electricity from natural gas, an interim fuel while the cost of photovoltaics continues to fall. Ironically, fuel-cell cars can generate electricity to feed the utility grid when parked. The typical car is parked 96% of the time, so every fuel cell car is a power plant on wheels, generating electricity and income for its driver while at home or at work. When all US automobiles are converted to fuel cell technology, the total electric generating capacity will be five times the existing national grid capacity. Large-scale power plants will be forced to close long before that time comes.

In a similar way, there are many other highly centralized industries that can be out-competed by smaller, more decentralized facilities. For example, consider any of the recycling industries, such as scrap iron, aluminum, glass, paper, or plastic.

There is an inherent inefficiency to producing a product like a glass bottle in a centralized location and shipping it several hundred miles to the point where it is filled. The bottled product may be shipped hundreds of miles again before use. Afterwards the scrap glass must be shipped back hundreds of miles to be recycled into new bottles. The cost of returning the glass—or any other recyclables—is so high that it is often cheaper to dispose of it, or to recycle it to lesser uses. Used glass is often ground up and added to asphalt to keep it out of the waste stream, but this is more like disposal than "recycling".

Fortunately, any time there is waste there is also an opportunity to close a loop and make a profit. The cost of the resources or energy involved in shipping goods all over the country may not be enough to make the alternatives competitive, but the labor cost in all that work can make the difference.

It is far more efficient to mass-produce smaller mills to recycle waste close to the point of origination. Most recyclables are essentially free for the cost of extracting them from the waste stream, and even that can be free if you put bins outside your "mini-mill" to accept recyclables. A small, mostly automated glass bottle factory can be placed in every town where glass bottles are bought and filled to reduce the transportation loop. Even better, build a right-scale mini-mill right next to a bottling plant, and the waste glass can go from the recycling bin through the bottle factory and on a conveyer belt straight into the bottling plant without the need for human hands, packaging or transportation at all. Closing these kinds of loops in the economic ecosystem vastly improves the profitability of recycling and greatly reduces or eliminates damage to the natural ecosystem. There is a tremendous opportunity to be had in mass-producing mini-mills for glass, aluminum, metals, paper, plastic, or any other recycled commodity. Until someone fills that niche, there is also great opportunity to be had by designing and building your own right-sized mini-mills from off-the-shelf components.

Automated Production

As we enter the 21st century we are transitioning from an industrial economy where people use machines to produce material wealth to an automated economy where computers use machines to produce material wealth. Increases in production from computer-assisted automation may be the biggest factor behind the booming economy that began in the 1990's.

Computers were in use before 1990, but they were expensive and didn't do very much. New computers and computer networking, especially the internet, led to many increases in production. An obvious example is Amazon, which offers customers many more books in one store. Customers do the work of placing orders via their own computers, while Amazon's computers do the work of automatically monitoring inventory, ordering books, paying bills and routing the customer orders to the right bins in the right warehouse. Amazon sells more books with less labor, so they are able to offer discount prices on many books that you would not get through traditional booksellers.

In the coming decades we will see increased automation in every sector of the economy. Already there are printing services that can keep an author's books in storage on a computer and print only as many copies as are ordered. If only one copy is sold today, then only one copy is printed. Soon we may see businesses like Amazon where paper and ink is delivered and put in place, but otherwise computers do everything from taking the order to printing, packing, and dropping it in a bin for the post office.

Given the unique nature of computers, automated companies can vary in scale from minor to major investments. As an author I can and will make this text available as a downloadable product off the internet without any human intervention at all. All businesses, large and small, will find ways to incrementally automate their companies, especially to eliminate the paperwork of monitoring inventory, ordering and billing.

Starting a full-scale automated company may be a bigger task than you are prepared to tackle directly, but you can still participate via the stock market. Today more and more middle class Americans are transitioning into jobs as bankers, by investing in new and promising ideas. People are finding that it is simply easier for to recognize a good idea and invest in it, than to hatch their own idea and bring it to fruition.

Mass-Production of One

Mass-production reduces the amount of labor required to produce goods and services by making thousands or millions of identical copies. A business invests vast sums of money and time to build all the tools necessary to mass-produce a product, then manufactures and sells enough copies to pay for the initial investment and make a profit. The next step in mass-production is "mass-production of one".

Better computers and advanced materials are making increasingly flexible production tools, so that mass-produced goods can be individually customized. Levi was one of the first businesses to provide customization, though limited in form, by opening a shop where people could have their measurements taken and fed into a computer. The computer makes a pattern customized to fit and sends the specifications off to the factory where the material is automatically cut. All the tools of mass-production are brought into use to produce a single, individualized item.

One of the limitations of traditional mass-production is that it was so expensive to tool up before a single item could be produced, but mass-production-of-one technology is reducing those costs dramatically. For example, automotive companies had to laboriously sculpt clay, carve wood, or machine steel to make prototype parts for new designs, but new technology allows them to design parts on a computer and "print" them in 3-dimensional form.

3D printing was started in 1984 by inventor Charles Hull using ultraviolet lights and light-sensitive plastics similar to the ones dentists use to seal and protect your teeth. Hull attached a 3D light to a computer-guided arm, then pointed the light beam into a vat of polymer, hardening a thin layer of plastic wherever the light moved. A platform under the hardened plastic then dropped a millimeter, submerging the item under more polymer, allowing subsequent passes of the ultraviolet light to build 3D objects. Hull's first test product was a tea cup.

Today 3D technology is used to make prototypes for hundreds of industries from automotive parts to dentures, heart valves, and lightbulbs. The technology enables "3D faxing" because an idea originated on one computer can be sent electronically to another computer and "printed" in 3D form. But this is just the beginning. The latest 3D printing technology under development eliminates the prototype and mold stages to print final products.

Like ink-jet printers, these gizmos spray out thousands of microscopic dots per second, but in this case there is no paper to print on. The printer heads whir around spitting out gobs of material, thus printing objects in layers. The first 3D printers used only hot plastics, but next generation printers are being designed to build objects from metal, paper, ceramics, or composite materials. With this kind of technology there is no longer the need to tool up big factories to mass-produce millions of identical copies. A factory can consist of a 3D printer able to print anything you instruct it to. Desktop models will enable kids to design and print their own toys, or to download and print toys off the internet. Desktop models may be available as early as 2010.

These kinds of technologies may radically change or eliminate the need for retail stores like Walmart, since individuals can print their own goods. Larger items can be ordered and delivered from 3D factories via the internet. Entrepreneurs will find ample opportunity for profit by building or selling 3D printers and the related goods and services. The individual working with limited resources will not be left out though, as anyone can innovate useful products and sell their designs on the internet.

Self-Replicating Production

The next step in technological development, beyond the ability to mass-produce a run of one item, is to build products that build themselves. For example, just imagine completely automated solar cell production, where solar powered robots mine desert soils (or the surface of the moon) and use the minerals to self-replicate, producing more solar panels and more robots, exponentially spreading across the landscape until switched off. All the technological hurdles have already been crossed to produce such a system. It could cost up to $100 billion dollars to integrate the technologies into one coherent system, but when set loose in a place like the Sahara desert, it would cost nothing more to maintain. A colony of self-replicating solar powered robots covering just a little over 10% of the Sahara desert could provide three times the world's current energy supply[10]. Any future expansions of the energy supply on this planet or elsewhere would be as free as taking a few robots from one colony and transporting them to start a new colony.

Self-replicating technology is inevitable and it will radically change the nature of the world we live in. After all, if the energy is functionally free, then it will be economical to desalinize vast quantities of sea water for drinking or for mass-irrigation projects. Likewise, we can expect gizmos such as self-sustaining tunneling machines that bore through entire mountain ranges, melting the waste material into glass walls to line the tubes. Such tunnels might be used for either high-speed transportation, or simply as pipes for massive irrigation projects.

Instead of reclaiming places like the Sahara or the Middle East with good stewardship, developers will likely turn to technology to pump hundreds of millions of gallons of desalinized sea water inland for irrigation. Saudi Arabia already irrigates the desert this way, but their desalinization plants are powered by their essentially unlimited supply of low-cost petroleum. Self-replicating solar powered desalinization plants will give them the tools and energy to complete what they've started.

Self-replicating solar-powered technology is nothing new, since that's what plants are. Researchers are working on the microscopic level to understand how photosynthesis works in plants on the molecular level. Already they've reproduced several steps in the process using artificially-made molecules[11]. Ultimately we may have microscopic self-replicating solar panels even before scientists find the funding to build the larger robotic version.

Either way, self-replicating solar cell technology will eliminate any remaining pollution from fossil fuels, helping to close that loop of the economic ecosystem. On the other hand, it will greatly increase the throughput of material resources and energy. We are already really good at building things. What we really need is the technology to recycle all this stuff we keep building!

Self-Replicating Molecular Machines

The greatest obstacle to recycling is that it is often easier to make materials than to unmake them. A typical couch, for example, consists of a wood and metal frame plus polyurethane foam pads and a fabric of synthetic acrylics, nylon, and rayon or natural wool and cotton, or some mix of the above. It is highly impractical to separate out all the raw ingredients to recycle them into something new. So the worn-out couch is hauled off to the landfill and buried for future generations to deal with. But just imagine if you had the ability to disassemble the old couch atom-by-atom, sorting each element into its own pile.

Nanotechnology has always been the stuff of science fiction. Molecular machines are so small that you could fit thousands of them on the head of a pin. Such machines may seem to small to do anything, but the truth is they are small enough to do everything. If you can manipulate matter on the atomic level then you can build or unbuild absolutely anything you could dream up—from a silk spider web to a glittering diamond—as long as it doesn't violate the laws of physics[25].

Molecular technology is not as farfetched as it seems, because it already exists in all living organisms. Plant cells are filled with gizmo's that manipulate matter on the atomic level, transforming water, gasses and elements from the earth into living tissues. The cells in our own bodies perform similar molecular wizardry, but utilize living tissues as the raw ingredients.

Scientists are still years away from building molecular machines, but meanwhile they are finding innovative ways to harness existing nanotechnology imbedded in living organisms. Insulin for diabetics, for example, is produced by genetically-engineered *E. coli* bacteria. The necessary machinery existed in the bacteria, and scientists merely switched the programming that tells it what to produce. Research will eventually eliminate the need for the bacteria, so that the insulin can be produced by non-living molecular machines.

The exciting part about live nanotechnology, such as that found in plants and animals, is that it is able to manufacture complex materials at normal temperatures from simple resources with no toxic wastes. As Janine M. Benyus pointed out in her book, *Biomimicry*[14], spiders take flies and crickets in one end and produce a superstrong silk out the other end, five times stronger than steel per ounce of material. The silk is also much stronger and more elastic than Kevlar, found in bulletproof vests, yet Kevlar must be manufactured from petroleum products boiled in a vat of sulfuric acid at a temperature of several hundred degrees.

Spider silk has to be strong and stretchy to withstand the impact of catching insects in flight. Reportedly, if spider silk were reproduced at human scale and used to make a fishing net, it would be strong enough to catch an airplane in mid-flight without breaking! This is just one of many materials produced in nature that will give us new and better materials in the coming decades. Researchers are experimenting with spider silk now, trying to transplant the genes into *E. coli* bacteria.

Similarly, scientists are finding ways to use living molecular machines to disassemble some of the messes we have made in the past. Toxic wastes that have leached into the ground are a particularly sticky problem. Traditional treatment options included excavating the contaminated soil and hauling it to a "containment site", or drilling wells and installing pumps to circulate neutralizing chemicals through the poisoned ground. A much more simple method for decontamination is to employ specialized bacteria that break down substances like PCB's into their simple and nontoxic components.

Producing these toxic-eating bacteria doesn't necessarily require genetic engineering, as there are already plenty of highly specialized microorganisms in nature, billions of them in a single teaspoon of soil. Scientists search contaminated sites for signs of useful bacteria, then mass-reproduce them in vats for release on a larger scale.

Commandeering the micromachines inside living organisms is only an intermediate step towards being able to produce our own similar technology. Scientists are already building simple gears atom-by-atom, and some expect that we will build the first molecular machine as early as 2010. As with the industrial revolution, each new piece of machinery becomes a tool to build other more complicated machines. According to Eric Drexler in his book the *Engines of Creation*[25], the "holy grail" of nanotechnology is to build a "general assembler and disassembler".

A general assembler would be a programmable molecular machine capable of making whatever it was told to make, including an exact duplicate of itself. An army of assemblers could produce sugar from air or diamonds from carbon. But even more exciting is that an assembler could be programmed to build something much more complex, like a rocket.

Programming an assembler requires an instructional code much like our own DNA, but with many more redundancies to prevent mutations. Consider that the DNA in a single fertilized egg contains all the necessary information to build an entire human being. Micromachinery within the cell grabs the necessary building blocks as they float through in fluid. The egg builds itself into a complex living, breathing human.

It is sometimes said that if you were to load a tank full of car parts and shake it to eternity, that it would never assemble itself into a car. Yet, ironically, that is essentially how some of our products will be built in the future. A single assembler, planted as a seed in the bottom of a large fluid-filled tube would grab the necessary ingredients as they floated by and build itself into whatever it was programmed to make. With this kind of technology it is possible to manufacture products as radical as a rocketship of pure diamond, designed for superior strength with minimal weight.

Equally important to the ability to build anything is the ability to disassemble or recycle everything that we do build. General disassemblers would do just that, separating any kind of garbage into its constituent atoms. Waste will completely cease to exist when nanotechnology comes of age.

Of course there is also a certain risk to working with machines that are so small that it would be virtually impossible to find one if you dropped it. What would happen if disassemblers got loose and started disassembling the planet and everything on it? In the *Engines of Creation* Drexler outlines a plausible safeguard against these kind of disasters, and I encourage you to read it for more details.

It is difficult to predict how soon the first molecular assembler will be built, although it could happen even before 2050. It will only take a year or two after the first one is built to be able to make anything and everything else that doesn't violate the laws of physics.

While it is important to know what is coming, it is perhaps more important to know and more effectively utilize what is already here. We have essentially all the necessary technology to close the loop on waste in the economic ecosystem, to create a world of abundance without pollution. You can profit now, and make the world a better place, by applying the appropriate technologies to the appropriate tasks to produce the most real goods and services with the least possible waste.

"If Americans were as energy-efficient as Western Europeans or Japanese, we would save $200 billion a year. That's about enough to wipe out the federal deficit, or to put an extra $800 a year back into the pockets of every woman, man, and child in the United States."

—Rocky Mountain Institute

3-4

Energy
-Squeezing Useful Work from Every Calorie-

Energy is the tool that runs all other tools. In the broadest sense, every action we make, from smelting ore to flexing a muscle, uses energy. All action, all wealth is ultimately based on energy. We cannot attain real wealth without expending real effort.

In the developed countries we are wealthy partly because we harvest and expend so many fuel calories—the energy equivalent of 100 to 300 people working 24 hours a day[16]—to produce our goods and services. Fuel calories are like cheap slave labor, and therefore our future prosperity is partly contingent on whether or not fuel calories remain cheap.

If usable energy is scarce in the future then our lifestyles would have to change. If, on the other hand, usable energy is abundant in the future then we will be able to continue supplementing our lifestyle with a significant influx of fuel calories. Since matter itself is energy, and since there is quite a bit of matter in our universe, the future really looks pretty prosperous. But before studying the supply and flow of energy through the economic ecosystem, lets consider the supply and flow of energy in nature.

The flow of energy through the natural ecosystem is often illustrated as an "energy pyramid". Land and sea plants convert the sun's energy into living tissues and form the base of the pyramid to support all other life. Plant-eating insects, fish, birds and mammals consume the plants to utilize their stored energy. But with the conversion from plant matter to animal flesh there is inherently a loss of energy. For example, a feedlot cow consumes about sixteen pounds of grain to produce just one pound of beef. There are further losses of energy when predators kill and consume the plant-eaters, and again with the predators that eat the predators. Ultimately every last residue of left

The Energy Pyramid

Plants capture and store the energy of sunlight, forming the base of the energy pyramid. Energy is lost as low-grade waste heat through each conversion as plants are consumed by plant-eating animals like cows and the meat is consumed by flesh-eating animals like humans. For example, a feed-lot cow consumes 16 pounds of grain to produce just one pound of meat. The ultimate limit to growth is determined by the amount of energy captured by plants at the base of the pyramid.

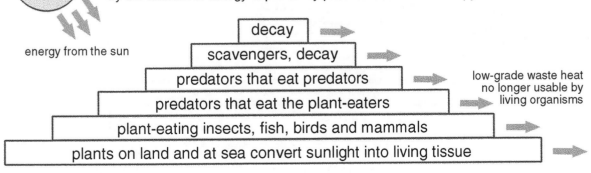

energy from the sun

decay

scavengers, decay

predators that eat predators

low-grade waste heat
no longer usable by
living organisms

predators that eat the plant-eaters

plant-eating insects, fish, birds and mammals

plants on land and at sea convert sunlight into living tissue

over energy is consumed by the scavengers and the organisms of decay. The amount of activity throughout the pyramid is determined by the amount of energy captured by plants at the base.

The world food supply is included in the energy pyramid, and hunger experts point out that we can provide for a much larger human population by transitioning to more energy-efficient diets. In many developing countries the farmers are exporting corn, soybeans, and other grains to the industrialized nations to fatten cattle in feedlots, even while there are people starving to death at home. Feedlot cows may require 16 pounds of grain to produce a pound of meat, but other livestock have more efficient conversion ratios, such as pork (6:1), turkey (4:1) or chicken (3:1)[48]. Switching to meats with better conversion ratios, or eating the grains directly, increases the energy efficiency of the pyramid, so that the same food base can support a much larger population.

As is often the case with energy efficiency, there is more to this story than meets the eye, and beef can be one of the most efficient sources of food energy. True, fattening cows with grain in feedlots is senseless waste, especially since most of the fat is later trimmed off by the butcher, or on the side of the plate at home. Grass-fed beef, however, can achieve a higher conversion ratio than pork, turkey, or chicken, because those animals require nutritionally dense foods like grains, whereas cattle are able to convert otherwise useless range grass into meat. Cattle can utilize range-lands that could not or should not be converted to croplands, and in brittle landscapes the hoof impact is required to keep the land productive. With proper management, cattle and other livestock can halt the process of desertification, encourage soil-building, and expand the food supply, without utilizing any precious grain crops at all! Those who are concerned about the environmental and social impacts of eating beef need not quit, but merely need to switch to grass-fed beef.

In the economic ecosystem there are many similar opportunities to maintain or increase prosperity while using the same or even far less energy than before. As was illustrated with beef, energy efficiency can require re-examining seemingly simple math problems from new and different angles. But first it is important to remember that the economic ecosystem is not limited to the same photosynthetic base as is the energy pyramid of the living ecosystem. Only "biofuels" like wood, ethanol, and methane or methanol are provided from the living energy pyramid. Other energy sources, like solar, wind, hydro, tidal, geothermal, fossil fuels, fission and fusion, are not tied to the energy pyramid at all. Yes, it is important to wean ourselves off of polluting fossil fuels and dangerous nuclear energy, but that doesn't mean we are restricted to biofuels.

In many places it is better not to use biofuels at all, such as in developing countries where fuel-starved peoples are stripping the land of every twig and cow patty for fuel, when the organic matter is desperately needed to

The Industrial Energy Pyramid

As with nature's energy pyramid, there are losses from the initial energy input with every conversion in the system. Most of the energy is lost in the process of generating the electricity, but other losses occur through the power lines, in motors, gears, pumps, and pipes. The losses compound, so that each step loses a percentage of the remaining total (i.e.: 30% comes out of the power plant and 9% of that is lost in transmission). In a typical industrial pump only 9.5 units of work is performed out of an initial input of 100 units of fossil fuel.

In such an inefficient system there are many opportunities for improvement and profit. Saving a small amount of energy at the end of the chain translates to a big savings of fossil fuel at the beginning.

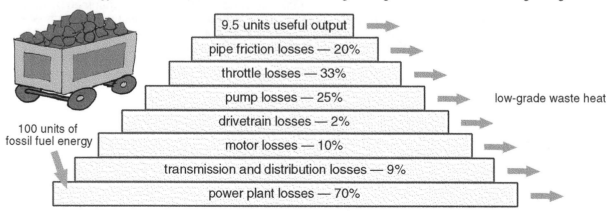

100 units of fossil fuel energy

9.5 units useful output
pipe friction losses — 20%
throttle losses — 33%
pump losses — 25%
drivetrain losses — 2%
motor losses — 10%
transmission and distribution losses — 9%
power plant losses — 70%

low-grade waste heat

(based on "A Typical Industrial Pumping System". Natural Capitalism, 1999. Pg. 121.)

restore the health of the soil. Nearly a third of the world's population is cutting firewood faster than the natural ecosystem can replenish it[45]. In other places there are still many opportunities to use biofuels sustainably and at a profit, but be careful to avoid falling into the trap of thinking that economic growth must be restricted to the energy supply photosynthesized by plants at the base of the pyramid. The economic ecosystem runs off of a different energy pyramid, which we could call the industrial energy pyramid.

The base of the industrial energy pyramid consists of all the energy sources listed above. Each form of energy has immense, sometimes mind-boggling potential, as you will see by reading the sidebars throughout this chapter. The only reason we have relied on fossil fuels so much is because it was the most economical energy source, but that is changing rapidly. For example, as the price of photovoltaics continues to fall, the quantity demanded grows exponentially. Already solar capacity is increasing by 70% per year (1999). The cost of producing solar cells is expected to fall by another 75% in the first decade of the new millennium[48]. When the cost of solar falls below the cost of oil then we will almost instantly be transformed into a solar society.

However, there is no need to sit around and wait for the solar revolution to come. There are immense opportunities at home and at work right now to increase energy efficiency and save money while reducing the impacts of global warming. When the solar revolution does come it will not take so many photovoltaic panels to

Biofuels Potential

Biofuels (fuel from living matter) has the potential to provide a large part of our energy supply, since just the amount of wood waste produced by the environment each year is estimated to be the equivalent of 50,000 terawatts of power, roughly equal to the total world energy consumption in 1970[19]. In my own community there is enough wood waste (branches, stumps, fence posts, lumber) thrown into the dumpster—and hauled away at an expense—to easily supply the energy needs of a small factory or our local school. The fuel is "free" for the cost of a small power plant to burn it in. Look around your own community for wood wastes. Any waste is a potential opportunity to close a loop and make a profit.

The problem with using wood for fuel is that there may be higher potential uses for the materials. For example, in rural places like my home town, there is plenty of available deadwood fuel in the surrounding forest and many of us depend on it to heat our homes. But every time we burn a tree we lose the opportunity to produce lumber from it. Even wood chips have potential higher uses in the form of chipboard or paper. Equally important is the value of the organic matter rotting into the soil, which we lose by turning it to ash. If a resource is to be utilized then it should be applied to the highest end-use practical, which is often where the greatest profit potential is. To optimize resource use in our home we make energy-efficiency improvements every year, steadily decreasing the throughput of firewood, while also saving time cutting it and feeding the fire. We utilize scrap wood as much as possible, rather than cutting whole trees from the forest.

Methane, also known as "biogas" has high potential too. Every person produces about $40 worth of potential gas each year, which can be captured at a sewage plant by digesting sewage with anaerobic bacteria. Multiplied by six billion people that works out to a $240 billion world asset which is virtually untapped. When you see a gas torch above a sewage treatment plant, it means they are burning the methane to dispose of it. We made simple modifications to our septic tank, and positioned it under our chickenhouse, so that we will be able to capture the methane gas from household sewage and chicken manure.

It should be noted that methane is a greenhouse gas, like carbon dioxide, but 21 times as effective per molecule at trapping heat in the atmosphere[39]. Methane is reportedly responsible for 18% of the effects of global warming[61]. Feedlot animals fed on rich diets significantly increase the production of methane gas. The gas can be captured and used at a profit from feedlot manure, although it is even better to raise grass-fed beef. Burning the methane destroy its greenhouse gas properties. The manure slurry left-over after gas production is still a rich fertilizer which may be applied back to the land. Watch for large manure piles at farms and feedlots along the road. Every manure pile is an opportunity to close a loop and make a profit.

Methane gas is being used as fuel to some extent already, especially where the gas is being captured from old landfills. This will supplement our natural gas supplies for awhile, but will probably not be heavily developed for other uses, because while the potential is large, it is not significant enough to consider processing it into methanol and retooling the auto industry to run on it. Methane is best used in small-scale applications at the site where it is produced. For this reason, home-scaled methane plants, similar to septic tanks, are becoming popular in developing countries.

Ethanol, or grain alcohol, is another potential biofuel, except that grain production causes soil erosion, increased pesticide use and other inputs of fossil fuels. Ethanol production is heavily subsidized, and may not even produce a net energy gain unless the grains are organically grown. Still, there is a potential for some ethanol production, especially for on-farm applications. For example, after threshing and winnowing, wheat farms end up with large quantities of cracked wheat mixed with chaff that is not salable, but could be used for ethanol production. A higher and better end-use would be to use the waste as chicken feed.

provide the energy you need, once again saving you money.

Business owners may wonder how it could possibly be economical to worry about energy efficiency when the cost of energy amounts to only one or two percent of their expenses. It hardly seems like the weak link compared to other expenses.

However, energy efficiency requires a whole-systems approach which typically leads to other cost savings as well. For example, most engineers design industrial pumping systems quickly, putting tanks where convenient, then adding pumps and pipes as needed after-the-fact (see illustration: "The Industrial Energy Pyramid). But Eng Lock Lee, an engineer from Singapore, does design work in reverse[39]. He lays out the pipes first, using the shortest possible lengths with the greatest practical diameters to reduce friction. Shorter, fatter pipes reduce friction enabling smaller, less-costly pumps. The new plants cost far less in materials and labor to build and incidentally use energy three to ten times more efficiently. In an increasingly competitive global marketplace these savings on materials, labor and energy can determine the difference between which company survives and which one doesn't.

Hydroelectric Potential

Hydroelectric power is a form of solar energy, since the sun creates the weather that delivers water from the oceans up to the mountain tops. Water flowing back downhill to the oceans is one the cheapest and most reliable sources of power. Electric-intensive industries like aluminum smelting often locate their factories near hydroelectric power plants to take advantage of the low-cost energy.

Most of the largest and best sites for generating hydroelectric power have already been exploited with dams and turbines. Unfortunately, interfering with natural stream processes has decimated fisheries in many locations, leaving once abundant species teetering on the brink of extinction. Part of the problem is that dams historically released water through the turbines as needed to meet power demand. Some dams are now being removed to restore ecosystem health, while others are adjusting the output of flow volume to better maintain the health of the fisheries.

Small streams offer some of the last and best sites for new hydroelectric developments. Instead of installing large dams, small hydro typically utilizes pipelines to divert a share of the water flow. The water flows downhill in long pipes before being jetted through a turbine and back into the streams. Two such power plants in our local streams generate enough electricity on average to supply all the needs of our three local communities, about four hundred people total. Even knowing the power plants are there, it is difficult to tell the difference in missing volume from the local streams. Many other small hydroelectric opportunities abound, especially for home-sized power sources in rural areas. Hydroelectric power is also available in ocean currents, which may be harnessed with underwater sails.

Wind Power Potential

Wind power is also a form of solar energy, since the sun creates the temperature turbulence that generates wind across the globe. The total wind potential on earth is in the range of 200 terawatts[19]. Wind power has been used mechanically to lift water from rural wells. An estimated million such windmills were used in the U.S. in the 1920's.

Wind-generated electricity was growing rapidly back in the 1950's before the Rural Electric Administration (REA) subsidized the distribution of centralized power to rural areas. The positive intention of supplying low-cost power to every rural family had the unfortunate consequence of killing research and development of affordable wind systems. But wind power is back in vogue today, increasing capacity at an incredible 26% per year[39]. Any site that has some wind most of the time has great potential for wind power development, but over-development can trash the landscape and kill birds.

Ocean Thermal Energy Conversion (OTEC)

The ocean absorbs about 75% of the energy that strikes the earth. The temperature difference between the warm surface and the cold depths of the ocean (about 40°F) provides the opportunity for sea thermal power, with a total potential of roughly 100 terawatts of power[19]. The warm water vaporizes a low-boiling-point fluid such as ammonia (evaporates at 78°F). The vapor drives a turbine to generate electricity. Cold water pumped up from the ocean depths condenses the vapor back to a liquid to restart the process. The pumps bring nutrients up from the sea floor and may invigorate sea life in the vicinity. Sea thermal requires large facilities to be efficient, so it will be most useful to heavy industry and cities located along coast lines. The greatest advantage to sea thermal is that the process also desalinates water, a resource even more valuable than energy. A 100 kilowatt test plant built by Tokyo Power generated a net of 31.5 kilowatts of electricity (the rest was consumed in the process) until a typhoon destroyed the pipes[5].

Ships can also be equipped for OTEC, and the electricity used to split sea water to make hydrogen gas. For safety the hydrogen can be combined with nitrogen extracted from the air to make ammonia, which may be used as a fuel with some modification to gasoline-powered cars. About 2,000 OTEC ships could provide enough fuel for all U.S. cars, at an estimated cost of $1.60 (1995) or less for the equivalent of a gallon of gasoline[9].

Whether you are building a home or a business you too can cut your materials, labor and energy expenses several times over by taking extra time up front with smart designs. Retrofitting after the fact can also be highly beneficial, although never quite as lucrative as doing it right the first time.

The amount of energy we consume says surprisingly little about the amount of real wealth we produce with it. We may all employ the fuel calorie equivalent of up to 300 people working for us, but what are all those "workers" actually producing for us? It is easy to consume lots of calories—but actually producing something with all that energy is another matter.

For example, the industrial farmer may harvest 300 calories of energy for every one calorie of food consumed, but he also burns up 5-10 calories of fossil fuels to produce each of those food calories. If you imagine all calories as gasoline then it would mean we expend up to ten gallons of gasoline to put one gallon of gas on the table. Given this, one could argue that the environment, and our finances, would be better off if we just ate the petroleum straight!

By comparison, Masanobu Fukuoka, with his "do-nothing" approach to farming raises some of the highest yielding crops in Japan—with little effort expended in food or fuel calories. According to his estimates, natural farming produces about 100 calories of food per calorie of food energy expended[32]. He does not use any fuel calories in his process. There are a few farms in the U.S. now, practicing natural farming on a big scale, using machinery for the seeding and harvesting. It would be interesting to study their caloric consumption/production ratio.

Principles of Energy Efficiency

Whether you are an enterprising homeowner or a business person, there are several keys to smart energy use you should know about. Whole systems thinking, (as described with industrial pumping systems) may be the most important. Whole-systems thinking should include these elements: 1) apply end-use or demand-side management, 2) compare life-cycle costs instead of up-front costs, 3) match energy sources to end uses, and 4) match complimentary energy uses. Effective use of energy will enable you to more easily achieve your Dreams.

1) **Apply end-use or demand-side management.** You have probably heard at one time or another that if you converted an ordinary American home to photovoltaics, the cost could be $40,000 or more. While that state-

Solar Power Potential

The total solar radiation striking the surface of the earth is equal to about 350,000 terawatts of power[19]. Additional solar energy strikes the outer atmosphere and bounces back into space. An area the size of the White Sands Missile Range in New Mexico could provide enough solar electricity to meet the current electrical demands of the entire nation[10].

Solar energy will likely become our number one source of fuel in the coming years. As the price of photovoltaics continues to fall the quantity demanded will grow exponentially. Already solar capacity is increasing by 70% per year (1999). The cost of producing solar cells is expected to fall by another 75% in the first decade of the new millennium[39].

The great advantage to photovoltaics is that it doesn't usually compete with other land uses. The panels can be installed on just about any bare surface, even incorporated into the roof shingles of a house, the body of a car, or the paint on the wall. Solar panels can also be placed in space where they can collect solar energy twenty-four hours a day, without interference from the atmosphere or nightfall. The energy can be transferred down through a focused microwave beam, using minor adjustments to communications satellites now being launched into space.

Solar energy includes solar electric and solar hydrogen gas. Hydrogen gas is produced with an electric current or high heat by splitting water apart into hydrogen and oxygen. Hydrogen gas is most useful as a substitute for poor battery technology. Solar electricity can be stored as hydrogen gas then converted back to electricity through fuel cells to power homes or automobiles. Early fuel cells have been used in some civic bus systems since the mid 1990's. Hydrogen gas can be made from natural gas while the price of solar continues to fall.

Sometime in the 21st century we can expect to see completely automated solar cell production, where solar powered robots mine desert soils (or the surface of the moon) and use the minerals to self-replicate, producing more solar panels and more robots, exponentially spreading across the landscape until switched off. All the technological hurdles have already been crossed, but it could cost up to $100 billion dollars to integrate the separate technologies into one coherent system[10].

There is no need to twiddle your thumbs while waiting for the cost of solar to become competitive enough to add to your roof top. Solar cells are very nearly competitive after most other increases in energy efficiency have been exhausted. Invest in saving energy in your home and business, and you can immediately benefit from real economic and environmental savings. When your building is as efficient as possible then you will be ready to install photovoltaics as they become affordable.

Closing the loop on wasted energy can be profitable for you and the environment.

ment might be true, it says more about the quality of our houses than it does about photovoltaics. Simply put, builders are not rewarded for resource conservation. They have little motivation to design or build houses to save any energy beyond federally mandated standards. The higher cost of some energy efficiency improvements will be repaid in only a few months or a year's time, but that is too long for the builder who intends to sell the structure and move on. Other efficiency improvements can cost nothing at all in extra materials or labor, such as facing more windows south than north, but may require extra thought and care in the design phase. Again, builders have little incentive to make such improvements. The result is that the typical American home is riddled with so many leaks that it is like buying a sinking ship!

A few innovative and conscientious builders are turning the tide by building highly efficient homes and marketing them as such. Some promise to pay homeowners utility bills if the cost is more than advertised to heat their homes. These builders are setting a new standard in the building industry that helps to educate home buyers to demand greater energy efficiency. Once you have lived in an efficient structure it is hard to go back to an energy waster!

Spending tens of thousands of dollars on photovoltaics to power a home is much like installing pumps on a sinking ship without ever repairing the holes. If you plug the leaks first then you may find the pumps or panels are not so necessary, and a whole lot less expensive. Whether you are building, buying, or already occupying a structure, the key to saving money on energy is to incorporate this kind of "end-use" or "demand-side" management. Focus on what the service you want, such as "a warm, dry place" and choose the least expensive means—either plugs or pumps—to achieve your goals. Plugs are usually more economical than pumps.

2) **Compare life-cycle costs instead of up-front costs.** Would you rather have $100 to spend today or $100 to spend a year from today? Obviously you could do much more with the money sooner rather than later. You could spend it immediately to improve your quality of life, or invest it to increase your future wealth. Because money is worth more now, people instinctively discount it's future value. Given a choice most people would rather have $100 today than even $110 a year from now. Unfortunately, such short-sightedness leads to much greater losses all the time.

For example, consumers choose 40¢ incandescent lightbulbs rather than $16 compact fluorescent bulbs

---

Fossil Fuel Potential

Fossil fuels, including oil, natural gas, oil shale and coal, are organically derived, but not "renewable", unless you have a million+ years of patience. Fossil fuels are mostly dirty and primitive compared to other fuel sources, but easy to use and sufficient to give birth to the industrial economy. At the dawn of the 21st century there are still enough fossil fuels to power the economy for hundreds of years to come, but we must transition to cleaner fuels to halt global warming, acid rain, and city smog.

Natural gas is cleaner than other fossil fuels and has much potential as a transitionary energy source, especially for the first generation of ultralight, fuel-cell powered cars. Natural gas can be used as a substitute for solar hydrogen gas until the cost of solar technology drops sufficiently to replace it. Fuel-celled vehicles can utilize existing natural gas lines to homes and businesses. An added bonus is that the parked cars can convert natural gas to electricity and feed it back into the power lines, generating a profit for their owners. If all US automobiles were replaced with fuel-celled ultralights, the total electrical generating capacity would be about 5-10 times the capacity of existing power stations[39].

All fossil fuels are still potential sources of energy, if the carbon and other pollutants are vastly reduced or completely stripped. For example, it may be possible to close the loop completely so that the smokestacks of industry run horizontally to other factories instead of belching into the atmosphere. If industry can extract the waste smoke for useful properties then it would be possible to burn fossil fuels without endangering the environment. Nevertheless, as with trees in the forest, there are higher end-uses for fossil fuels than turning them to ash, and we would be better off to save our fossil fuels for the many other products we can make from them.

because incandescents cost less in the present. The compact fluorescent bulb uses barely a quarter of the energy of an incandescent to put out the same amount of light and lasts many years longer, saving up to about $40 worth or electricity over its lifetime. Choosing the cheaper incandescent bulb only insures that the customer will have less money in the future too, so that when the bulb burns out they will still not have the money to spring for the more expensive unit. Poor economic investments beget additional poor economic investments, while sound economic investments bring a positive return to enable even better future investments.

The power bill is one of those major expenses that comes around month after month, year after year, throughout a person's life. Fortunately, you can do something about it in your home and/or your business. You can invest in energy efficiency so that you have the same end uses, but while consuming less power. This will save you money which you can then spend elsewhere. Remarkably, investing in energy efficiency can yield even better returns for you than the stock market.

For example, Rocky Mountain Institute has demonstrated that a $20 investment in a low-flow shower head can more than pay for itself in savings in one year. Low-flow shower heads use less water, so less energy is employed to heat the water. Your savings comes to you through smaller power bills. RMI documented that a $20 low-flow shower head can yield a $17 to $25 energy savings every year with a gas water heater or a $47 to $71 energy savings with an electric water heater. (Based on switching from a 4 or 6 gallon per minute shower head to a 2 gallon per minute shower head at energy costs of $.075 per kilowatt hour for electricity and $.53 per therm for gas.) RMI compared this to a certificate of deposit and a savings or now account. A $20 investment in a CD would yield only $1.60 in a year, and the same investment in a savings or now account would yield only $1.20[67].

Eliminating your expenses through energy conservation can be profitable for you and for the environment since fewer fossil fuels need to be burned for energy. It can also be beneficial to the utilities. Power plants are expensive to build, and it is often cheaper for them to help their customers use less energy than it is to pay for new power plants. Then more customers can be served without the utilities having to expand their capacity. Because of this, the utilities often have special programs to help customers use energy more efficiently, such as free energy audits, extra insulation for water heaters, and often reduced rates on compact florescent lightbulbs

3) Match energy sources to end uses. If you want to create a small temperature difference, such as heating your home in tens of degrees, suggests Amory Lovins, author of *Soft Energy Paths*[38], then the need should be met by a source that provides that heat in tens or hundreds of degrees, rather than in the thousands of degrees with a coal-fired plant or in the trillions of degrees with a nuclear reactor, which is "like cutting butter with a chainsaw". The "soft approach" according to Lovins is to use highly refined energies such as electricity and gasoline only for the tasks that require high-grade energy. Lower grade energy should be used for all other tasks.

Consider, that when a utility generates electricity it has to burn three units of a lower-grade energy, like coal

---

Geothermal Power Potential

Our planet is a slowly cooling ball of molten matter covered by a thin, floating crust. Heat escaping from this vast mass of molten rock beneath our feet is what gives us hot springs, volcanoes, and geothermal energy potential. The entire energy potential of the earth's core is awesome, as it will be cooling for billions of years to come, but the readily harvestable heat from existing vents totals about 10 terawatts of power annually[19]. Water in the earth's crust is heated by the hot magma below.

Geothermal power is cheap and easy to develop. Most of the larger sites have already been harnessed, but many smaller hot springs still exist. The biggest problem with geothermal power is that it prevents other scenic or recreational uses of the thermal water. However, many hot springs have excess hot water that can be developed for small power systems while maintaining the existing pools. Even more lucrative, the warm water left over from power generation or bathing can be piped through houses, businesses or greenhouses for radiant heat. Geothermal greenhouses can produce large quantities of vegetables in northern climates without the cost or impacts of fossil fuels. Although the income potential seems obvious, many small hotspring owners have yet to take advantage of the opportunity.

Tidal Power Potential

The ocean tides are generated by the pull of the moon's gravity. The world-wide potential for tidal energy is only about 1 terawatt of power[19], but some locations are very lucrative. One of the best tidal energy sources is in Canada's Bay of Fundy where the tide rises and falls by fifty feet every day, but developing the site would likely destroy the local ecology. Tidal power is being developed especially in coastal countries where fog may limit solar potential.

or oil, to produce only one unit of high-grade electricity. Two-thirds of the potential energy is lost as waste heat in the conversion. This is why electric space heating is so expensive. You have to burn three times as much fuel to generate enough electricity to heat your home or business as you would if you burned the coal or oil directly. As a result of this kind of backwards energy use we burn up 27 years worth of stored, fossilized sunshine in this country every day[40].

Granted, coal and oil are very dirty, so it is nice to burn it hundreds of miles from home. But you can switch to the relatively clean natural gas for more efficient energy use. Better yet, compare the cost of a natural gas furnace with the cost of investing in better insulation, weather-stripping, and super-efficient windows. With the aid of a simple solar hot air collector attached to the house, you may be able to slash your energy consumption, even while

Fission and Fusion Potential

The Big Bang created a universe of only hydrogen and helium. These original materials were squeezed into heavier elements under the massive gravitational pressure found in the cores of the stars. Our own solar system is built from other stars that have long since collapsed under their own weight and blown their debris across the vast emptiness of space. Radioactive materials are among the heaviest elements, which slowly "decay" into more stable forms. Their "half-lives" are determined by the amount of time it takes to decay half of any given amount of material. They've been decaying for billions of years since being blown from the last stars. Our planet was initially much more radioactive at the dawn of life, and there were likely many spontaneous nuclear explosions.

Nuclear power plants control the decay of radioactive elements, especially uranium-235 and uranium-thorium, releasing vast amounts of energy from small amounts of material. Although non-renewable, the energy potential for nuclear fission is very high—at about 100,000,000 terawatt hours[19].

Nuclear **fission** has been around since the 1940's when the first atomic bombs were developed. It was once touted as being the energy of the future that would be "too cheap to meter". Today nuclear electricity is the most expensive form of conventional electricity we have because it takes so many calories of food and fuel energy to safely build and operate the facilities. The net efficiency of a fission reactor is a paltry 12% since so much of the energy produced from the process is consumed in mining, transporting, processing, using, and disposing of the uranium. Fission may always be prohibitively expensive here on earth, simply because it is too dangerous. We still have not found a safe and practical method to dispose of the waste material. Many nuclear power plants are being moth-balled at a young age because it is more economical to close them down unpaid for than to continue generating such expensive electricity.

The exponential spread of solar energy would seem to seal the fate of fission forever on earth, but there are applications off-world where fission still has potential. For example, it is theoretically possible to build a solar powered rocketship, just not very efficient to do so. A "solar sail" on a star ship can be unfurled close to the sun, such that the sun's light will quickly push it up to a fantastic speed, allowing it to "coast" to another star system. The only problem is that such a device would take a thousand years or more to get to the nearest star. That's not a bad speed for interstellar travel. In fact, it ranks among the best proposals we have for that task. Conventional chemical rocketry, including hydrogen fuel, is similarly limited in speed. The travel time to our closest neighboring planet, Mars, is about six months. Travel time to the nearest star system is still measured in thousands of years. You can speed things up a bit by carrying more fuel, but the "catch-22" is that more fuel means more mass to propel, and thus you have to carry more fuel just to propel the added mass, a no-win situation. Nuclear fission can greatly lighten the load to enable rocketships to travel farther and faster.

Nuclear **fusion** may be another source of energy for the not-too-distant future. Fusion is the process of the sun, the reverse of fission, where lighter elements are fused to make heavier elements. Fusion experiments here on earth involve tritium-deuterium extracted from sea water. Like fission, the source is non-renewable, but the earthly supply dwarfs the imagination, with a total potential of 300,000,000,000 terawatts of power[19].

Given the high potential and that the ingredients are found in common seawater, fusion is often touted like fission once was, as being the fuel of the future, "too cheap to meter". Whether it will happen that way or not is hard to say for sure. Taxpayer-subsidized researchers have spent billions of dollars and decades of effort attempting to achieve a sustainable fusion reaction, but without success. They will undoubtedly someday achieve fusion, but the economics of it may be questionable. In December 1993 at the Princeton University Plasma Physics Laboratory researchers generated 5 million watts of controlled fusion power in a one second burst. Incidentally, they consumed eight times as much energy getting the plasma reaction hot enough![2] Fusion will be a viable technology once scientists are able to sustain the reaction so that it fuels itself. It is believed that a fusion "pulse rocket" could reach the next star system in only 50 years—a heart-beat compared to the thousands of years required by our best technologies today.

Fusion will be economical here on earth only if it has a much higher net efficiency than fission. That may be achievable since the cost of supplying the fuel—sea water—is virtually nil. The primary factor left effecting the efficiency of fusion reactors will be the ratio of how much power is consumed building and operating them relative to the amount of power they produce over their lifetimes. Fusion reactors may be especially useful in cold, cloudy climates where solar potential is limited.

keeping the inefficient electric heat for backup.

Likewise, an electric clothes drier relies on high-grade electricity when low-temperature heat is all that is really needed. A gas clothes drier is therefore much more appropriate to the task. It is just too easy to plug in electric gizmos, so we use electricity to do many tasks it is not required for. Switching to alternative fuel sources wherever possible immediately saves the two-thirds of the energy that is otherwise lost to produce electricity. By matching energy types to the end uses, and by installing efficient appliances, you can meet the electric demand of the ordinary American home for only a few thousand dollars worth of photovoltaics, with a pay-back rate that makes it almost equally competitive with grid-delivered power. It may be cost-prohibitive to throw out all the old appliances at once, but you can sure replace them as they wear out with newer, better alternatives.

4) **Match complimentary energy uses.** The other key towards effective energy management is to match complimentary energy uses together. For example, a refrigerator consumes energy to pump heat out from the inside, leaving cooler air behind. The heat removed from the refrigerator, plus extra heat given off by the pump, is radiated into the room. Meanwhile, down the hall, the water heater is burning more fuels to heat water, and the air-condi-tioner may be working to remove all this extra heat from the house! A single appliance that pumps heat out of a refrigerator, or out of the household air, and into a water heater, would effectively accomplish two jobs with only half as much energy. Granted, an all-in-one appliance would be difficult to fit in an existing house, but new houses could be designed with such an appliance in mind, and the energy savings would be worth the extra design work. Another option that would fit in many existing structure would be a clothes dryer that generates hot water from waste heat for an adjacent clothes washer that needs hot water.

Complimentary energy use may be cost-pro-hibitive in most existing homes, but it can be essential to keeping costs down in businesses that otherwise have power bills running in the hundreds, thousands, or even tens of thousands of dollars. Just about every business in this country, from restaurants to laundromats to major industrial plants, utilizes energy to serve their customers and discards the low-temperature "waste heat" back into the atmosphere. But this waste heat can be used in many ways, for simple heating tasks, like greenhouses, homes, and water. In fact, many industrial plants vent hot steam that could otherwise be used to generate electricity!

> ### Energy Glossary
> **Barrel**—A volume of crude oil measuring 42 gallons, the equivalent of 5.8 million BTU's.
> **BTU**—British thermal unit. The amount of heat required to raise the temperature of one pound of water one degree Fahrenheit, or 251.996 calories.
> **Calorie**—The amount of heat required to raise the temperature of one gram of water one degree Celsius, the equivalent of 4.184 joules.
> **Joule**—A joule is the same as a watt-second. It is the work done when a force of 1 newton acts through a distance of 1 meter.
> **Watt**—1 watt is equal to 1 joule per second or 0.239 calories per second or 3.4192 BTU's per hour. A 100 watt lightbulb uses 100 watts of electricity per hour.
> **Kilowatt**—One thousand watts. Utility bills are measured in kilowatt hours. A typical small, portable heater uses 1.5 kilowatts (1,500 watts) per hour.
> **Megawatt**—One million watts. A typical coal-fired power plant generates 1,500 megawatts of electricity.
> **Terawatt**—One trillion watts. Used to describe the total potential of energy sources.
> **Quad**—One quadrillion watts. Used to describe the total potential of energy sources.

By adopting all these kinds of energy efficient technologies and strategies, Rocky Mountain Institute documented that we could reduce our electric consumption by 75% across the country at a cost less than we pay now to produce it! We can reduce our oil consumption by 80% at a lower cost than we can drill for more, and we can cut our emissions of greenhouse gasses in half at a profit[39].

"I too had woven a kind of basket of delicate texture... and instead of studying how to make it worth men's while to buy my baskets, I studied rather how to avoid the necessity of selling them."

—Henry David Thoreau, *Walden*

3-5
Money
-Financial Ladders & Cultural Relativity-

Money is the grease that keeps the economy moving. It facilitates the exchange of goods and services between individuals. Money can be a powerful tool to help you achieve your own personal and professional goals, but be forewarned, too many people get caught up in the illusion of money and lose sight of real wealth.

Most people seek to climb the ladders of financial success through an ever increasing supply of money. We took the opposite approach. Our starting route to success was to work towards not needing money. To our way of thinking, money is representative of calories, and the fewer we expended the fewer we would need to earn. In essence, we applied a conservation/efficiency ethic towards the money we earned at our jobs. Instead of expending a lot of effort attempting to bring home more money, we simply worked to achieve needing less. It is similar to the idea of producing "negawatts" of energy or "negagallons" of water. By reducing our expenses we produced "negadollars" and "negajobs", so that we do not have to work so hard to earn a living. We closed the loop on wasted dollars so that we can apply our time and money towards more fulfilling ends.

To understand this better, imagine for a moment that you are in charge of a dam, and your assignment is to keep the reservoir full behind the dam. Given this, what would you do if there was a leak in the dam? Would you plug the leak or would you find a new source of water to pour into the reservoir to replace the water spilling out? I think most people would choose to cure the problem rather than mask the symptoms.

Yet, each of us does caretake a dam of sorts, and for most of us there is hardly a drop of water in the reservoir because it is all gushing out a split in the dam. The liquid behind our dams is our wealth, and like water, our wealth can sustain us and it can help us to grow prosperous—but we cannot use our wealth if it is flooding away uncontrollably through rent, energy, food, and other expenses. Most people see their wealth flooding away, and they respond by working harder to bring home more wealth to throw behind the dam. To many people this is normal; to me it is absurd.

To my way of thinking, a home is a business just like any other business, and the same basic rules apply to both. In either, we always have a **gross income** from our jobs, and we have a **net income** from that, after we have paid all our expenses. Unfortunately, most of us, whether we make $5,000 or $50,000 a year, find that our gross incomes and our expenses are nearly identical, leaving us very little net wealth to invest in our hopes and dreams.

Part of the problem we can run into as we try to fulfill our dreams is that we often believe there is only one ladder of financial success and that the only way to climb that ladder is to make a higher income tomorrow than we made today. We often believe that the only way to move upward in the world is to increase our gross income by getting a raise or by selling a greater number of products. It is human nature that we tend to think that having just a slightly higher income will solve all our financial problems—regardless of which financial bracket, rich or poor, we are in now. Meanwhile, most of us neglect to ask what is at the top of the ladder, or even if there is a top to the ladder. We strive to climb to the next rung on the ladder, but we do not stop to ask how that rung is different or better than the one we are on now.

The conventional ladder of success has some serious shortcomings, and I would like to offer an alternative way of thinking. Our experience has shown us that there is not just one ladder of financial success, but many. We can be financially successful with a very small amount of wealth or with a very large amount. A person with only a small amount of wealth may be at the top of a short ladder, while a person with vast wealth may be at the top of a ladder that is simply taller. Attaining the top of a ladder actually has little to do with how much money we make. A higher gross income does not necessarily bring us up any ladder, rather it brings us across to ladders that can be climbed higher. It is our net income that brings us up the ladders of financial success.

A person who makes a lot of money may have a nice house and a lot of toys, but that does not necessarily mean they have reached the top of any particular ladder. They may have a significant gross income, but that means little if they also have big debts. What would happen if they lost their job tomorrow? For that matter, what would happen if they merely decided not to show up for work? Would the bank come and repossess everything and put them out on the street? A big gross income can put us at the bottom of a ladder that can be climbed very high, but it does not explicitly put us at the top.

On the other hand, a person might have only a modest income, say ten or twenty thousand a year, but they can be at the top of their ladder if they have few or no expenses. For example, Renee and I do not make a lot of money, but much of the time we can choose whether or not we want to go to work. We have a certain level of financial freedom, or perhaps, freedom from finances, that allows us to be in control of our lives. We can hang out around the house if we choose to, or we can take off on a camping trip. We can take extended vacations from work without fear that our home will be repossessed or our power or phone shut off. We periodically go to work climbing on our short ladder, but then we hop off the ladder and back onto our little "cloud" at the top (see illustration "Financial Ladders"). We have only a modest gross income, but we keep most of that as net income since we have few expenses.

Our net income is what we have once all of our expenses are paid from our gross or total income. Our net income is ours to use as we please. We can choose to simply stop working and use our net income to pay future expenses. We can stay on our cloud at the top of the ladder until we run out of money. If our wealth is like water then we have it contained fairly well, so we can use it when and where we please.

If your dam of wealth leaks then you are forced to return to your job to earn more wealth to replace what you are losing. But if you fix the dam then you can do whatever you want to. If the dam is not leaking then you can take a vacation; breathe for a while. Or you can continue working and accumulate a surplus of wealth to use however you please. Pour your surplus wealth onto the crops you

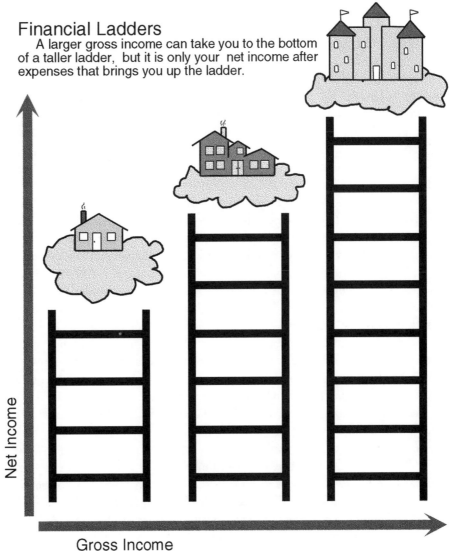

Financial Ladders

A larger gross income can take you to the bottom of a taller ladder, but it is only your net income after expenses that brings you up the ladder.

Net Income

Gross Income

99

want to grow, and reap your bounty.

It is simple logic, but in every day life we sometimes miss it. Most of us turn up the thermostat when the house is cold, but does it not make more sense to plug the leaks to keep the existing heat inside? Either option requires an expenditure of wealth and makes the house warm, but one option eliminates the problem while the other only prolongs it.

A hunter-gatherer harvests two or three meals of food for every meal consumed, whereas the modern farmer harvests about 300 meals for each consumed, and yet the farmer works more than the hunter-gatherer. It may seem like the farmer should work less because he can produce food so easily, but he works more because he has to trade all that food for farm equipment, a house, a car, a satellite dish, and all manner of other things that hunter-gatherer peoples have no use for and no means of producing anyway. Now consider, what might happen if the modern farmer, or anyone of us, maintained an industrial level of production, but only a hunter-gatherer level of consumption?

As part of our strategy for climbing the ladders of financial success, we invested our resources towards paying off our house and land so we would never have to pay for them again. At the same time we made our house energy efficient so that we would not have to work all our lives to pay high energy bills. We invested our wealth to eliminate our expenses, so we now have the comforts of our industrial culture, while our bills are not much higher than they would be if we lived as hunter-gatherers.

Henry David Thoreau, unknowingly perhaps, took advantage of this particular equation when he spent two years and two months conducting his "experiments into the economy of living" at Walden Pond in the 1840's. Agriculture at that time was essentially based on farming with oxen and plows, which as you may recall, translates to about 33 meals produced for each meal consumed. At each of his jobs Thoreau earned wages equitable to the production capabilities of his culture, but he maintained a level of consumption barely above that of hunter-gatherer peoples. For example, conventional houses in Thoreau's day cost about $800 (a fifteen year mortgage at that time), but Thoreau built his simple cabin for twenty-eight dollars, twelve and one half cents. He earned wages at the same rates as his neighbors, but had a much more primitive life-style. With his basic cabin, a simple diet, and almost no possessions, Thoreau found he could work six weeks per year to earn a living (plus additional time tending to home chores). Thoreau only had to work six weeks per year and had 46 weeks left over each year "free and clear for study".[79]

Now imagine what our work year would be like if we adopted a life-style similar to Thoreau's, but maintained a modern level of production (more than ten times as productive as in Thoreau's time). We would hardly have to work at all.

Granted, few of us want to give up our houses, telephones, electricity, and plumbing, among other things, to live a Spartan life as Thoreau did. Indeed, even Thoreau went home two years and two months later, when he finished his "experiments" into the economy of living. Nevertheless, the concept of what I call "relativity" between economies can be very useful to us today. For instance, imagine an average married couple saving money to buy a house or land. They might rent an apartment, or a trailer, and pay all the usual expenses for power, water, telephone, food, etc.. They might spend 95% or more of their incomes on their living expenses, sacrifice the movie and the night out, and put the remaining 5% or less of their incomes in savings to eventually realize their dreams. Our own approach was just the opposite.

As you may recall, Thoreau worked six weeks per year for a living, and vacationed for the other 46 weeks. Thoreau could have worked all year long to save up extra calorie dollars to invest in either consumption or production, but he chose not to because that suited his goals. However, the Mennonite and Hutterite colonies in our country today are highly successful because they do maintain a minimalist level of consumption, while working hard. They are able to reinvest almost all of their incomes into production, buying more tools and land, occasionally splitting off to form new colonies. Their modest life-styles enable them to thrive and expand while neighboring farms and ranches succumb to bankruptcy.

Renee and I also minimized our consumption so we could allocate most of our incomes towards buying land and building a house. We started out together, working towards a common dream in the fall of 1988. Our combined annual income from all sources totaled between $8,000 and $14,000 each year, with an average of about $10,000 while we were building our home. That may not seem like a whole lot of money for one year, but imagine what you can do with it when you have the whole wad in your hand at once. Renee and I adopted a pseudo hunter-gatherer life-style to temporarily minimize our expenses. We taught primitive skills and lived on the trail, in our car, or with our parents when we came home. About 5% of our incomes went towards our expenses, while the other 95% went into savings. In one winter we saved up almost $10,000, which gave us a good start towards fulfilling our dreams. Later, when we bought land, we moved into a tent while we built our house. We continued living a hunter-gatherer life-style of sorts, and we continuously put about 90% of our incomes into our house and land.

Living a pseudo hunter-gatherer life-style in a tent or a camper trailer, etc. is certainly not for everyone, and certainly not for indefinite periods of time. It may be adventurous for a while, but it can also become tedious, and it can be hard on marriages. As I said, even Thoreau eventually went back "home" to a conventional life. However, living as "hunter-gatherers" can be a temporary measure to rapidly store up capital to achieve your dreams. Together Renee and I believed in our dream so much that we were willing to give it everything we had. I was further motivated by my strong dislike for being employed. You see, the couple that saves 5% per year has to work for a long time to achieve their dream. I personally do not like being employed, and I am willing to go to great lengths to avoid it.

What might happen if we maintained our industrial level of production while temporarily living a "hunter-gatherer" level of consumption?

Looking back, I can say it was very worthwhile for us to live a "hunter-gatherer" life style for the time that we did. By the age of twenty-six we had built and paid for a very nice home, and we could do pretty much anything we wanted, which for us, is the way it should be. You too can get a jackrabbit fast start by maintaining an industrial level of production while temporarily adopting a hunter-gatherer level of consumption.

Today we still have a modest income, and we have adopted three children, plus many critters. Our expenses are higher now that we are spending for five, but we still have freedom. Few people could survive on an income like ours, but we are able to get music lessons for the kids and go on extended family vacations. With our house and land paid for and low power bills, we are able to live a comfortable life-style. Only a small part of our income goes towards required bills. The rest of it we have available to spend in any way we choose. To us it is a lot like winning the lottery—every year!

Our experiences have shown us that anyone can win the lottery and climb the ladders of financial success. Anyone who has an income has the winnings already, it is only a matter of plugging the leaks that drain those winnings away. It is the net caloric income that brings you up the ladders towards financial freedom. At the same time, however, a bigger gross income can be helpful because it gives you a larger income to net calories from. For example, we live quite comfortably on our income, but we also enjoy spending money. We like to travel and go to movies and buy books and art and we like computers, and a newer car would be nice, as would an arboretum and an observatory! We can do all those things on a modest income; it would just be easier with a greater income.

Consider a gross income of $25,000 annually, which is still modest by most accounts. On that income a family could spend fully $15,000 on living expenses, much more than we spend, and still net $10,000 a year as profit to spend on hopes and dreams. A higher gross income does not explicitly bring one higher up the ladders of financial success, yet it does provide a greater resource to net from.

Each of us does have tremendous resources even if we only make a few thousand dollars a year. For example, what would you do if I gave you ten or fifteen thousand dollars to spend any way you wanted? You could really go on quite a shopping spree! Chances are, however, you may already have that much to spend every year. That is an amazing amount of money, especially when you consider that billions of people around the globe make less than one or two thousand dollars each year.

The important part is how you choose to spend your wealth. The decision to make a purchase may bring you a specific gain, but it also costs you the opportunity to spend your money in other ways. When you spend $6.00

on a movie you are giving up the opportunity to spend that $6.00 on food, or a stereo, or real estate. You also lose the opportunity to avoid working to earn the money in the first place. Thus the true cost of an item is not measured in money, but in terms of the opportunities forgone to make the purchase. In economic lingo this is called **opportunity cost.**

For our purposes it is useful to think about three types of opportunities: disposables, depreciables, and appreciables. Every choice you make with your wealth as a consumer is an investment, fitting into one of the three categories. With each investment you will realize a specific gain, while simultaneously losing the opportunity to invest in the alternatives. In a nutshell the three types of opportunities can be described this way:

1) **Disposables.** You spend your dollar and it is gone the instant you spend it.
2) **Depreciables.** You keep your dollar when you spend it, but it depreciates in value.
3) **Appreciables.** You keep your dollar when you spend it, and it maintains or grows in value.

Disposables: People spend most of their money on the first investment option, the disposable purchase. The disposable purchase is the black-hole of finances where money goes in, but never comes out. Included here are the "survival" expenses (rent, energy, food, telephone, interest on loans, etc.) as well as entertainment-type expenses, such as movies, recreation, and travel.

There is nothing wrong with spending money on these types of expenses, as long as you are getting what you really want. I am not sure, however, that most people do get what they really want out of the money they earn and spend. For instance, a person who drinks two 50¢ cans of pop each day spends $365 in one year. It is pretty easy to fritter away hundreds of dollars when it is spread out as a dollar or two or three a day, but most people would make different choices in their spending if they had the whole wad at once.

For example, what would you do if I put $365 in your hands right now to spend however you wanted? Would you say, "Wow! Just think of all the soda pop I can buy with this!" or would you say, "Wow! I am going to put this towards something really special!" Presented this way, few people would choose to invest in soda pop. However, the truth is, at the rate of a few dollars here and there, most of us do choose to make major investments into many minor things; soda pop is only one example.

Similarly, imagine if you were a person who spent $1,000 a month renting a nice apartment. Most people have to work awfully hard to earn that much money every month. An apartment with half the rental cost might not be as luxurious, but it would free up $500 a month, or $6,000 per year to invest somewhere else.

You could then choose another disposable investment, such as a classy vacation, or you may choose to put that money into a depreciable or appreciable investment, something that will continue to benefit you in the years to come. The choices you make are entirely up to you. What is important is that you are getting what you really want with your money and your time.

Most people seem to assume that they have to work every day of their lives, and they spend money like they are trying to dispose of it. It appears as if the objective were to get rid of all the money before the next paycheck comes! People seem to automatically get up and go to work without ever questioning why they do it. This is the epitome of do-somethingness. It is important to realize that you always have a choice.

Depreciables: The depreciable investment is primarily represented by things and gadgets, such as cars, stereos, recreational equipment, appliances, clothes, etc.. These depreciate dramatically the instant you buy them and then continue to depreciate gradually until reaching the landfill or the recycling center. This is the category where people spend most of the money that is leftover after they make their disposable purchases.

Just imagine how your car might look and run if you took the ten or fifteen thousand dollars saved by not buying a new car and invested some of it into fixing up the one you have now.

For the most part, any investment in things or gadgets, when these are what you really want, are best done second hand, after the initial depreciation. For example, a new car can cost $20,000 or more. By making monthly payments you may pay half again or more the total cost of the car just as interest. By the time you complete your loan payments you will likely have a vehicle worth little more than the one you are driving now. On the other hand, you can save a bundle by buying a used car. Even better yet, just imagine what your existing car could look and run like if you invested some of the ten or fifteen thousand dollars saved by not buying a new car into fixing it up. Fixing the car you have can be the best option of all—as long as it is not a gas guzzler or a lemon.

One way or another, if things and gadgets are high on your priority list, if you do want that new car, then you can make the choices so that you have several thousand dollars or so each year to spend in this way. With a steady job and income you could establish a continuous, albeit non-growing, money supply to support these choices.

Appreciables: You can also choose the third type of investment and let your money grow. This will give you more income later on to purchase depreciable things and gadgets and disposables, like vacations—and maybe you could even do away with your job. Some of the investments you might choose from could include: a higher education, a new business, stocks, bonds, or other interest type accounts, or you could invest in eliminating your expenses.

A higher education can be an invaluable investment that may pay off. Unfortunately, most investments into college-type educations will teach you how to get a job, as opposed to learning how to not need a job, which is, in my opinion, far more worthwhile. If you do not already know what you want to do, then a college-type investment may at least yield some new ideas.

Alternately, an investment in stocks, bonds, or other interest type accounts will yield steady growth. Unfortunately even in a booming economy, many of these choices yield profits at a rate only slightly greater than the rate at which inflation devalues that profit. You might be able to make money and eventually realize your dreams, but perhaps it would be better to start living your dreams now.

One of the greatest payoffs can come from investing in the elimination of expenses, so that you can free up more funds to invest elsewhere. This may include some of the expenses you are presently incurring as rent or energy bills. Consider the amount you presently spend on these each month. How would it be to have that amount available every month to spend or invest on anything you wanted? Working to eliminate these expenses is the true do-nothing approach to real wealth. When you eliminate your expenses you become free to do whatever you want!

In a good economy or a poor one, having few expenses in both your home and business means you can drop your prices lower than anyone else's. You can afford to lower your prices if your break-even point is lower than everyone else's. Lower prices are helpful to the consumer, and that means more customers and more profit for you. You can make a profit at prices that your competition cannot afford to match as long as your expenses are lower than anyone else's.

Also, the freedom of not needing an income can allow you to run a business which you might not otherwise be able to afford to do. For example, you may have a hobby, which you would like to be able to work with full time. You could achieve the freedom to do that by turning your hobby into a business, except that not all hobbies-turned-businesses have the same amount of income potential. The freedom to not need much of an income can allow you to make your hobby your business, even if you do not especially profit from it. This is true for us, in the case of our school and my writing.

Primitive living skills is a fascinating hobby for us. Operating our school allows us to turn a hobby into a business and gives us the freedom to practice our stone-age skills more often. We could not always afford to run our school if we had to make a real income from it. For one thing, many of our customers make only a "stone-age income" themselves; they could not afford to come if our prices were any higher. Not needing much of an income allows us to market to people who have only modest incomes themselves. This way more people can afford to come to our classes, and we can afford to keep practicing what we enjoy so much.

Likewise, I have a passion for writing, and the desire to make a significant income from it. We do not need a greater income, but I intend to invest in businesses that will further help to make the world a better place. Besides, there are about ten thousand acres of land near home that I would like to purchase and protect with conservation easements for future generations to enjoy. But I would not have the opportunity to express myself in writing if we

Eliminating Rent Payments

The mortgage payment is the biggest monthly and yearly expense for most people and businesses. It is a big expense that returns month after month, year after year, often for twenty or thirty years, and frequently for a person's entire lifetime. If you can permanently reduce or eliminate this one expense then you have really accomplished something. Without a big mortgage payment or high maintenance bills you can have a significant chunk of money available each month every year to spend however you please.

Eliminating mortgage payments is a challenge, but a very rewarding one, and there are many routes you can take towards that end. The most important requirement, however, is that you buy your house or business space, rather than rent. If you rent then you pay for someone else's mortgage and your money is irretrievable. If you want to keep your money then you have to buy your own place.

However, many people are shocked after spending tens of thousands of dollars in mortgage payments to find that they have built up only a few thousand dollars equity in their property. For example, consider a $50,000 loan at 10% interest over 30 years. Your monthly payments would be $431.31, but on your first payment only $22.31 goes towards principle. The other $415.00 is lost towards interest. This ratio changes slowly over the years so that you gradually pay more principle and less interest, but after ten years you will have paid out $51,757.20 but gained only $4,266.21 on the principle. You will have lost $47,490.99 in interest. That does not seem like much of a deal and I agree.

Fortunately you can make additional payments on most loans to pay off the balance early. There are many ways you can do this. One popular method is through the process of making two principle payments each month.

In the example above you will have paid out a total of $157,431 for the $50,000 loan over 30 years. But you can save a bundle if you make two principle payments each month. As I said, the principle portion of the first payment is only $22.31 while the rest of your payment is lost as interest. That changes slightly on the second month so you pay $22.50 to the principle and a hair less than before towards interest. You can add the second month's principle on top of your first monthly payment and you will have made two payments.

Do not be mistaken here, you still have to make a full payment next month and every month, but you effectively lower the total balance in one month to the amount it normally would have been after two months. Each time you lower your total balance then you pay less towards interest and more towards principle, so the faster you make payments the better off you will be. In ten years on this schedule you will have paid $16,853.89 in principle instead of merely $4,266.21. By that time you would be making your regular payment of $431.31 plus an additional principle payment of $160.86[34].

By making double payments every month you can pay off a 30 year loan in 15 years, and in this example, you would save $53,610.87 that you would have otherwise paid out in interest. A schedule like this can work very nice because your payments start out low and then grow little by little over time, presumably as you move up in the world and make more money, thus making it easier for you to make the larger payments. Even more important is that the schedule is non-binding. You are only required to make the $431.31 payment each month; the rest is voluntary, so you can put your money elsewhere if an emergency arises. If you wish to make double payments then you may be able to obtain an "amortization schedule" of your loan from the bank, or you could make a spreadsheet of it if you have home computer. An amortization schedule is a payment-by-payment listing of a loan, listing your new balance after each regular payment is made.

It is not important how you go about paying off your home loan; just remember that the sooner you pay it off, the sooner you can use your money elsewhere, and there is usually no limit to how quickly you can pay off the loan. For example, one way to pay off a mortgage quickly is by buying a property with a smaller mortgage. If the banker says you can afford a $500 monthly payment then buy a house with a $250 monthly payment, and then pay the full $500 every month. You will own your property free and clear in no time at all. Finish paying it off, then you will have $500 a month, every month, to spend as you please. Also, buying a property this way allows you to build up equity quickly; you put most of your money into principle from the very beginning. You can then use your equity to buy a bigger property later, or to make some other type of investment.

Our own strategy was to put every penny we could afford towards our home to pay it off in only a few years. Also, we built our own home so we did not pay interest on the house itself; we just bought the materials as we could afford them. Of course, the advantage to a loan is that you can buy a house or business building all at once and completely assembled. You can start using it from day one. Buying a house one piece at a time as we did meant that we did not always have all of the pieces. Among other things, we had the opportunity to experience a full Montana winter with no door on our house (that was one of the smaller leaks). Living that way for a short time was indeed an adventure, but is was also an income. By not paying interest on a conventional home mortgage we probably saved at least $150,000. That is not a bad wage for a couple years of roughing it!

You can use any of these strategies or some of your own to pay off your home or business mortgage quickly. Even a system as simple as making a once-a-year extra payment from your tax refund can help a lot to whittle down the mortgage. With your mortgage out of the way you can pay yourself each month thereafter, instead of the bank.

were struggling every day to pay our bills.

Effective use of our limited calorie income has allowed us to pursue business choices which are truly meaningful to us. Effective use of your calories will likewise allow you to achieve your own success. Eliminating many of your personal and business expenses will give you the stable economic foundation you need to launch a prospering

Reducing Your Taxes

It is funny that collectively we vote to enact taxes, yet individually we do almost any thing we can to avoid paying them. It seems that we should eagerly fork over as many tax dollars as we can, especially knowing that the money can go to some of the good programs we all support. Our tax dollars can be spent on jobs programs, education, and programs to help the environment. That seems worthwhile, does it not?

On the other hand, I know that I can accomplish the same good even more directly. I can spend my money in ways that help the environment and creates jobs, while also making my own life more prosperous. I can study products and make environmentally sensible choices. My purchases create jobs, and the items I purchase contribute to my own prosperity. I can even go on to invest my money in starting a new, environmentally sensible business and that way I can create even more jobs. No bureaucrat can accomplish all that as efficiently as I can. For me that is the primary motivation to minimize the amount we pay out in income taxes. Every dollar that I can avoid paying in taxes is another dollar that I personally can invest directly in making the world a better place for all.

As for strategies, there is one surefire way to avoid paying taxes—simply do not earn very much money! Indeed, our tax laws encourage you to earn less money, just as welfare checks encourage many people to earn no money. There are many people who would rather do nothing and be paid $300 a month than to be paid $1,000 and have to work for it. Welfare is a disincentive to work and taxes have a similar effect. Every person has a threshold where they value their time for themselves more than they value trading their time for additional income. Taxes push that threshold lower. Let me explain.

If you earn a low enough income then you do not have to pay any taxes. If you have a low income and children too, then you can take advantage of the Earned Income Credit (EIC) and get a refund up to two or three thousand dollars—even if you paid far less than that in taxes. Earn too much money and you will lose the earned income credit *and* you will have to pay additional taxes. The more you work the less reward you get for your efforts!

Granted, this tax strategy is a bit unorthodox, and you do not want to go to your boss and tell him or her to cut your $30,000 salary in half, simply so you can avoid paying taxes! No, the more conventional tax strategy is to go ahead and earn more, but to deduct much of that income as expenses.

For example, by turning your hobby into a business, big or small, you can deduct most of your hobby expenses. Suppose you have an interest in medicinal herbs. If you start a small business wild-crafting herbs and selling them then you can deduct your business expenses—for books, classes, supplies, computers and office supplies. Items like a computer can only be deducted to the extent that you are using them in business, but even if you only deduct half the cost of a computer for business purposes, you still have 100% of the computer for entertainment purposes. You can even deduct some of your travel expenses if you happen to drive 1,000 miles to wild craft herbs in some mountain range that you've always wanted to explore—as long as the primary purpose of the trip is business related . You can spend thousands of dollars on your hobby without paying any taxes for all that fun. The "catch 22" is that you still have to work and make some sales from your business to pay cover all those expenses, but there is a genuine tax savings if you would have spent the money on your hobby anyway. By deducting expenses you can make more money and spend more money, but still be taxed at a lower bracket.

Filing tax forms is tedious and it does not produce any real wealth, but the way our tax laws are written there is a real incentive to take the time to do the research and the paperwork. If you do enough research in advance (at the beginning of the year, rather than afterwards) you can always find ways to spend and invest your money wisely, so that you can pay little or no taxes. Indeed the richest people in the country often pay little or no taxes at all. The tax laws change constantly, so it always takes some research to find the best strategies for your situation and to keep up with the changes.

In spring there are always articles in the personal finance magazines pointing out the latest tax changes and offering tax tips. There are also many excellent books at the library that nitpick through the tax forms and tell you exactly which forms to use and how to fill them out. Some guides will even help you organize your paperwork throughout the year to make tax time easy. There are also computer programs to help you file your taxes. You do have to buy an updated program for each tax year, but these programs do make it easier to go through the paper work. Still, I recommend going slowly, learning only one or two new tax forms each year. The first time through is the hardest because you have to figure out which lines to fill in or leave blank. But the next year you will likely use most of the same lines. This means you can put the new form next to a copy of your previous return, and fill in all the same lines using the new figures.

Use good tax strategies to plug the tax leaks in your financial dam. You may find that doing the paperwork is one of the most profitable things you can do all year. Closing the loop on your annual tax bill will free up even more wealth for you to invest in creating the world you believe in.

enterprise. A stable economic foundation underfoot makes it that much easier to sow your calories in your hopes and dreams and to harvest your bounty.

Fledgling businesses often experience lean times in the beginning, and it is much easier to start a business if you can survive without an income. If you need to earn $20,000 from the business to survive, then you are immediately plunging the enterprise $20,000 into the red. But, if you can live on only a few thousand dollars a year then you have a much more stable foundation on which to start out.

Having a stable foundation will help you through the lean times in your new business. It will also help you through the ups and downs of the local, national, and global economy. Recessions, for instance, have little meaning when you are not heavily dependent on the health of the economy. When a recession comes along you may simply make less money. Your assets cannot not be repossessed if you have no debts. If you have to you can simply go on vacation and wait out the recession until times are more prosperous. Having few expenses means you control your life; you are not a puppet of the economy. When you require few calories then you can afford the risk of harvesting few.

You do not need to build a house as we did to close the loop on wasted money. There are many ways to lower expenses just by taking advantage of the "relativity" between industrial and nonindustrial economies. Consider, people in our country enjoy vacationing in less-developed countries where prices are so low that we can live like royalty with only modest amounts of money. People in poorer countries will work all day to provide products and services to us for only a few dollars. They may not particularly like doing that for Americans, but they do like the influx of money. They only work so cheaply because, as a whole, they do not produce as much as we do per calorie of food and fuel energies expended. One year's wages in our country can be enough to retire on in another country. I do not necessarily advocate such a route to wealth; it does not seem respectful to move to other countries and have people become your low-paid servants.

Many people, however, do approximately the same thing right within the borders of our own country. People's homes on many parts of the east or west coast have an average value high enough to buy hundreds of acres of land in more rural parts of the country. Montanans have a certain dislike for all the "rich Californians" that keep coming in and buying up all the land. At the same time every local business person drools over the influx of new, wealthy customers into their store. There is a certain animosity towards people from California, much as there is a degree of animosity in poor countries towards Americans. There often becomes an underlying sentiment of "I don't like you because I have become your servant, but I want and need your business anyway."

Fortunately, you do not have to make an enemy of yourself to take advantage of the economic relativity between different parts of our country. There are many small, rural towns throughout the country where you can purchase a decent, usually older home, for as little as $25,000 or so. You may not be able to find a job locally that would enable you to make the payments on such a house, but you can go "hunting and gathering" to other parts of the country to easily make that kind of cash. Purchase the house, put a little money aside, and you can hang out and live for awhile. More importantly, people in small towns generally like to have new neighbors, particularly when the towns are declining and other people are moving away.

I meet quite a few people who do this sort of thing already. They go to Alaska and work on a fishing boat, or they get a high-paying job in the city. They quickly earn a pile of money and then come back home to live for awhile. I met one young couple who were hired as a team to drive semi-trucks. They expected to take in more than $30,000 apiece in a single year. More importantly, they would have virtually no expenses because they would be living on the road. Their dream was to build a cabin in the country and go hunting and fishing. Their plan was to save up for a couple years and then "retire".

Even a teenager fresh out of high-school with no job skills can go into virtual retirement within about five years. The military may not be every person's first choice for employment , but a kid can earn a decent income, gain useful skills and discipline for free, and the military will pay part or all of his or her meals, housing and clothing to boot! Any kid that resists the temptation to spend tens of thousands of dollars on car payments, bar-hopping and other shallow frills will quickly have enough money to buy a decent house in a small town, plus an okay used car and all the other basic necessities of life. Just imagine the freedom of having all that and no monthly bills! When you have few expenses then you can do whatever you want—including to jump into the global economy and make your fortune—if that is what you desire.

"If you are interested in the arts, or music, or any creative field then you need to fight not to get a job."
—A musician who bought a $4,000 house in Butte, Montana (1980's)

3-6
Labor
-Adding Caloric Value-

All the worldly goods of an individual in a hunter-gatherer society could be transported from one camp to another in a backpack or by travois. Their entire accumulation of material wealth stacked up like a single grain of sand on the beach compared to the vastness of the natural world around them. Today a majority of the population lives in a man-made world and many live their entire liveswithout leaving the matrix of human society to find out what the real world is really like. The amount of stuff our species has built is truly astonishing, even within the walls of a single home, and it was all built by the labor of human hands! Even in this newly emerging age of automation, the world's most sophisticated technology still requires human labor to design, build, and install it. Labor is the tool that built this world. Your labor is the tool that will build your world. Whether you are a home-owner or a business person you will need to make decsions every day about how to most efficiently allocate labor to achieve your goals with the least work possible. Sometimes it will be more cost-effective to "out-source" jobs out to somebody else, but other times it is most economical to buckle down and do your own work. Unfortunately many people enter adult life ill-equiped to do anything for themselves.

Since the dawn of humanity it has been parental instinct for each generation to help their offspring become established in life. In many past cultures people entered adulthood with pretty much everything they needed to get along in the world. Sometimes an entire community would pitch in to help a new married couple start out. The parents might divide off a section of the farm for the newlyweds and the neighborhood might pitch in and build an entire home in a few days. Even today children are still typically well supported through the transition into adult-hood. Children used to be married off as adults when they were only twelve to sixteen years old. Now adulthood may legally begin at age eighteen, but kids are often supported throughout college and more. They may live at home until they are in their late twenties or in their thirties. Directly or indirectly kids may receive many thousands of dollars of parental subsidies after they are legally adults, but before they are fully supporting themselves. Even so, young people today do not necessarily enter adult life as well prepared as kids did in the past.

Kids in the past may have started adult life young, but they often started with virtually everything they needed to survive and few bills to pay. In many stone-age and primitive farming cultures it was customary for the community to pitch in and build a new hut or home for the newly married couple. Young people often started their adult lives with no house payment, no land payment, no power bill, no water bill, few taxes, and certainly no phone bill! They may have paid for water by bucketing it from the creek to the house, and they may have paid for fuel by cutting wood, but neither is a horrible price to pay. More than that, though, they often entered the adult world with a viable trade.

People in the past were typically exposed to a trade from the time they were toddlers, and they often worked in that trade from the time they could walk. The kids of a stone-age culture entered adult life with all the tools and all the skills they needed to survive. From shooting a bow and arrow to tanning hides to cooking, they had done it all already, mimicking their elders. In other cultures they may have grown up in the trades of carpentry, or farming, or black-smithing, etc., but one way or another, they typically entered adult life knowing more than merely how to flip a hamburger.

I am not saying that the past was better. On the contrary, the past was often a rough, tough place and people worked hard. Young people today have infinitely greater opportunities awaiting them throughout their lives. The only real advantage that people in the past had was that they often started out with most everything they needed, including a trade. They started out on a stable foundation. Children today may still have parental subsidies, but they often leave the nest with six-dollar-per-hour skills to enter a world with twenty-dollar-per-hour expenses. The first step in the ladder of adult life can be the biggest.

It can be hard to get a good job when employers will only accept experienced applicants. It is a paradox of sorts that to be hired we must have experience, yet to gain that experience we first need to be hired. We start out at a disadvantage in life when we earn low wages for our work, but pay other people high wages for their work.

Going to college for training does not always make the transition to adulthood any easier. Most students may be able to get low-interest loans to cover their costs, but they still end up working six-dollar jobs to live on through school. They absolutely have to get a high-paying job when they graduate, because they may be tens of thousands of dollars in debt from their education.

The first step up the ladder was more than just big to me in high-school; it was ominous. I dreaded the thought of working a job, and I despised the idea of working my way up the ladder one-dollar-per-hour at a time. It could take years to work up from a five-dollar-per-hour job to a twenty-dollar-per-hour job. I did not think I could survive employment that long to begin with, and besides, it seemed like a lot of sweat and tears just to reach a level where I could break even. That was a future I could not accept. I knew that whatever happened, I would fight to not get a job. I understood that I would have to get jobs for awhile, but I was determined to make sure that any work I did was as a means to eventually end needing to work. Renee and I worked around the handicaps of inexperience by, first of all, avoiding the need to be employed as much as possible, and secondly, by "hiring" ourselves whenever we needed work done for us.

Working for ourselves allowed us to boost the value of our original income. Our income may not represent very many calories, but we traded those calories for materials. Then we invested additional calories in the form of work and sweat, to transform those materials into a valuable product, our home. We started with little, but we invested ourselves and came out with more than we started with.

We wanted a nice house, but the house we built, because of its unique nature, could have cost a couple hundred thousand dollars if we hired professional stone masons, loggers, carpenters, plumbers, and electricians to do the work. We could not have afforded this house on our meager incomes, so we "hired" ourselves. There were no applications to fill out, no taxes to pay, and we could "earn" almost as much as professionals; I say almost because we generally worked slower since we usually did not know what we were doing until we were done. Hiring ourselves effectively boosted the value of the income we did earn. Our W-2 forms indicated that we earned only about $10,000 per year, but we "earned" much more by hiring ourselves to build our own home. A stone mason might make ten to thirty dollars per hour, and that is effectively the wage we earned by building our own home, not bad for a young couple who previously had no experience. Hiring ourselves was the easiest way for us to earn top wages with no previous skills.

In addition to earning good "wages", we also gained experience so that now we can do construction contract work—we are professionals now. In a sense, working for ourselves was like going to college, only better. It cost us less to build our house than it would have to pay college tuition and to rent a place to live. We graduated with a degree in experience which we can use to start our own construction business, or to write books. Our diploma was a house, built and paid for.

Each of us is both a producer and a consumer. We produce goods and services through our work, and we consume goods and services both in and out of work. As producers we need to choose between employment for ourselves and employment through someone else. As

You can effectively earn an additional "income" by investing your own calories of energy into the products you need.

consumers we need to choose between hiring someone else to work for us (i.e.: cleaning our carpets, cooking meals, painting the house, etc.), versus doing that work for ourselves—or not consuming at all.

This is a basic exercise in weighing **costs and benefits**. If, for example, you are capable of getting a high-paying job then it can be to your advantage to take the job while hiring other people do to work for you, such as building your house. If you can only get low-paying jobs then it can be more advantageous to work a job just enough to buy materials, and then to put in your own labor to use the materials.

Similarly, you have the option of starting your own business at any time, with an income potential that may be quite significant or rather modest. From that you will need to decide when to hire jobs out to others (like painting your home or business) and when to do those jobs yourself.

There is a benefit from any choice you make, but there is also a cost in forgone opportunities—choosing any one opportunity means you have to give up the alternatives. This is not a permanent choice of course, but one that is re-decided moment-by-moment as the relative costs and benefits change.

As with all economic decisions there is more involved here than simply achieving the best monetary outcome. You must always check your opportunities against your total goals. For example, to achieve my goals as a writer it may be advantageous for me to choose to do extra work writing at two dollars per hour, even while paying someone else twenty-five dollars per hour to fix something on my car that I could have fixed myself. I might be able to save a lot of time and money by doing my own automotive work, but only while forgoing the opportunity to write. If, on the other hand, the repair bill would be so high that I would feel compelled to get an outside job (versus going into debt), then I might be motivated to do the work myself as the best option to allow me to remain unemployed so I could continue to write.

People who are just getting started in life typically have few skills, and therefore few opportunities to make a significant income. Ultimately you must consider your Dream and choose the most direct route towards achieving it. If your dream is a specific career then you might work at any job and spend most of your income on the education you need to get that career. If this career is really important then you may forgo the opportunity to pay off all debts, or even to avoid working in the first place. Even after you achieve your career goal you may find that the income potential is, and will always be, minimal. For instance, perhaps you want to aid people in the under-developed countries. It is okay to not get rich, as long as you are meeting all your goals and Dreams.

Of course, if your situation is like that of most people then your Dream will include both material

You can hire yourself in many ways, for big jobs or little ones. For example, a garden-in-a-bottle takes a minimum of effort to keep you supplied with salad sprouts in winter.

wealth and a fun and fulfilling career. In that case you have to continually weigh the relative importance between material wealth and your career against the opportunities you perceive are available at any moment. For instance, as a writer, I need to choose between spending the income from a magazine article on consumer goods (groceries or new furniture), or on goods for production (more RAM for the computer).

There is no secret to this process of weighing costs and benefits. Each of us operates this way instinctively as we pursue the options in life that we perceive will yield us the greatest advantage towards achieving our individual wants and needs. It is as basic as standing in the candy isle of the store choosing between a Hershey Bar and a Butterfingers—which opportunity will yield the greatest satisfaction, and what other opportunities do you have to forgo to get it?

The purpose of discussing costs and benefits here is to teach you to think consciously through the process so you may discover additional choices that you would not otherwise have realized. For example, if you happen to be an adult standing in the candy isle and you are looking for a quick pick-up because you are tired from working at a job that is not your Dream, then you may find that not buying the candy bar will allow you to not work your job, so that you will not be so worn out that you need a pick-up after work!

Surprisingly few people ever truly realize that most of the time they have the option of not working a job. Most people grow up expecting to work all their lives because that is what everyone else is doing. (I happened to be in my formative years at a time when every person close to me was doing their own thing, and no one was formally employed.) Now I have come to believe that the reason most people are continuously broke is because they have jobs. After all, there is a certain incentive to dispose of this week's paycheck as long as you know you have another one coming next week!

I am not suggesting that everyone should go out and build their own home or do all their own repair work. There are plenty of houses in the world already, and chances are yours needs some work, from plumbing to landscaping to insulating. Instead of paying someone else to do that work, you could "pay yourself" to do the work. Are you too busy working, or do not know how to do such jobs? Does it seem like that might not be the most effective or economical use of your time when you have a high-paying job and no time for such distractions? Consider this:

Many high-paying jobs actually pay out very low hourly wages by the time you factor in all the added time and monetary expenses that come up outside the workplace. In their book, *Your Money or Your Life*[24], authors Joe Dominguez and Vicki Robin give an example of this with a person who earns $440 a week and works a standard 40 hour week. By conventional calculation that works out to a wage of $11 an hour. But they argue that the time and monetary costs associated with work, but not in the workplace should also be included into the calculation. Commuting, for instance, adds time and costs money every day. So does "costuming", the buying and putting on of clothing, jewelry, and cosmetics for the workplace. Many expensive meals out and coffee breaks can also be necessitated by a job. Likewise for "decompression time", and "escape entertainment". You spend time and money outside the workplace to recover from working. Each of these activities adds time to the 40 hour week and reduces the pay you bring home. In their example, the authors show a 40 hour, $440 week becoming a 70 hour, $280 week. That works out to only $4 an hour, instead of $11.

When you put your adjusted income up against the cost of hiring a professional to come in and do home or car maintenance, you may find you can afford the time to learn to do that work yourself. Working for yourself may turn out to be the most profitable work you do!

Furthermore, as I mentioned, there are no taxes to pay when you work for yourself. This point bears special attention. Let's say that someone offered to paint your home for the cost of the paint, plus $300 labor. You go to your job and earn $300, but then you have to earn almost another $100 to cover city, county, state and federal taxes, including income taxes and sales taxes, plus you need additional money to cover the costs of going to work (commuting, dining out, etc.). By doing the painting yourself, you "earn" a savings of at least $300. You did some work and you gained from it, but you were not paid in dollars, and therefore you cannot be taxed on that income.

Economists often consider this type of work to be part of the "**barter economy**". Most people think of barter as being a non-monetary exchange of goods and/or services between two or more people, but here the term barter economy has a broader scope. The barter economy includes "under-the-table" transactions, any exchange that cannot be traced and taxed. In addition to non-monetary trades of goods and services this also includes informal jobs and money income from such things as one-day jobs, or garage sales. Working for yourself is part of the barter economy too, because you work and you receive a reward for your work, but your gains cannot be traced as income.

To understand that better, consider an example given by author Jude Wanniski in his 1978 book, *The Way the World Works*[81]. Suppose that a man hires a woman to clean his house (or vice-versa). He pays her out of his income and the government levies a tax on that income. Then they fall in love and get married. She continues cleaning house, and he continues bringing in the income, but she no longer has a formal "job". Realistically, she is still getting paid, but government records indicate that a job was lost and the IRS can no longer levy a tax on her income. The newlyweds gain a tax savings as a result.

We gained in a similar way by doing so much of our own work, from building our own home to fixing the car and cooking our own simple meals. We would have needed much higher paying jobs if we were to pay someone else to do all that for us, and that would have pushed us into a higher tax bracket. We would have paid out many thousands, perhaps tens of thousands of dollars in taxes, which we saved by working for ourselves.

This relationship between the taxable money economy and the non-taxable barter economy is very useful to understand. In Wanniski's book he writes that higher taxes in the money economy push more and more people over into the barter economy. The barter economy becomes more attractive each time taxes are raised. Beyond a certain threshold, raising taxes can actually lower tax revenues as people jump out of the money economy. Conversely, lowering taxes can bring people back into the money economy and result in a net gain in tax revenues.

Unfortunately, such information has not reached our Congress. If it has then it seems that Congress is reacting not by lowering taxes, but by finding ways to tax the barter system. There are forms to fill out and taxes to pay just for hiring the baby sitter. There are even tax laws covering some barter exchanges, where goods are traded for services (i.e. a refrigerator is traded for dental work). These kinds of taxes are hard to enforce because they are not very traceable. But the future implications are nonetheless worrisome. How long will it be before we are taxed on the money we save by painting our own homes?

In any case, you can save thousands of dollars every year, not just in taxes, but in labor costs as well, by "hiring" yourself to do your own work. You cannot do everything yourself, like making rubber, tanning leather, and using them to make your own shoes, but you can do a lot, from wallpapering to common automotive repairs like changing the spark plugs and more.

Last, there is one other advantage to hiring yourself to do your own home, vehicle, and other maintenance work. By doing the work yourself, instead of hiring it out, you can be employed less, which means you can be more choosy about the jobs you work. Having lots of bills means you have to work all the time to pay them. But if you keep your bills down by doing things yourself, then you may not have

Time Management
-Closing the Loop on Wasted Labor-

Studies show that even highly successful businesses typically waste more than 85% of their time in the process of getting goods and services to the customer[42]. The idea of better time management isn't about trying to work faster and harder; it is simply about closing the loop on wasted effort. For example, when United Electrical Controls, Co. in Watertown, Massachusetts, studied process flow in their factory, they found that one product traveled a whopping twelve miles within the confines of their 50,000 square foot facility. All that mileage added labor and cost to the temperature and pressure sensors and controls they manufacture. The problem was that the products were arranged around the processes, so that each item had to be transported around the factory from work station to workstation.

Company vice president Bruce Hamilton corrected the problem by rearranging the work stations around the products. For example, instead of bringing all their products to a centralized welding station, the company spread the welders around the factory as mini stations along each assembly line. Stream-lining the process this way greatly reduced the distance the products traveled and reduced the lead time on customer orders from 10 to 12 weeks down to a couple of days—without making anyone worker harder or faster. The company reduced the travel distance for the one product from twelve miles down to only forty feet!

The key to effective time management is to mentally separate your actions into two categories—those that create real wealth and those that do not. For instance, assembling a part or writing a service contract helps generate real wealth, but transporting goods within the company or filing sales reports do not. Effective time management is about minimizing the calories of labor expended for chores that do not contribute to the final goods and services.

Of course time management also applies at home. Just consider, how much time do you spend looking for things each day like your keys or shoes and socks? If there is any non-productive action that you do on a regular basis then there is an opportunity to close the loop on wasted time, giving you more freedom to do the things that are meaningful and important to you. Putting your shoes and socks and keys in the same place every day, so you know right where to look, is a simple way to become a more effective time manager.

Another form of time management is to simply make sure that if you do have to move a product from Point A to Point B, that you never come back empty-handed. It doesn't matter whether you are making a trip across the state or across the house. If there is something that must be transported from one place to another then try to find something that requires transportation back the other direction. For example, if I am going to walk the 30+ feet to the cellar to get canned goods for dinner then I always check the kitchen counter for recyclables that can be transported to the cellar, since I am headed that way anyway. Such "efficiency" may seem trivial, but if you can think this way in and around your house then you can think this way in business when dealing with trips that may be hundreds or thousands of miles long.

More importantly, if you give it some thought you may be able to eliminate the need for some trips or discover that there is no urgent need to go at present time, so that you can wait until a more pressing item on the agenda sends you that way. I have found this kind of time management is especially important while living in the country. Through careful time management I've been able to reduce my required trips to town—sixty miles away—from once or twice a week down to once or twice a month. Every trip to town seemed to consume a whole day of my time, so I have effectively gained about an extra month of free time each year to do whatever I want, while also saving money and reducing air pollution. People who live and work in town have easy access to many stores, but consequently waste even more time and resources making quick dashes downtown for certain items that are usually not all that important anyway. One or two twenty minute trips each day of the week really adds up over the course of a year.

to work a job every day. That means you can have the freedom to choose higher paying or higher quality jobs. There are all kinds of good paying short-term jobs that last only a day, a week, or a month, and to take advantage of these you have to be available. If your expenses require that you have a steady income then you may have to work a steady $7 per hour job and miss out on the short-term $15 or $25 per hour jobs that only come around once in awhile. But, if your expenses do not require that you work all the time then you can be more choosy about the jobs you do take on and you can take advantage of those golden opportunities.

Our annual income may be quite modest, but we usually earn reasonable wages when we do work. When I got out of high-school one of my first jobs paid $100 a day (1980's), which was not too bad at that time for a kid with no experience. I was building stair railings on apartment buildings in the Seattle area with my brother. He bid on the job and I worked with him. It was a cream job on the construction site, and I earned more per day than many seasoned carpenters working there—but my job was done after twenty work days. I could have stayed on afterwards and earned half as much per day, but one of the nice things about having few expenses is that you can work when you choose and take only the most golden opportunities. When my job in Seattle was done I simply went home and went camping.

As with everything you do in life, it is essential that you keep in touch with your goals when you choose to work for yourself. It is especially important that you check in with your need for "quality of life". You cannot do everything, and it is not healthy to work all the time, so that should be factored into your decision of whether or not to do the work yourself. You need to tune into yourself to know what you need to do to maintain your quality of life.

I maintain my own quality of life by not being employed, therefore I have not minded working on the car and other such jobs as a means to remain unemployed. That does not mean I like fixing the car. I definitely do not. But I prefer that to getting a regular job. I will gladly out-source that job to someone else if I can afford to pay for it without having to get a regular job. Now that we are more financially stable and have our own businesses I find that I do less and less of the work on the car and truck, and hire more of it out. It is all a matter of choices, and believe it or not, you have choices in everything you do.

"It is difficult to begin without borrowing, but perhaps it is the most generous course thus to permit your fellow-men to have an interest in your enterprise."

—*Henry David Thoreau, Walden*

3-7

Credit

-Calories to Start On-

Every person's Garden is unique. You may have a small corner plot that you work by hand to raise the few calories you trade away for the goods and services you want. Or perhaps you have an acre or two or three, and you farm with modest lawn tractors, sowing and harvesting your crops. You may even have a hundred or a thousand acres, with big machines and a big harvest. On the other hand, you may be working in someone else's fields, bringing in their harvest for a share of the calories. Every person's situation is unique, as is every person's Dream. Achieving your dream is a matter of assessing where you are in relation to it and choosing the best route there.

Your dream may require many calories or very few. In the terms of financial ladders, you may already be on a ladder that is tall enough to reach your dreams. In that case, reaching the top is just a matter of carefully allocating your harvest towards your dreams.

If your Dream is big, however, then you will need to move across the financial ladders to one that is tall enough to reach that dream. You will need to expand your garden to bring in a greater harvest of calories. There are two ways to do this. The slow and careful route is to reinvest your calories as you earn them, gradually expanding your production capability without going into debt. A faster but more risky path to expansion is to borrow the calories you need to get started from another source. This can put you at the bottom of a ladder than can be climbed higher. Either approach towards expansion is equally valid, as long as it enables you to achieve your dreams.

Imagine for a moment being so poor that the only job you will work at all day long is to find enough food for you and your family to make it through until tomorrow. Every day there is a question of whether you will find enough food or not, and even on good days your family is malnourished from a poor diet. If you have no goods or services to trade then there is no way to enter the economy and better your situation or break the cycle of poverty. For a billion or so of the poorest people in the world, every day is literally a question of "making a living" or not.

In 1976 an economics professor in Bangladesh decided to try an experiment. Muhammad Yunus offered loans to the poorest of the poor in his country[45]. He offered small loans, averaging just $67, to those in need— especially women with children, who would be strongly motivated to build a better life for their families. The average annual income in Bangladesh was $150 at the time, and over half the population qualified as poor, owning no more than a half-acre of land. Now, $67 may not seem like much money, even when adjusted for inflation, but for those who have nothing, it is a chance to enter the economy in a small way and earn a reliable living to keep the family fed and sheltered. Just $60 is enough to start over 500 different types of small businesses, such as growing crops, agricultural processing, sewing, weaving, garbage collecting, vending, shoemaking, blacksmithing, carpentry, fishing, crafts, leather work, food preparation, and vehicle repair. With tools as simple as a hammer, a saw, and a tape measure, impoverished peoples have the resources they need to enter the economy and earn a living.

Muhammad Yunus' loan experiment was so successful that he expanded the program to form the Grameen Bank with more than 400 branches serving 8,000 villages by 1987. The bank has handed out more than $54 million in "microenterprise development loans" to more than 400,000 borrowers, with a repayment rate of an astounding 98%. Through the Grameen Bank people can apply for loans at interest rates of 1-4% per month versus the 10-20% per day that was previously charged by loan sharks.

Those who apply for loans do not have to be able to read or write, and there is no collateral requirement. To apply for a loan, fifty people of the same sex must form a support network in groups of five. With the aid of bank personnel, they cooperatively evaluate the strength of each loan request. When an agreement is reached the loan money is given to two of the five members of each support group. After six weeks, if repayments have been made on schedule, the next two members of each support group get their loans. Six weeks later the fifth person in each group gets their loan. Those who borrow are also required to save a few cents per week into a special bank account, which is used to make new loans. Due to this program, borrowers saved roughly $4.3 million and own 75% of the bank. Grameen Bank has been so successful that more than a dozen similar programs have started in other impoverished regions of the world, including some in America's inner cities.

Like most young adults Renee and I started our lives with little money and few marketable skills. We did not have enough skills to start a business of our own, so we found the best jobs we could and immediately began investing almost every dollar we earned directly into our dream, our home. There were probably faster routes toward reaching our goal, but these were not necessarily better. For instance, investing in our house did eliminate the expense of a house payment, but it was still consumption. Perhaps we could have ultimately achieved our goal faster by building our first house on "speculation", selling it to gain a greater caloric harvest to pay for our own home. Perhaps we could have even borrowed money to build that first house, rather than buying the materials paycheck-by-paycheck. In this way we may have been able to expand our income enough that we could have built and paid for our own home in even less time than we did.

As I said, however, we started out with few marketable skills. We did not have any knowledge about running a business or borrowing money, and we had little construction experience beyond having read lots of books. Building our home gave us a safe opportunity to develop our skills before trying to market those skills to anybody else.

When you sow seeds and plant a crop you are gambling that the weather will be favorable and your crops will mature. But sometimes the weather is not good, and the economy, like Mother Nature is not very forgiving. About 400,000 new businesses start up in this country every year, and 350,000 of them go under in that first year. Few of the remaining 50,000 businesses ever become truly successful[13]. Many achieve minimal sustainability at best, and it can often take years for a new business to turn its first profit. Your first business may fail too, and that is okay, because you will survive. You can always turn around and try again. If you happen to listen to some "success tapes" of people who have made it, they will say the same thing. When you fail you just get back on your feet and try again. That is what eventually makes you successful.

I have listened to many "success tapes" over the years to compare what I am doing with what these speakers have to say, and to see if I can pick up anything new that I have not thought of. Often the speakers tell how they started with many business failures, and even failed miserably after they had already been successful. Many of them bounced from being broke to being millionaires and back again many times before they finally stayed successful. The speakers usually say the first time they became millionaires (before they lost everything again) was the hardest. The next time they became millionaires was much easier. You may not need to, or even want to be rich, but it is important for the management of your business to understand how some individuals can seemingly just jump up the money scale.

People often think that a business is started and grows gradually and eventually becomes big, but that is not necessarily the case. A business can have a gradual, even rate of growth, and that may make a business successful, but it does not make the business big.

As a farmer you might purchase a hundred acres of land and plant a crop of wheat; then you might plow part of the profits back into the business each year by buying and planting a few more acres. But the way businesses become big is by jumping from one level to the next. You may have borrowed money to buy that first one hundred acres. Learn to manage that land well, then borrow more, and jump to 500 or 1,000 acres. This is important to understand.

We started our business HOPS Homes with the idea that we would build just one house the first year, and then expand to two houses the next year, and maybe three or four the year afterwards, which is a relatively fast, but still a steady rate of growth. Our plan changed after completing that first house. Instead of building two houses the following year, I realized that we would be farther ahead by building none, while taking the time to do a little more research. Then we would test our product out by again building just one house in one year. This approach enables us to take the time to work the bugs out of our process. When we are completely satisfied with the process of building this one house, then we may choose to jump directly to building ten of them in a year, instead of just two. When we feel that we are good at building ten houses, then we will be ready to jump again.

A concern I have when I hear a speaker talking about their yo-yo route to success, making millions and losing it again, is that every time they failed they probably took a lot of other people with them. When you get into business, and particularly into big business, you are usually dealing with other people's money. They loan their money to you as an investment, and you can potentially lose it all for them. You might bounce back again, but what about them? It is my hope that this book and this chapter will help you to be successful the very first time out.

One way to help insure your success is to start out small. You might have this great brainstorm to grow peaches in Montana, but try a test plot first. Plant an acre of peaches. That way you can absorb the loss when they all freeze and die. That would be preferable to planting and losing a thousand acres of peaches. The only real difference between managing a small amount of money and a large amount of money is the number of zero's on the end. When you learn to manage $5,000 well, then you will be able to manage $50,000 too. When you learn to successfully manage $50,000 then you will be largely prepared to manage ten times that amount.

Our school has been a nickel-and-dime operation since the beginning, but that has given us the time to understand our product and our market. We know enough to become a full-fledged business at any time we choose. The same could be said of my books. I have been writing for years, and printing a few copies from time to time, but not trying to really print and sell lots of them. Now my writing and my business skills are where they need to be to allow me to successfully print and sell many more of my books. We have always had a relatively low income, but I now we are nearly ready to jump to a new income level. Given the direction of the many projects we have going, I have no doubt that we will someday be millionaires. We do not really need the money because we have everything we need now, plus most of what we want. The only use I would have for more money is to invest it in more businesses to make the world a better place to be.

I encourage you to move slowly and gradually too as you start your own business or businesses. Take some time to build a solid foundation. A good foundation will support a sizable enterprise later on. But a hastily built foundation can bring your work to the ground just when you thought you were finishing the roof.

For a hunter-gatherer to harvest some calories he must first expend a few calories to walk to the food supply, and then a few more to work at harvesting it. For a farmer to harvest some calories he also must first expend a few calories. He must plow his field, purchase some seed, and plant it. Your own harvest will similarly require you to make a start-up investment of calories. Like the hunter-gatherer, it is possible you will only need to invest a few calories of your own labor to begin your harvest. But more likely in today's world, you will be like the farmer, investing much more than just your own physical work. You may need a good sum of calories to start with so you can plant a big crop and look forward to a bountiful harvest.

It is possible that you have already stowed away a pile of calories, perhaps from working a job, or perhaps you inherited it. If you do, well that is terrific. It makes the whole process a lot easier if you are your own banker. It is more probable however, that you do not have a big supply of calories cached away. That is why you go into business.

In any case, a jump of any kind, big or small, requires calories of energy. If you do not have a surplus on hand, then you must find outside financing.

Credit, as you probably know by now, means that you borrow someone else's surplus of calories. You use them now to get what you want, then you earn some calories later and give them back. You are not really borrowing from "the future", because calories are a real and tangible thing. They have to come from somewhere in the here and now. Somebody has a few extra and they loan them out, on the condition that you pay them back, plus some, at some point in the future.

For a hunter-gatherer to harvest some calories he must first expend a few calories to walk to the food supply, and then a few more to work at harvesting it.

115

You use up those calories to get what you want, and then you go harvest some new ones.

The biggest problem with credit today is that it masks the connections between making and spending money. Young people who do not have a lot of experience handling money can get into some pretty serious trouble when they discover credit. Suddenly they can go out and spend money, and they do not even have to go earn any of it-or so it seems. Before long they are making monthly payments on a new car, a new TV, and several credit cards to boot. Credit can be a powerful tool, but you have to know how to handle it, if you are going to get what you really want. In a nutshell, credit is good if you use it to increase production, but bad if you use it to increase consumption.

In his book, *The Next Economy*[40], Paul Hawken talks about oil being more valuable to a poor person than a rich person. The poor person might buy a gallon of gas to put in his tractor; this works to increase his income. A rich person, on the other hand, might burn up a gallon of gas just running down to the store for a couple grocery items. This decreases his income.

Gas is made of calories of energy, and money is a token to represent calories of energy. If you borrow someone else's money to buy a gallon of gas, then you should try to use that gas to increase your production. Consumer debt is generally bad, while producer, or business debt is often good.

What this means in our day-to-day lives is that debt is bad when it is on your home, but often good when it is on your business. It also means that a home equity loan is bad if you take the money on vacation, but good if you use it to start a business (assuming that business is successful).

We did not use credit at all in the initial steps of our path to success. We found jobs and invested our income home directly in house materials one paycheck at a time. There were advantages and disadvantages to this approach. One disadvantage is that we were often out of money when we were trying to build. Our construction work would nearly come to a standstill. In particular, we often wasted nice summer days when we had no money, then ended up working inefficiently at some point in the middle of the winter we did have money. If we had borrowed a couple thousand in the summer, then paid it back in the winter, we would have progressed much more quickly-at least in theory. On the other hand, we were novices at construction, and going slowly gave us time to thoroughly explore all our options at every step, before diving in. Moreso, having a very tight construction budget meant we had to be resourceful every day. We figured our lumber orders down to the exact inches, with virtually no waste. We took the time to salvage old lumber and to make do with whatever we had.

At the very moment we got our pay checks we would suddenly become looser in the way we handled it. Having access to money affected our judgment as to how we used it. If we had actually borrowed enough money to build our house, then we may have also spent a lot more. Our house could have been much more costly.

The most important thing for you to do as you manage your own money is to keep your Dreams in mind at every moment. Hold onto that thought about what it is that you really want, and never let go of that thought; then you will successfully manage your money to make your thoughts into your reality. The following is a list of some of the more common sources of start-up and/or expansion capital.

Credit Cards: Credit cards are easy to get—amazingly easy. Once you pick up an application and get one card, the rest happens on its own. You can use that card and build up a credit rating, and other companies will automatically access your records and send you pre-approved credit applications. If you accept them then you can, within a couple years, accumulate tens of thousands of dollars worth of credit cards. It amazes me just how loose these companies are with their money, but I guess they make enough money on all of them to recover their losses on the few individuals who go on a berserk shopping spree and run with the goods.

If you are using the cards for business investments then it may be okay to carry a balance and pay interest. But generally you want to avoid carrying a consumer balance. One way to avoid that is to take your checkbook along when you use your credit card. Deduct your consumer purchases from your checkbook balance sheet as soon as you spend it. Then at the end of the month, when the bill comes, all you have to do is write out the check for the full amount and send it in. This helps you maintain fiscal responsibility, because your purchases immediately show up as negative numbers in your checkbook if you spend more money than you actually have. It might make more sense to just cut up the credit cards and use checks, but using the credit cards will help you establish a credit record.

We sometimes allow the debt to run on our cards when we know that we have money coming. For instance, we lived on our credit cards for a few months when we finished building a spec house and were waiting to sell it. We had the money to pay the debts off, it was just tied up in the house. It was kind of like having money in the bank, just not as easy to get at. We ended up paying some money out for credit card interest, but we were able to put our profits from the spec house directly back into an addition we were adding onto our own home. Instead of sitting around waiting for the house to sell, we were able to go to work, getting the essential work done on our addition before winter set in.

Credit cards are famous for their usurious interest rates, and you generally do not want to use them for any long-term debts. Six months or a year is about as long as you would ever want to carry a business balance on your credit cards. Surprisingly, however, credit cards often offer a lower interest rate than you can get at a bank, particularly for short periods. Many credit cards offer a promotional low interest rate; anywhere from 2.9% to 9.9%, running for three to six months. They encourage you to transfer your balance from another credit card over to this new card. You get to pay the lower interest rate for awhile, then they sock the original 19% or 20% back on you once you are sucked in. For short-term loans you can often get a lower interest rate this way than through a bank. If you have enough cards then you can bounce your debt back and forth between the cards to whichever one is currently offering a "promotional rate". But you do always have to be careful to read the fine print so you do not get "stung" with high-interest or balance transfer fees.

Banks: Banks can be amazingly difficult to get a loan from. Banks have extremely stringent guidelines for their loans, and either you meet their requirements or you don't. It is really kind of amazing, considering that credit card companies (banks) will give

Credit cards are an easy way to get loans, but you have to handle them carefully. (These have been digitally altered.)

money away left and right to people they never even meet, but store front banks do not normally lend money unless you can prove you do not need it.

They main piece of proof the bank asks for is your tax return. The bank needs to see your tax return to be sure that you are already making enough money to be able to make the monthly payments. For many entrepreneurs (including us) that puts an end to it right there. We have been successful not because we've made a lot of money, but because we have strategically put calories of energy to use. But banks do not care. The bankers themselves may be great people who are genuinely interested in what you are doing, but their hands are tied by the written rules of the bank they work for, or so they claim. In a situation like ours, even if we have $100,000 in assets to put a lien on, the bank will not do the loan as long as our tax return says we only make $10,000 a year.

If your financial situation is similar to ours, then it is possible that the only way you can get a loan through a bank is with a co-signer. You get someone else to sign your loan, who does meet the bank's qualifications. In the case of our construction company, we got the loan through my mom. She took out a loan in her name, and handed us the money. As one banker said, "Don't let pride get in the way; if you have someone who can get a loan for you, then by all means, take advantage of it."

Family: I should emphasize that "not letting pride get in the way" does not mean that you always accept financial aid from your family. Families can be a great source of financial and moral support, but always remember to keep your priorities straight: family relationships always come first. Borrowing from family members is the greatest business risk there is, because you have the potential to lose a lot more than their money. Before you ever

117

consider borrowing from family members you should be certain of your business venture and equally sure that you could repay the loan, even if your venture fails.

When we started HOPS Homes we had only marginal credibility from a business standpoint. I knew inside what we were doing, but from the outside, including from my mom's perspective, I'm sure the picture looked quite different. I personally felt okay about it though, because I knew that even if the business failed, we could not lose money on the venture. We were not contracting anything out, and we borrowed twice as much money as it took to build our own home. If we were to fail it would have been in taking five years to finish the house instead of one. I think that from my mom's perspective though, the only way we got the loan was because she had made a similar loan to my older brothers years before when they started a construction business. She could not refuse to do the same for another son. Anyway, always remember, family comes first. Do not let money come between you and the ones you love.

Partnerships: A partnership is when you pool your resources with one or more other people. Together you all share in the vision, the rewards, the work, and the risk. The advantage of a partnership is that you have multiple people working on all fronts to make the business work. The biggest disadvantage to partnerships is not that you have to share the rewards, but that you have to share the vision. A team of people working together towards a common vision is an incredibly powerful force, but a team working towards all slightly different visions is a disaster.

SBA Loans: The Small Business Administration can be a great source of capital for starting or expanding your business. The SBA gives out many loans that you could never get through a bank, totaling some $3 billion dollars a year.

I find that any type of bureaucracy is stifling to deal with, and dealing with the SBA seems intimidating. But then again, we manage to file our taxes each year, and that is an incredibly stifling bit of bureaucracy, but also one of the most financially worthwhile uses of my time. Working with the SBA may be equally worthwhile. Chances are we will probably finance one of our ventures someday with the aid of the SBA. Anyway, there is a book out called *SBA Loans: A Step-by-Step Guide* by Patrick D. O'hara that should make it easy to negotiate through the paperwork. According to the book, a loan can be approved in as little as three weeks. Also be sure to check out the SBA site on the world wide web.

Grants: Grants are a great source of capital, especially because you do not have to pay them back. But you will not find the money laying around for free. You have to expend a few calories of effort to get that "free" money. You can start your research on grants at the library or on the internet.

If you do pursue grants as a source of funding then I would recommend that you use them for start-up only, rather than relying on them to get you through every year. Partly, it is a matter of survival, because free money does not come around forever. But also it is a matter of principle. We live in the era of "entitlements" where everyone thinks they should be paid whether they do anything or not. There are thousands of non-profit organizations and private businesses always looking for a handout. The idea of helping should be a two-way street. If you are working to make the world a better place to be, then your help should include direct compensation (rather than subsidized compensation) for your efforts.

Grants can be much easier to get for non-profit projects. Our local grass-roots group received two $800 grants for agricultural projects with youth in our community. With these grants we were able to use horses and sheep to do experimental weed control and reclamation work in our community. Local kids have had the opportunity to learn about livestock, and we've been able to accumulate some essential experience that will eventually make this project sustainable on its own. We hope to create an opportunity for kids to earn money by herding sheep though weed-infested pastures around town.

Creative Financing: Any type of financing quickly becomes creative, but some financing is more creative than others. For instance, *Real Goods*, a California company selling environmental and energy products, needed money for expansion. They borrowed not just once, but twice from their customers, once for $150,000 and once for $100,000. They printed a blurb in their mail order catalog asking to borrow money for two and three years at 10% interest. They were flooded with money from their established clientele. The company had to send back the excess checks[13].

One retail store, called *Earthwise* in Virginia raised start-up capital by soliciting money from friends, relatives, and acquaintances. They asked for $100 from each person to use to stock the business. In exchange, for each $100 received, they issued a certificate good for $120 worth of merchandise, redeemable 90 days after the store opened[13].

One nice thing about these forms of creative financing is that individuals benefit from directly loaning out their money. I think that is fundamentally more desirable than having the profits go to seemingly faceless banks and other institutions. Banks make a profit when they use your savings account to loan money out. They pay you a couple percent interest for your money, then loan it back out at a much higher rate. I think the world would be a better place if it were more convenient for individuals to loan directly across to other individuals, while by-passing the banking system. In this day of the information super-highway, perhaps there is a business opportunity in setting up such a system.

Part IV
Turning Dreams into Reality

". . . if one advances confidently in the direction of his dreams, and endeavors to live the life which he has imagined, he will meet with a success unexpected in common hours."

—Henry David Thoreau, Walden

4-1

The Sum of the Criteria
-Creating Your Personal Vision-

Success at anything always begins with a goal. Defining clear goals is the most difficult step along the path to success for most people. Achieving a goal can be comparatively easier than defining it. People may say, "I want lots of money.", but that is not a goal. A goal must be consistent with all of your being mentally, physically, and spiritually. A goal won't work if it doesn't fit you just right. You may find a way to sabotage your success if some part of your being is not totally consistent with your goal.

Goals can be remarkably uncomfortable subject for many people to talk about. Sometimes people do not think they have goals, and so they may wince a little at the word, as if they have shirked in their duties. More often than not, however, it is simply that they do not have a mental file labeled "goals". Amazingly enough, few of us were taught to use that particular word. The subject of goals is seldom taught at home or at school. Most people do have goals; it is simply that they are usually stored under the file name "hopes and dreams".

We all have hopes and dreams. You probably do not access them in their entirety each time I use those particular words, but it is likely that you at least get a "warm, light, fuzzy feeling" when you read those certain words. They are indeed nice words. Our hopes and dreams embody all that which is really meaningful to us. It includes our personal aspirations and our best wishes to our friends and our families. Our hopes and dreams represent to each of us what living would be like if we lived in the ideal world. For each of us our dreams are many and diverse.

Every person has hopes and dreams.

It would be a little obstructive if we brought out all of our hopes and dreams upon reading those words. Fortunately, our minds are more effective than that. Instead of pulling up the entire file each time we read the words, our brains shorten the sequence. In our minds we basically go to the file labeled "hopes and dreams", and instead of drawing upon the whole file, we simply check if it is a pleasurable file or not. If it is a good file then our brains simply give us a little dose of good feeling drugs, and we read on to the next word.

I use the words hopes and dreams because virtually everyone has hopes and dreams, and it is almost invariably a pleasurable file for people to access. The word "goals", on the other hand, tends to be a bit more complicated. Actually, our hopes and dreams and our goals are pretty similar; there is not a lot of difference between them.

Another problem with the word goals is that many people have negative beliefs and feelings associated with the word. There are many environmentally and spiritually minded people who associate the word "goals" with money-hungry individuals who live only in the future and who will do anything to get ahead. People do not always realize that goals can be about anything, including spiritual enlightenment, a more peaceful world, or musical achievement.

Remember, money is not useful in itself. It is only when we get rid of it, in exchange for something else, that money becomes useful. Therefore, money is usually a means or a tool to a particular end, but is not an end in itself. We may have hopes and dreams of becoming a millionaire, but it is not the millions of tokens which we really hope and dream of. Rather there are many appealing qualities of life that we often associate with millionaires. Those qualities may be some of what we hope and dream for. Setting well-formed goals simply means defining what we value and the quality of life we want. When we have defined what we value, then we can take steps every day to achieve that.

Goals are often associated with distant future events, but the true purpose of goals is to help us live better today. Certainly, many goals extend beyond the end of one day, but the next day will be "today" soon enough! Every day we can strive to immediately fulfill our happiness, while also taking steps to ensure our continued happiness in the many todays yet to come.

To ensure happiness, any good process for setting and achieving goals should include a statement about values, and a system for testing actions against those values. Values become the core of the goal, and all future actions ultimately support that goal. So far I have discovered two separate decision-management models that utilize both a values statement and a testing system to ensure congruity between one's values and the actions that follow.

I am most familiar with Allan Savory's *Holistic Resource Management* (HRM)[74]. Savory's process was originally designed as a model for making land management decisions, especially regarding livestock.   HRM includes a model of the natural ecosystem, how it functions, and how our actions effect it. The model also includes the social and economic aspects of decision making, hence it is a "holistic" process. Holistic management starts with at three-part goal that includes a quality of life goal, a production goal, and a landscape description goal. The quality of life goal is the ultimate goal, for example, to be healthy and happy, to be part of a loving family and a caring community, and to produce enough material wealth to support a middle-class lifestyle, including occasional family vacations to tour foreign countries, etc.

The production goal is a generalized statement about what the individual or family wants to do to generate the necessary income to achieve the quality of life goal, such as raising livestock, raising crops, or serving as a guide and outfitter. Last, the landscape description goal is a statement about how the ecosystem must function (i.e. the level of succession required) to sustainably produce the income needed to support the desired quality of life.

Establishing a workable goal requires that you first understand what Savory calls the "foundation blocks of the ecosystem". You need to establish a mental concept of how the ecosystem functions and how each of the possible actions or "tools" affects it. The model includes a set of guidelines for testing the accuracy of an idea, plus additional guidelines for implementing the idea and monitoring the results. The holistic management model enables land managers to work with the ecosystem processes to restore the health of the land to a level of greater abundance, stability and prosperity. It is good for the land and good for the pocketbook. You may have noticed by now that the structure of *Direct Pointing to Real Wealth* is patterned after holistic resource management, except that the purpose of this text is to understand and manipulate the economic ecosystem rather than the natural one.

Although HRM can be used in any management situation, it can be cumbersome when agriculture is not involved.   It is difficult, for example, to use the model in managing a restaurant, when so much of the information in the book applies directly to livestock and grass! The reality is that most people in the modern world, myself included, do not earn their living directly off the landscape. My family owns five acres of land, and I consider HRM indispensable for managing the property, just not very functional for running businesses which have little or nothing to do with the five-acre parcel.

Recent adaptations to the HRM model have made it more functional for croplands and other agricultural situations, and more user-friendly for management situations where agriculture is not directly involved. If you are involved in making any kind of land management decisions beyond the scope of city lot then I highly recommend you pick up Savory's book. I especially recommend it for farmers and ranchers, public land managers, and individuals who want to comment on public lands management. The book is simply in a class of it's own.

The other decision-making model that utilizes a values statement and a testing system for congruity is Charles Hobbs' *Time Power*[43]. I should point out that we have never adhered strictly to either model. In the past we have stumbled along intuitively, achieving considerable happiness and prosperity without written values or goals. We have always had strong values and fantastic goals—we just never wrote them down as such. Nevertheless, the process we intuitively used had much in common with both the HRM and Time Power models. We were able to achieve many of our Dreams that way, although I have no doubt that we would have been even more effective in our endeavors had we used a decision-making model. Today we rely more and more on thought-models to better facilitate communication and cooperation, especially as we work less by ourselves, and more on joint projects with other people.

Contrasting between the two models, I think the HRM model provides a better framework for creating an overall vision, with more comprehensive guidelines for testing and implementing actions, while the Time Power model provides a better system for prioritizing and achieving those actions. I have taken parts and pieces of both models, and added much of my own material to put together the process out-lined in this book. Please note that the process out-lined here is designed for personal and business goals management and does not apply to land management at all. Please use the HRM model for that.

Self-Unifying Principles

Self-unifying principles are essentially a personal code of behavior, a description of what you value and how you want to act towards yourself and others[43]. It is pretty easy to establish your own code if you just think about how you would like to be treated by others. If you treat all other people the way you would like to be treated yourself, then you are doing pretty good. Nevertheless, even the most disciplined people have trouble up-holding their ideals all of the time. A written code of self-unifying principles makes a difference because it forces you to take the time to focus on your values and define them clearly. Moreover, a written code is a specific, tangible goal against which you can check your progress. Most of the time you will only need a simple statement of what kind of person you want to be, but some ideals may be harder to live than others. If you have trouble living up to your ideals, then try clarifying each of your values with a paragraph of explanation, and prioritizing them in order of importance. Clarifying and prioritizing your values will enable you to focus more on specific issues until you can make your behaviors congruent with your beliefs.

Quality of Life Statement

Defining the quality of life you value begins with eliciting specifically what qualities of life you hope and dream of. For example, I value my freedom to do what I want when I want to. Freedom is a very important quality of life to me, one of many, and I take steps every day to enjoy my freedom. Every day I also take steps to maintain that freedom into the many todays to come. That is only one small example of my own values; what qualities of life do you value?

One good way to elicit your values is for you to take some time and dream, either now or when you finish reading this book. Go into your ideal world and live your dreams. Spend a little time fantasizing, living your life as you would if you and your family had all the choices in the world. Enjoy your fantasy, and meanwhile, notice what qualities of life you enjoy in your dream world for yourself, for your family, and for your community. WRITE THEM DOWN.

As you do this exercise, be sure to include your family and your community in your dreams. It is important to have a vision that extends beyond yourself. Many personal values, such as peace and security, can only be had when you extend those values to your community. For example, if you seek those values only for yourself then you may decide to post a security guard at your door; but is that really peace or security? On the other hand, if your vision extends out to your community then you would be more likely to work with your neighbors to create a more peaceful and secure environment for all, thus eliminating the need for security guards.

Likewise, another example, and a very personal one, is the quality of open space. Many people move to Montana and buy twenty-acre "ranchettes" because they value the wide open spaces of Montana, and they want a piece of it. Typically, each person thinks only of themselves

A goal is a way of defining and achieving your quality of life for today and for the many todays to come.

and wants to get the best piece. As a result, in my lifetime much of western Montana may become a sea of houses on twenty-acre tracts. Then nobody will have the wide open spaces. If each person instead valued space for the whole community as much as for themselves then they would be more likely to locate as part of existing communities, rather than chopping Montana up into bits and pieces. That way many millions of people could still move into the state in the coming years, and there would still be a Montana here for everyone to enjoy.

I have provided my own goals in the sidebar "Tom's Personal Vision" as an example. Do not be concerned or ashamed if your own goals are less fluent. Goals must be continuously evaluated and updated. It doesn't matter what you start with. The important thing is that you start. Also please note that it is important that a goal be created by all those who are instrumental in carrying it out. I have only published my personal goals here; we also hold regular family meetings to establish our common values and common goals.

Action Statement

An Action Statement is a goal of verbs. It is a goal of what actions you would enjoy doing, both personally and professionally. In terms of your profession, the Action Statement is a description of what you would like to do to produce the necessary income to support your desired Quality of Life. Basically, you need to invest your calories in actions to produce products or services. Then you trade your products or services to other people for their calories. The return on your investment is what you exchange for the products and services you need to sustain your desired quality of life. Thus the action statement is simply a description of what you would most enjoy doing to earn your living.

As I said, setting and achieving goals is essentially a matter of making your ideal world the real world. With that in mind, then, the substance of your Action Statement is to be found, once again, in the ideal world of your hopes and dreams. Take some time, either now or later, and enjoy your fantasy of what your life would be like in the ideal world where you have unlimited choices. Get into your fantasy and live in it for a short time. Then step out of

---

Tom's Personal Vision

Self-Unifying Principles

My personal code of behavior is to treat all people as equals and with respect. I aim to be a caring, compassionate, and honest person. I want to give loving support to my family, allowing each person to create and achieve a unique personal vision. I want to strive for excellence and make a positive contribution to our local community and to the world as a whole. I want to be responsible, while also retaining a high-level of personal freedom to do what I want, when I want. I want to live with a feeling of peace in my heart.

Quality of Life Statement

I desire a happy, healthy, and fun quality of life for myself and my family. I want our family to have enough wealth to live comfortably and without worry. I value a clean and beautiful home and landscape, with an abundance of habitat for wildlife and nutritious home-grown foods for ourselves. I want to travel frequently with the family, with at least one trip to a warm climate during each winter. I want to maintain a close relationship with the natural world.

Action Statement

I seek to produce a profit while making the world a better place for all, especially through the media (books, videos, etc.), but also through classes and other products. Specific actions that I enjoy include: primitive living, reading and writing, speaking, learning and teaching, alternative technologies, traveling, quantum physics and spirituality, construction, politics, gardening-farming, space exploration, raising animals, and entrepreneuring.

Description

According to the criteria set down in my Self-Unifying Principles, Quality of Life and Action Statements, there are many opportunities to achieve my Dreams, both in my personal and my professional life. I can learn with or teach my family about many subjects, from primitive skills to science. We can garden and raise animals together and travel and talk about politics. Professionally, I can read and learn and write and speak and teach about the subjects that interest me-from primitive skills to alternative construction and quantum physics. The logical framework for my diverse interests is HOPS, a school of "primitive living skills and contemporary lifestyles", with an emphasis on publishing and presenting new and useful information that will help make the world a better place to be.

your dream world and analyze it. Think of your fantasy as being on a movie screen. Sit in the director's chair and observe what types of actions you are doing. WRITE THEM DOWN. Your actions are verbs, and verbs are your production goal.

As you do this exercise, it is important to write down your Action Statement in general terms. For example, if you notice that you are skiing in your fantasy, then simply write down "skiing". This gives you more options than if you wrote down a specific job, such as "ski instructor". There may not be any openings for ski instructors, or the income from that job may not meet the needs of your specified Quality of Life. The less specific word "skiing", on the other hand, is fairly general and therefore leaves you many options besides being a ski instructor. You could open a ski shop, or a resort, or a manufacturing company, a touring company, or a thousand other options.

Another reason to write your production goal in general terms is because you will most likely find many different actions in your fantasies. Specific descriptions may preclude each other, but generalizations leave many opportunities to mix and blend your interests and to come up with something new. I will discuss this further in the next part of the vision process. Just remember, at this point it is important to keep your goal general to give yourself unlimited options.

Description

When you have defined your Self-Unifying Principles, the Qualities of Life you value and the Actions which excite you, then you are ready to formulate a combined Description. The Description is the sum of the criteria from the first three statements.

For instance, consider a sampling of my own criteria. My Self-Unifying Principles include such values as: respect for others, inner peace, and closeness to my family. My desired Quality of Life includes values such as freedom for myself and a close relationship with the natural world. Some of the Actions that excite me include: stone-age skills, writing, teaching, speaking, helping the earth, resourceful construction, doing art, and involvement in space, to name a few.

Formulating a combined Description is a matter of "brain-storming" ways to meet all of your criteria, or as much of it as possible. It is part fantasy and part realism. Fantasize what you might do to meet all your criteria, then review it in context of reality as we know it. This process is different from the dreams and fantasies you started with in the beginning. You may have started with many unrelated fantasies, such as sailing the seas, being a knight in armor, or becoming a rock music star. Then you elicited the qualities of those fantasies that you value, and you elicited the actions. Setting a description goal is a matter of rolling those values and actions into, more or less, one single fantasy. This step takes some time and imagination.

You may think that it would be easier to have only a few values and actions on your list of criteria, but actually more criteria is usually better. You originally expressed each individual criteria in general terms, to provide flexibility, but now, your description goal needs to be fairly specific. The goal is the sum of the criteria, so the more criteria you have the more specific your goal will be. For example, stone-age skills is one of my criteria, and teaching is separate criteria. Either is general, but together they become specific. Adding in the rest of the criteria only makes the description goal more specific. An interest in stone-age skills may initially seem entirely opposite from, let's say, a fascination with space, but when these criteria were combined with all the other actions and values I had, the result, HOPS, had a surprising amount of continuity in terms of "primitive living skills and contemporary lifestyles".

Brain-storming new ideas is truly the fun part of the process in achieving your goals. Use your imagination and toss out all the ideas you can think of to help you to produce your Dream. It doesn't matter how wacky or zany the ideas are; anything counts at this point in the game. You can eliminate the bad ideas later.

Please note, when you are working as a team it is important to have a high level of trust and respect within the group. Each person needs to feel free to express their ideas without getting "shot down". Every idea, no matter how far-fetched, should be put in a list for consideration. The brain-storming process should facilitate the free flow of ideas.

Next, as you switch from fantasizing to criticizing you should continue to entertain even the wild ideas. Do not shoot down an idea if it merely seems impossible. Starting an international corporation may seem impossible, but such corporations exist, so it is definitely possible. Flapping your arms and flying, on the other hand, may indeed by impossible-although I would at least keep an open mind to the possibility! If it is physically possible for a human being, in the known context of physics, to do what you are imagining, then the idea is within the bounds of realism.

Do these exercises. Fantasize, elicit the qualities of life you value and the actions that excite you. Write these down as the criteria of your quality of life goal and your action goal. Then think up a new fantasy, where you fulfill each of your criteria through means which are physically possible. The summary of your criteria is your goal and your primary blue print for fulfilling your life for today and for all the todays to come.

Intermediate or Project Goals

Every task you undertake, whether you are learning an instrument, starting a company, or baking bread, must be chunked down into individual steps. You have to play "Mary had a Little Lamb" before you can play Bach.

If you followed through with the exercises in this chapter then you may have an out-line of your own personal symphony. Now you need to learn each instrument and play each note. Big goals can be unmanageable all at once. Chunking down your goals makes each part manageable. In little chunks you can be successful every step of the way.

You do not need to chunk down your whole goal all at once. Chances are you will not even know what all the chunks are. Just start with the smallest piece you can find and work your way up. For us, building a house was a goal, but not an end goal; it was only one of many steps we are taking towards all of our goals. Chunking our larger goals down into smaller pieces, including our house, has allowed us to be successful already. Likewise, chunking down the house into many smaller goals allowed us to be successful every day, with each stone mortared in, and every board nailed in place.

The process for defining and achieving the individual chunks as goals is much like the one used to create your personal vision. The individual chunks can be thought of as "intermediate" or "project" goals. As with your personal vision, your intermediate goals should include the ideals that you value, the actions that excite you, and a description built on the criteria you describe.

Renee's Dad and Mom...

For example, let's say I envisioned opening a restaurant. I would start defining the restaurant by considering my personal values, including my self-unifying principles and the quality of life that appeal to me. The self-unifying principles would describe how the customers, employees, and suppliers should be treated, for example, with honesty, promptness and respect. The quality of life, or more accurately, the quality of experience, would describe the kind of atmosphere the place should have-such as to be aesthetically pleasing, to have an aura of nature, and to be a healthful place to come into.

Next, I would define an action statement similar to the one in my vision, but more specific. For instance, some of the elements I might want to actively produce in a restaurant would be: reasonable prices, profit, a garden-like atmosphere, energy efficiency, and quality foods (including local domestic and wild plants and animals). Each of these items becomes part of the criteria, along with the criteria from my values.

Finally, the description is a way of describing the project in detailed terms. The criteria is already established. Now I would dream up ways to meet that criteria. Up to this point the criteria should be fairly general, although more specific than was stated in the

...realizing their Dream of building their own log home.

personal vision. The criteria should be fairly general to start with, because you may not have all the information you need to make it specific.

For example, consider some of the criteria we had for designing and building our home. In addition to our values, we also had quite a list of actions to produce, including such things as: low cost, low maintenance, durability, energy efficiency, water efficiency, fire resistance, earthquake resistance, natural feeling, and openness, to name a few. Writing a description goal to match all our criteria meant we had to research our criteria. For example, we had to research energy-efficient construction, and we had to pick out the aspects of energy efficiency which were also low cost, low maintenance, and natural feeling, etc., etc.. Our research gave us even more specific criteria, such as that the house should be bermed in, at least on the north side, with most of the windows on the south side, and a heat source right in the middle. Thus the criteria starts becoming pretty specific.

Pretty soon, as more and more criteria is added in, the sum of it all becomes a well-defined description. For instance, the list of criteria for our home may have totaled to a hundred or more specific points, many of them very precise, such as putting most of the windows facing south, and having the kitchen sink positioned with a view, and next to the kitchen stove, which is a wood cookstove (which we selected for the qualities of living it contributes), and of course the cookstove had to be in the center of the house since was also our heat source, and that meant the open loft had to be over the stove to distribute the heat around the house, etc., etc.. Part of the reason we spent four years drawing house plans was because we had such specific criteria that it took us four years of drawing to come up with a plan that met all that criteria. It is possible that there was only one working combination, and we had to try many, many combinations before we arrived at it.

The description goal is a description of how to meet all, or as much as possible, of the criteria you establish. From my example it may sound like a lot of specific criteria could be cumbersome, since it took us four years to draw our house plans, but I disagree. In fact, many people who build their own homes do not consider all of their criteria adequately. As a result their project may be more expensive or more work than they imagined, or they may not be satisfied with the results when they are finished. I am sure that the same could be said of many businesses and other projects which are begun without all the criteria being fully considered. We took the time to meet our criteria, and we feel good about that every day that we are in our home. It will be important to you to meet all of your criteria too.

This process of setting your project goals should be a fun one. As you go through the process just switch back and forth from dreamer to realist. Float along with your imagination and see what you can dream up. Then play the part of the realist and rework your dreams to make them possible. This process is very important.

Many people skip the dreaming and start out as realists. For example, most houses are built square and sterile; they are designed by adults who only think in "realistic" terms. A child, on the other hand, would design a house that was entirely fantasy, of indoor forests and ponds, slides and swings; exciting, but hardly functional. Ideally your own project goals should reflect both the imagination of a child and the realism of an adult.

To sum up, let me say that defining your goals is a process of dreaming and realism. First you dream and fantasize, then you analyze as a realist to elicit the qualities of living you value and the actions you enjoy. Then you dream again, rolling all of your general criteria into a single fantasy, and you examine that fantasy as a realist to come up with a tangible plan.

It is important to point out, however, that you can create your own Personal Vision by any method that works for you. There are many approaches to a similar out-come. Use any kind of a process that feels right. Indeed you may already know very clearly everything that you want to do. The important thing is that your Vision must include a strong statement of values upon which you base all of your actions.

Also, it is okay if you do not come up with a grand, all-encompassing Vision the first time you sit down to think about it. In fact, you might want to keep your options open and continue to explore all life has to offer, without committing to any one specific life goal. That type of freedom is a goal in itself, and should be expressed in your Quality of Life. The Self-Unifying Principles and the Quality of Life Statement are the only truly essential parts of the goals process, because they are a description of your values. Define your values as clearly as you can right now, and the rest can wait.

Later in the goals implementation process I will give you a method of prioritizing your current commitments (family, work, debt payments, etc.) with your many other interests (riding horses, etc.) into a daily plan. Setting your priorities in order will establish some immediate and intermediate goals. Define your current priorities, and your long-term goals (children, career, happiness, etc.) will tend to fill themselves in over time, even if you never put together a comprehensive life vision.

"The cost of a thing is the amount of what I would call life which is required to be exchanged for it, immediately or in the long run."

—*Henry David Thoreau*

4-2

The Test of Time

-Planning for All the Today's to Come-

It is easy to sit here today and imagine doing a project tomorrow. Our brains give us the ability to create a movie of something we have never done. In an instant we can preview the basic sequence of just about anything, from driving across town to driving across the country, from building a bird house to building a people house.

In a matter of a few minutes you can imagine enough projects to keep you busy for ten lifetimes. It is therefore important to carefully consider the element of time when you set goals and brainstorm ways to achieve your objectives. Realize that when you start a project you begin to create commitments for yourself down the road. You set into motion a series of events that will require your attention, a little or a lot, at some point in the future.

Unfortunately the future sometimes seems pretty intangible, like something you imagine. Since it is like something imagined, then it is easy to also imagine doing a lot there. On the other hand, it is just as easy to not think about the future at all.

Eventually, the future always comes around. In fact, today is the future—or at least *a* future. When you set in motion a series of future events you should think about those events as if they were happening today. Eventually they will be happening today.

"Time," it is sometimes said, "is what keeps everything from happening all at once." That may be true, but some contend that everything does happen all at once, and time is just a perception we have to separate it out. I do not know if I have watched too many science fiction shows, or just read too many books on quantum physics, but to me everything does kind of happen all at once. To me there are only todays. There are todays we were active in, todays that we will be active in, and todays that we are currently active in, but they are all todays.

The purpose of this chapter is to remind you to think very carefully through the future consequences of your actions today. You may take on a project that seems important and urgent now, but how important will that project be in the tomorrows to come?

I have occasionally helped others with remodeling for their business ventures. Sometimes, when we

There are only todays...

are pulling walls down or putting them up, I get this sensation that there is no difference between putting them up or taking them down. I remember thinking, as we once installed special windows in a rented office space, that someday those windows would have to come back out. We did a great deal of work to prepare this office for use, having soundproofing put in, one-way glass installed, and carpeting laid on the floor. It seemed to me that the day would come when all that work would be undone. Sure enough, "today" came along after a couple years, and I helped pull out the windows and reframe the walls. In a sense we put the windows in today, and we removed them today. They may have been different todays, but they were still todays.

Having this kind of perception may make it a little difficult to get things done, but that is the point. It makes you think about the future impacts of your actions today. If the time and labor cost of tearing something down in the future is included with the time and labor cost of putting it up today, then you may adjust your plans.

I think about that sometimes, when I see a twenty, thirty, or fifty year old building being torn down, or just falling apart from the weather. The people who built those structures may well still be alive. They built something and then it was nullified. To me it is about the same as never having built the structure to begin with. What a waste of a person's time.

Granted everything eventually does return to dust. But we do not move forward as a species if every generation we have to build all new houses and every ten years we have to repair them. I like to think that my work benefits future generations. Building houses that out-last me and serve several generations besides will free up others to make their own positive contributions.

Likewise, people do not move forward as individuals if they are always attending to the same basic needs, like paying rent for a place to live, or paying high monthly power bills. One of the key reasons that Renee and I have been successful is because we have always searched for permanent solutions for achieving our objectives. We have strived to make long-term decisions that would benefit us for the longest possible time. Thinking about all of your todays together will help you make the choices that give you the most of what you want for each of your todays to come.

When you learn to think about all of your todays together you will be able to eliminate many projects that initially seemed urgent and necessary. You will be able to search for more permanent solutions to achieve your goals once and for all.

I always encourage people to take on big Dreams, to reach for their highest potential, but it is also important to recognize that there is a cost in achieving one's goals, just as there is a cost in not achieving them. Any dream, great or small, requires an input of your time and energy to achieve it. You have to make choices between many different possibilities to decide how you really want to live your life. Whatever kind of Dreams you have, from raising a family to starting an international widget corporation, you must give up your life to bring them life.

Of course, you will give your life to something, no matter what you do, so there is nothing wrong with giving life to achieving your dreams. You only need to be absolutely certain that your choices are really worth your life. At that point you will experience a whole new level of self-unification, and you will find an abundance of energy to achieve your Dreams.

Part V
Putting Your
Ideas to the Test

"If you have built castles in the air, your work need not be lost; that is where they should be. Now put the foundations under them."

—*Henry David Thoreau, Walden*

5-1
The Weakest Link
-Success One Task at a Time-

There is a story I once heard about a consultant who offered his services to the executive of a large corporation on a donation basis. His advice was simple: focus the company on one task at a time. Do not attempt to follow multiple goals at once. Achieve each single goal before moving on to the next. The CEO put this simple idea to the test, and he was so impressed by the results that he later sent a $25,000 check to the consultant who offered the sage advice.

In a world that is often overwhelming, the ability to focus on and complete one task at a time is vital to both success and sanity. It is too easy to be torn in a hundred different directions, to accomplish nothing at all. The weakest link is an analogy about a length of chain to help you identify which single task you need to focus on right now along the path to your Dreams.

In a chain there is always one link that is weaker than all others. That is the link that will fail when the chain is stretched to the breaking point. Metaphorically speaking, this is the chain you are using to hoist your Dreams to the sky. The purpose of the *Weak Link Guideline* is to remind you to always find and strengthen that weakest link before working on any others. You must focus on the single most important task between you and your Dream.

Quality of Life

Keep in mind that your Dream consists of many integrated goals. It is helpful to distinguish the different types of weak links between you and your goals and invest your resources towards strengthening that link. The weakest link may be personal or organizational, or informational. It may be in your quality of life or in some aspect of business, like product development or marketing. If you determine the weakest link in each category, then you can compare the results with each other to find the weakest link overall. The weak link may require you to work late at the office to put the final touches on a contract, but it might also mean that you need to take the day off and bring the family to the park for a picnic. This process will prevent you from becoming a workaholic, because quality of life is so often the weakest link. Strengthening your quality of life goal does not usually require much money, but it does demand that you spend quality time with those you are close to.

Personal

Although the weak-link analogy was originally developed for financial planning, it is useful as a guide in all aspects of life. Plotting the next step towards a production goal is relatively simple and linear compared to the dynamics of a relationship between two or more people. For every time I use the weak link guideline to assess my next step in business I probably use it twenty times or more relationships.

As a child I had difficulty expressing my feelings. I bottled my emotions inside until I couldn't hold any more and blew it all out in a single fit of incoherent rage. The result was that nobody understood what I was trying to communicate, and I never got the outcomes I wanted. The frustration of not being able to communicate forced me to separate my emotions, to deal with only one issue at a time. With years of practice I learned to take as much time as I needed to define my feelings, to figure out how to express them so that others would understand me, and to determine a clear and positive outcome before I acted. I dealt with the biggest issues first. The problems that nagged me the most caught my attention and became the weakest link in my emotional well-being. Often I would try to find a clear way to express myself, and I would try to find a positive outcome to work towards, but the process revealed that I was the one who was truly unreasonable. I would argue every side of the issue in my head until there was nothing left for my anger to hold on to, and I let it go. It was much easier to talk out the remaining issues with others once I stopped being so unreasonable myself! I am most successful in communicating as long as I deal with one issue at a time, define my objective and develop a plan before I open my mouth. It is a way of acting instead of merely reacting.

Organizational

The technical and physical aspects of achieving any particular goal are usually easy compared to dealing with the human dimension. In any venture from marriage to business to government, the weakest link is often a lack of effective communication and subsequently a lack of vision, consensus or cooperation.

The key to building an effective organization is to cooperate in creating a common vision, so that everyone feels that they have some "ownership" in the goal. That way each person is working towards something that is truly meaningful to them, rather than just working to fulfill somebody else's dream. While the idea of a common vision is simple in concept, it can be challenging to produce in the real world.

As a writer, used to working alone, I find the organizational process especially trying. I would much rather be a dictator and tell everyone else what to do! Often in a group consensus projects I feel like I have a good vision worked out already, and the process of communicating to build a common vision seems tedious and redundant. I would rather jump into the action of getting the job done. But usually I gain new and unexpected insights from other members of the team. Even when the outcome is obvious it is still important to go through the process, so that each member of the team understands and shares the vision. Even though I can recognize and write about the need for using effective organizational skills, it still remains a weak link for me in most group projects I am involved in.

The business world, which theoretically optimizes the efficient use of people, energy and materials, is unfortunately fraught with inefficiencies due to organizational weak links. One unbelievable, but relatively common problem in big companies is that leading innovators are often discouraged rather than encouraged. For example, some individual factories have implemented vision-sharing polices that led to much better morale and more efficient use of materials and energy, only to be thwarted by upper-level management for making their sister factories look bad! Instead of spreading the new and effective techniques to other plants within the company, the innovative factory is forced to revert to the old ways of doing business.

Businesses that have become so engulfed in their own bureaucracy are doomed to be out-niched by other companies that have more effectively addressed their organizational weak links. For instance, one East Asian factory consumed $7.00 worth of electricity to manufacture each hard drive they sold. They were out-niched by a more streamlined start-up company that used only 13.5¢ worth of electricity to manufacture an equivalent hard drive. The inefficient factory went broke two months after the new one opened[39]. Staying competitive in the market place requires good communication and vision throughout an organization.

Informational

Organizational and informational weak links are often related, since impaired communication often leads to a failure to look for or act on the best information available. In fact, people, businesses and governments often fail to do any meaningful research at all, but merely mimic what they see everyone else doing. In the effort to "keep up with the Jones's", people keep making the same mistakes the Jones's made! Consumers may study the price and quality of every fifty cent item at the grocery store, only to plunk $1,000+ down on a computer with almost no research at all. Houses are the biggest expense most people ever make, but home buyers spend proportionately less time researching the quality and efficiency than comparing prices at the store, before signing the dotted line. Businesses often make the same kind of choices, spending more time researching the cheapest source for office supplies like paper clips than evaluating the energy efficiency of a new office building or factory. More thoughtful design might save tens of thousands, even millions of dollars a year in energy costs, but the necessary information doesn't make it into the hands of the decision makers. Likewise, developing countries want the same prosperity that the industrial nations have, but they adopt expensive polluting technologies which those of us in the industrial world are already starting to replace with cheaper, cleaner alternatives. In the effort to boost their economies, they tie up the nation's capital for twenty years into the future and plummet the nation billions of dollars in debt.

In most projects research is the most profitable part of the work. I know that Renee and I literally saved tens of thousands of dollars in the cost of our home by researching house construction and design extensively before we started. More importantly, we got the house we really wanted.

Production

Besides weak links at the personal, organizational, and informational levels, there are also weak links at the production level. In the household it may be the need to cook up bigger stews and to freeze the extra for quick and easy future meals, saving on the cost of other instant foods. In business it may be a need to improve the quality of the products you make and sell, or the need to do more marketing. For example, as a writer I have to choose every day which is the weaker link between the need to write and the need to market my work. Often the weak links in production are organizational and informational in nature. When you are well-organized and well-informed then the weak links in production can be strengthened very quickly.

Crisis Management

The *Weak Link Guideline* is helpful to achieve any goal, but it becomes essential during times of crisis. When you feel overwhelmed and do not know where to turn, then turn to your Dream. Think about your dream and ask yourself what is the single weakest link between you and your objectives. Especially there may be times when you think you need to put your dream on hold, while you take on another job, or engage in other emergency actions to stabilize the situation at hand. But if you stop to assess your vision and the best route to get from here to there, you will often find that you are nearly on the right track, and only need to make a minor course correction, rather than plowing a whole new route. I have found that the times I was most depressed about a "lack of success" always came moments before my greatest surges of new inspiration and energy. It is easy to get lost in the middle of a situation, but when you hit bottom it is time to remember the Dream and assess the shortest route to achieving it. Upon review you will often find that the weakest links are not quite so weak after all!

"A few years ago I knew of but one place in the town where the hound's tongue was naturalized. I put a handful of its nutlets into my pocket with my handkerchief, but it took me a long time to pick them out of the handkerchief when I got home, and I pulled out many threads in the process. I afterward spent twenty minutes in clearing myself of them after having brushed against the plant. But I do not mind such things; and so, the next spring, not intending any harm, I gave some of the above-named seeds, gathered the previous August, to a young lady who cultivates a flower garden, and to my sister, wishing to spread it, it is so rare. . .

"I learned that the young lady's mother, who one day took a turn in the garden in order to pluck a nose-gay, just before setting out on a journey, found that she had carried a surprising quantity of this seed to Boston on her dress, without knowing it-for the flowers that invite you to look at and pluck them have designs on you-and the railroad company charged nothing for freight. So this plant is in a fair way to be dispersed, and my purpose is accomplished."

—Henry David Thoreau, *The Dispersion of Seeds*

5-2
Cause & Effect
-Finding Solutions Beyond the Symptoms-

If there is a single human behavior that threatens the survival of our species more than any other behavior, it would have to be our tendency to address the **symptoms** of problems while ignoring the underlying causes. The purpose of the *Cause and Effect Guideline* is first to ensure that we are addressing the **root cause** of the problem, and second that we must try to predict all the **effects** of our solutions.

For example, when crime increases we react by building more jails and writing tougher laws—without ever asking what caused the crime rate to go up in the first place. When we discover weeds where we do not want them we react with poison, without ever asking what allowed the weeds to take hold in the first place. In medicine we fight diseases as if they were the problems, when in fact most diseases are merely the symptoms—we are focusing on what makes people sick, while ignoring what keeps them healthy.

When floods wash away whole towns and ruin peoples' lives, we react by building more dams and dikes for flood control, but most floods are at least partially man-made, because poor land management across the continent and around the world causes water to run off the land when it should be soaking into the soil. If a town or city does not have enough water then we react by drilling more wells or building more dams to increase the water supply, without realizing that it is much cheaper and more effective to simply replace the inefficient, water-wasting appliances in the community.

If it is cold in the house then we treat the symptoms by turning up the thermostat, while ignoring the real problem of insufficient insulation. If there is not enough energy to serve everyone, then we react by building more and more power plants, without realizing that it is (once again) cheaper to merely replace inefficient appliances, so the existing supply will serve more uses. If we run short of money then we think we must raise our income-we may feel that we cannot survive on what we have—even while billions of other people in the world are able to prosper on far less.

As a rule, cause and effect in mechanical systems, like a washing machine or a house, is relatively simple and linear, when compared to cause and effect in ecosystem processes. If a washing machine breaks down you can find the problem, replace the broken part, and the whole thing should work again. Even in a house with high energy bills it is relatively easy to get beyond the symptoms to the true problem of not enough insulation.

Organic processes, like the natural ecosystem or the economic ecosystem, are inherently nonlinear, so cause and effect can be much more difficult to predict, as suggested by the quote at the beginning of this chapter. Plagues of grasshoppers are a good example. Some years there are "outbreaks" of locusts that strip the fields of almost every living plant. We have experienced the phenomenon on our own small property, where there are so many hungry grasshoppers that they eat anything they can find-even the needles off of the spruce tree and the black plastic off the garden.

Farmers may watch with horror as their fields—their very hopes and dreams—are stripped by tens of thousands of hoppers, and they automatically react to the "problem" by pouring their wealth into pesticides to stop the invaders. Unfortunately, by the time grasshoppers are mature enough to cause visible damage, it is too late in the season to make a meaningful difference with pesticides. Watching the grasshoppers die may provide the satisfaction of vengeance, but at an incredible expense, with little economic return.

A new method of grasshopper control utilizes a parasitic bacteria that consumes grasshoppers from the inside out, turning them to mush. The bacteria is spread through the population as other grasshoppers consume those that have already died. Introducing this predatory bacteria is more of an "ecosystem" approach, but it is expensive, and it must be applied early in the year to have any effect. There is some carry-over from one season to the next, but not a lot. Moreover, the bacteria has to be applied very early in the season to have any useful effect.

A few farmers see the fallacy of attacking a problem plague that has nearly expired itself anyway, and instead have the "foresight" to save next years crop by torching this years, thereby toasting all the hoppers before they can reproduce. Unfortunately, they do not realize the connection between the water cycle and grasshopper reproduction. Burning away the organic matter compromises the soil's ability to capture water and keep it in the soil, and that water is needed in the soil to rot the grasshopper eggs. Grasshopper plagues are naturally greatest when there is dry weather in the spring, so it is more essential then ever at these times that the soil is able to capture and hold moisture. Torching the fields only aggravates the true problem.

In ecosystem processes you may never find the solutions as long as you are busy dealing with the problems. As long as you attack grasshoppers as the problem, then you may never realize that healthy fields and soil are the solution! You have to adjust your farming practices to favor more organic matter in the soil to trap moisture and rot future grasshopper eggs. You need to work with the ecology to support more predators to kill and eat those grasshoppers that do hatch.

Cause and effect can be similarly convoluted in the economic ecosystem. Consider, for example, the OPEC oil embargo of 1973 and the resulting "oil shortage". People had to stand in line for hours at the gas pump to fill their cars, and the economy fell into a recession. There would seem to be a direct cause and effect relationship between the embargo and the effects to our economy, but that assumption is not correct.

The concept of "shortages" is not possible in a naturally functioning economy, because the **law of supply and demand** simply states that supply is always equal to demand. True shortages can only occur when artificial controls are imposed on the economy.

In the economy all goods are "scarce" and therefore must be rationed, usually according to each person's willingness to pay money. Ostrich meat, for instance, is quite scarce. The meat is more expensive than the available substitutes, and not many people are willing to pay the high price for it, but we never say that there is a "shortage". Gasoline is also "scarce", a fact which has nothing to do with how much or how little is actually produced. Supply and demand are always equal because we buy more when the price goes down and less when the price goes up.

Unlike ostrich meat, gasoline seems much more essential, and "should" be available to every person, but remember, there are always substitutes. Bike riding is a good substitute for the Sunday drive. Car-pooling or riding the bus is a good substitute for driving to work. When prices remain comparatively high for extended time periods, then alternative fuels also become good substitutes.

The only cause of the 1973 oil "shortage" was the price controls imposed by President Nixon[53]. The artificially low prices resulted in a demand greater than the supply, and hence, a "shortage", that caused people to stand in line for hours at the pump. It is simply impossible to avoid the process of rationing scarce goods. Artificially lowering the monetary price of an item only raises other nonmonetary costs of making the purchase. Instead of paying more money for gasoline, people paid more of their time—so they could be first in line when the gas stations opened in the morning. Rationing with money is arguably much more efficient!

With the question of the gasoline "shortage" understood, there still remains the puzzle of the "recession" that accompanied the oil embargo. Lay people and experts alike tend to believe that a rise in the price of energy results in an economic recession.

Government officials assumed that the increased cost of oil would inflate all prices at home, and therefore the Federal Reserve tightened the money supply to help forestall inflation. As you may recall, the Fed prints the money it loans out, which increases the number of tokens in relation to the number of calories in the economy, and results in inflation. The Fed fights inflation by raising interest rates, so that less money is being printed and borrowed. Unfortunately, higher interest rates mean less investment, and a greater possibility of recession. Thus the recession that followed the oil embargo was caused by a tighter money supply, and had nothing to do with the "shortage".

Consider that the Iranian revolution of 1979 also led to higher prices at the pump. The Fed again tightened the money supply to safeguard against inflation and caused another recession. Meanwhile, Japan continued to expand it's money supply through 1979-80 and experienced no recession, even though the country imports virtually all of it's energy. Conversely, since it is commonly believed that a rise in energy prices seriously hurts the economy, it is also assumed that a drop in prices should stimulate the economy, but that does not happen either. Oil prices dropped by half in 1986, which, in theory, should have generated a worldwide economic boom, but it did not. (The boom did not come until the 1990's.) The true cause of the oil "shortages" and the subsequent recessions was due only to the attempt to control the economy.

Cause and effect can be equally challenging to unravel in both the economic and the natural ecosystem, and therefore you will usually be far more successful in your efforts when you focus on solutions described in positive terms, rather than on the problems themselves.

For instance, what happens when the kids are fighting with one another, and we join the fight and yell a them for yelling at each other? In order to get real results, sometimes we have to leave the problem behind so we can find the solution—by sitting down together to work out a common vision for how each of us would like to be treated by one another. If each of us takes part in creating the vision and brainstorming ways to achieve it, then we may find the fighting can be resolved, without ever focusing directly on the "problem" itself. The *Cause and Effect Guideline* reminds you to make sure you are taking a solutions-oriented approach. Only when you have defined what you want to achieve, and described it in positive terms, can you plot a course to achieve it.

"I was more independent than any farmer in Concord, for I was not anchored to a house or farm, but could follow the bent of my genius, which is a very crooked one, every moment. Beside being better off than they already, if my house had burned or my crops had failed, I should have been nearly as well off as before."

—*Henry David Thoreau, Walden*

5-3

Marginal Reaction
-Comparing your Options-

You have walked out the door on a snowy winter day to go a mile through the woods and over the hills to Grandma's house. You thought you dressed warm enough, but a quarter mile down the trail you decide you are getting cold. Do you return to the house for more clothing or do you wrap your arms tight around your body and continue on your way, thinking of the hot coffee and apple pie waiting at the end of the trail?

The choices we have already made in life are considered **sunk costs**. We cannot pick up our foot prints and undo past decisions. We can only live in the present, on the narrow **margin** between the past and future. A step just taken is immediately sunk in the past, while the next step ahead remains a **variable** of the future. In economics sunk costs are said to be "irrelevant" to future planning, but this statement is highly misleading.

Your sunk cost in the walk to grandma's house is the quarter mile you have already traveled. But it doesn't matter where you have been. The only thing that counts is where you are. You have to weigh the expected costs and benefits from your present position. You expected the day to be warmer than it is, and you were wrong, but that is all part of the past. Now you have to weigh the expected costs and benefits of either pushing on towards Grandma's warm stove, or returning to the house for more clothes. You would benefit by walking onward and getting there sooner, but at the cost of being cold for 3/4 of a mile. On the other hand, you would benefit by returning 1/4 mile for warm clothes, but at the cost of having to walk 1 1/4 miles from your present position to get to your final destination.

Where you have been in life has no bearing on where you will go in the future. It does not matter if you have been a student, a beggar, a criminal, or a hundred thousand dollars in debt. Your past actions are sunk costs which merely determine where you are in the present. The thing that counts is the choices you have from your present position. You have to compare options and weigh the expected additional costs of each potential action against its expected return.

In matters both minor and major, we deal with **sunk costs and marginal decisions** every day in life. Six dollars spent at the movies is a sunk cost, whether we like the movie or not. We expect a good movie, but that is irrelevant to future decisions. Forcing ourselves to watch two hours of a bad movie does not mean we get our money's worth; it only means we raise the sunk cost to six dollars plus two hours of our time. All future movies remain variables on the margin of decision until the moment we hand over our cash and sit through the show.

The idea that sunk costs are irrelevant is easiest to understand if you imagine a grocery store that has bought fifty crates of bannanas at $1.00/lb just before the price dramatically drops. If the competition starts selling bananas for 25¢ a pound then this store must also drop their price. It would be less of a loss to sell the bannanas at 25¢ per pound than to not sell them at all. In practice sunk costs and marginal decisions can be much more complicated.

If we decide to pay $5,000 for a used car we expect the car to run. When the car breaks down a couple months later and the bill is $1,500, we have to make a new decision. The original cost of the car is irrelevant to any decisions now. We have to weigh the expected costs and benefits of all the known options given the current situation. What do we expect from the car in the future? Should we fix the car and keep it? Should we fix it and sell it, or sell it as is? Should we try to bring legal action against the dealer, and what might the costs and benefits of such an action

Comparing Options

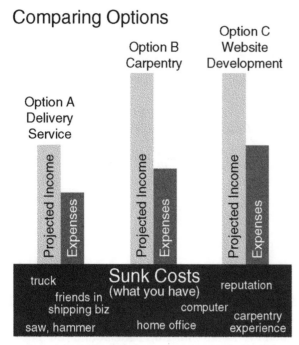

To compare options you need to consider the projected income against the projected new expenses. For example, an expense of starting a delivery service is the need to find clients. To get a job with a friend as a carpenter, you may need to purchase additional tools. To design websites you may need additional training.

Sunk costs are those things you have already, like past experience, your reputation, a computer or a home office, including expenses you have to make anyway, like car payments. In economics, sunk costs are "irrelevant" to determining future actions. This statement is both true and false.

A truck is relevant as an asset which may be used to produce an income, but it is also a sunk cost that is irrelevant to determining the best enterprise to undertake. The important question is, "What NEW expenses are incurred for each possible option?" The fact that you are still paying for the truck does not mean that using it in business is the best means to make those payments. After comparing all your options you may discover it is most profitable to get a job flipping hamburgers!

be?

Marginal decisions can be very difficult to make when your sunk costs are high. For example, many college students go through two or three years of schooling towards a particalur degree before realizing they would rather go after a different degree or none at all. Like walking to Grandma's house in the cold, you are part way there already. Do you keep going and finish what you've started, or chuck it all and start over?

Every day we make decisions on the margin, collapsing future variables into choices sunk in the past. By thinking through this process consciously we can more easily let go of the sunk costs and focus directly on the opportunities now on the margin. With every choice made you want to get the greatest reaction towards all of your goals. This is called **marginal reaction**.

The *Marginal Reaction Guideline* is a useful thought model for comparing a variety of possible courses of action, as illustrated here in "Comparing Options". Traditionally the guideline is used exclusively to compare numbers, for example, an automobile factory tooled up to produce an out-dated car must decide whether to retool a little bit, to make a more stylish version of the old car, or to retool completely to produce a new car from the ground up, or to produce something else besides cars. The sunk costs are relevant becuase it is a lot cheaper to retool a little bit than a lot, but the sunk costs are also irrelevant, because the important part is the expected *additional costs and benefits* of each enterprise from the current position. The factory would crunch a lot of numbers and then go with the option that seems to offer the best return for the new investment.

The real world is a bit more complicated than that, and you must include non-monetary assets, income and expenses into the equation. For example, knowing people in the right places can be an asset that lowers the cost to jump into a particular enterprise. But some occupations, like spraying pesticides on crops, can have health and environmental costs which must also be factored in, even if the numbers otherwise look good. Other options might offer very poor return financially, but may be very fulfilling to the heart. You have to make the choices that bring you the farthest towards your combined goals, with the least total expenses.

A high-paying job offer may be a quick fix for your financial woes, and you would often be wise to take advantage of it, but not always. I have walked away from many job offers, even when we were broke and had bills to pay, because I would have been working for money only, and I would have been neglecting other equally important goals, like raising my family and working on my writing. We have been successful because we always stick to our goals, even if our choices may seem to defy commonsense to others.

One short-coming to the illustration here is that it does not represent the **time dimension**. The length of time it takes to break even and turn a profit is vitally important to decision making. Sometimes an option with a short payback period, but less income potential is better than an option with a long payback period and higher income potential. After all, if you get a small but quick return on your investment then you can turn around and reinvest in whatever new opportunities you have discovered. You also have to factor in that some enterprises will have high start-up costs, but will bring in a steady income later, while other options have lower startup costs, but more long-term costs. As you can see, determining the optimal marginal reaction for your efforts is often a very intuitive process. But the more you think about each option in these terms, the better the decisions you will make.

Marginal Costs

Books Printed	Cost Per Book	Total Investment
1,000	$5.00	$5,000
2,000	$3.50	$7,000
3,000	$2.50	$7,500
4,000	$2.25	$9,000
5,000	$2.00	$10,000

The cost per book drops with larger orders, but there is a higher cost in opportunities forgone as more capital is tied up in inventory.

As my own publisher, I have to make choices about how many books to print at one time. More books cost more money upfront, but reduces the cost per book. If I pay out-of-pocket, then I have to pay the cost of forgone opportunities while my money is tied up in inventory—what kind of a return could I get on alternative investments? If I use credit to print the books, then I also have to pay interest on the borrowed money. I have to consider how long I expect it will take to sell all the books, and what would I do with my money or credit if it were not tied up in inventory?

All possible choices lay on the margin until the moment of decision. I make the choice I believe will yield the greatest reaction for my investments. For example, assuming I had $10,000 to work with, I might print 3,000 copies of this book ($7,500), spend another $1,500 on a wholesale purchase from other authors (to sell along side my own), and spend the remaining $1,000 on a quality canoe for the family. I would choose the combination I perceived would give the greatest reaction towards achieving my combined quality of life and production goals. Keeping all of your goals in mind may be the most difficult part of decision making process.

The *Marginal Reaction Guideline* is especially useful in making these kind of **incremental decisions** where there is a point of diminishing returns, and the best solution is a combination of investments.

Imagine that you are insulating your house to make it warmer. The first layer of insulation you put down in the attic will conserve a certain amount of energy, and the savings from the power bill will help recover the cost of the insulation. Each additional layer of insulation will cost the same amount, but will contribute incrementally less to the efficiency of the house. *Marginal Reaction* reminds you to add insulation only to a depth that will recover it's costs within a reasonable amount of time. Adding more insulation beyond that point will not bring a good return on the investment. Moreover, *Marginal Reaction* requires that you test all available options to find the best action, or the best combination of actions to help you achieve your goals.

The author searches for the point of diminishing returns.

If your project goal is to make your house warmer—with best possible "profit" for the investment (in terms of a lower power bill)—then you have to consider each of the available technologies to achieve that goal. Weather-stripping the doors and windows may prove to bring a greater profit reaction than insulating the attic. More likely, however, is that a combination of some weather-stripping and some insulating would provide the greatest overall savings for the investment.

It is too easy to react impulsively to the situations at hand without considering your actions in terms of your Dream. If someone offends you or causes you injury, accident or not, you may want to react by telling them off or suing them. That may take you away from your quality of life goal. You need to choose your thoughts, your words, and your feelings carefully, to help you achieve and maintain your desired state of mind. Whatever your situation is, taking the time to carefully weigh your options will help you get the greatest marginal reaction for your subsequent efforts.

"Many men go fishing all of their lives without knowing it is not fish they are after."

—*Henry David Thoreau*

5-4

Energy/Wealth Source & Use
-Looking Out for our Children's Grandchildren-

We live in a world of abundance. The resources are here to sustainably give every person on this planet a life of prosperity and comfort. Prosperity for all is easy to achieve as long as we think and act in terms of Real Wealth. Real wealth is any investment of our resources that benefits ourselves or our communities in tangible and lasting ways.

People get caught up in the numbers and think wealth is money. They forget that true wealth is the products, services and environment that sustains us. Businesses too often sell gimmicks in the pursuit of paper dollars, without working to create useful products and services. Corporations work to expand their incomes through leveraged buyouts or by starting credit services. Governments also fail to look towards real wealth to build an economy. Instead governments seek to stimulate the economy through manipulating the numbers supply, by raising or lowing interest rates, or by affecting the number of tokens in circulation. We have reached a point in time as a culture where we commonly believe that wealth is numbers, and that we can increase our wealth by investing in the numbers. Remember, our abundance has to come from somewhere. Someone has to take the raw materials of the earth and modify them into the products that sustain us.

As a consumer you have the power to vote with your money. Products and services exist on the market only as long as there are consumers to buy them. You control whether or not we invest our collective resources in real goods or real waste through the purchases you make. You will always make the best choices possible as long as you ask these simple questions:

1) Does this choice help me achieve my Dream?
2) Does this decision represent a worthwhile and useful application of the earth's resources and energy?
3) What will happen with the materials when this product is no longer useful for it's intended function?

As a producer you have even more power to choose how material resources and human labor are utilized. You will use resources wisely as long as your goal includes a vision that extends beyond yourself to the world around you. Businesses only waste resources when they chase after the partial goal of money.

I remember when the movie *Jurassic Park* came out. Months ahead of time manufacturers started producing all kinds of dinosaur toys and candies and general gimmickry to market with the "dinomania" that followed the movie. I recall one spokesperson for the movie saying in a television interview that there would be a "lasting market", or some such words, and in the same breath he indicated that "lasting" meant about six months. He and others expected to sell millions of dollars worth of products in only a few months before people lost their interest and the market faded. You will do best by making goods that are truly useful to the consumer.

People who market gimmickry do it on the assumption that the consumer is going to be bored with their purchases within a few hours, days, or weeks of having spent their money. They have to trick the consumer and sell to them when they are caught up in the fads and emotions of the moment, before they have the opportunity to really consider their goals. When a business markets gimmickry they are selling something people ultimately do not want. Most of the time that is a hard sell. Only a well organized fad, such as those that follow some movies, can really guarantee a market for gimmicks. But even when entrepreneurs make money from gimmicks I am not sure that they truly profit from it.

Such entrepreneurs may come out with more paper dollars than they had, but everyone, including them, end up paying the higher costs of depleted resources and bigger landfills. Likewise, we all suffer from lost opportunity when human minds are directed towards producing products to be put in landfills, rather than innovating and producing the new goods and services that will carry our species successfully into the future.

Today there is a greater awareness about environmental concerns than ever before, but unfortunately this has only led to the environment becoming another hot item to sell. I am reminded right now of the great grocery bag caper that was pulled on millions of consumers across the nation. The consumers of America were subjected to a massive guilt trip over the paper versus plastic issue, and then grocery stores cashed in by selling canvas "earth bags". Now there is nothing wrong with reusable canvas grocery bags. We use them at least part of the time. The problem was simply that the grocery stores were taking advantage of consumers when they were emotionally charged and feeling guilty and vulnerable about using paper or plastic bags. Millions of people bought canvas earth bags, and these bags were embarrassingly ugly. They had the stores names, along with some poor graphics and some earthy acronyms, blazoned all across the bags, each proclaiming to be genuinely concerned about the environment. People bought them because the felt guilty over the issue. They bought them impulsively without thinking through their decision. Many people had not yet reached the point where they would make the adjustment in their routines to bring the bags to the store with them. Additionally, many of those who were ready to make that adjustment may not have followed through, because the bags were too ugly for people to be proud of carrying around. Today I would bet that most of those bags are either in landfills or in closets, which is where people put them when they feel too guilty to throw them in the trash.

The great grocery bag caper exploited the resources of the earth, it exploited people's emotions, it cost consumers money, and it may have contributed to the despair people often feel over environmental problems. Many people bought the bags out of a feeling of guilt over environmental problems; having those bags sit around unused for years only prolongs the guilt, and eventually throwing the bags into the trash does not help either. The grocery stores may have won some immediate sales, but I think the losses to the whole far out-weighed the gains made by any few individuals. Most of all, consciously or subconsciously, I think those kinds of marketing tactics lead to an atmosphere of distrust in our culture. It does not have to be that way.

The American economy of our time is sustained by gimmickry with businesses tricking consumers into thinking they need products they really have little use for. The environment is only the latest gimmick on the market, and it is a waste of incredible opportunity and human potential. Businesses are putting up flashing neon signs proclaiming to be "green", and it may sell, but eventually people see through it. Numbing the consumer into indifference does nothing but blow the sales in the long run. Let me propose a different approach.

The approach I propose is simple. Basically, instead of selling people on their guilt, how about selling them on your merits? Instead of merely proclaiming to be a "green business", how about actually demonstrating it?

For instance, the first step in demonstrating greenness is to create a green atmosphere. Instead of merely putting green neon signs outside, how about planting real living trees out there, in the seas of asphalt we call parking lots? How about putting shrubs, and trees, and vines, and flowers everywhere they can be squeezed in, such as in planters along the face of the building? Setting out a lot of plants is not merely a green facade, it genuinely provides habitat for insects, birds and other small creatures, and all those plants help to clean the air we breathe.

The inside of the business should also be as green as possible, creating an atmosphere that is inviting to be in, so that people come simply because they like being there. Ideally, but not essential, the building itself could be built of largely natural materials, such as stone, adobe, rammed earth, or some other material. These have a much more natural appeal than many conventional materials like cinder blocks.

In addition to appearance, a green business might have a genuine ethic of conservation, perhaps installing energy and water-efficient fixtures and posting informational signs where people can read and learn about the conservation efforts undertaken. Many businesses also have roof tops which are conducive to mounting solar panels, perhaps solar hot air panels for space heating, or panels for solar hot water, or even photovoltaic panels for generating solar electricity. Additionally a green business can provide bins where customers could drop off their recyclables, particularly for anything that might have been purchased at the store.

A green business might also provide informational displays, giving the background of some of the products, where they are made or grown, or what materials they are made from. Many people want to live a lifestyle that is more in tune with the ecosystem, and they might like the opportunity to learn more about the resources they use in their daily lives.

Of course, being a green business also means making sure that the products or services you produce or sell are as environmentally sustainable as they can be with our present knowledge. More than that, however, it means providing the customers with the information they need to make decisions that they will feel good about today and down the road. Most businesses today do not give customers information; they only strive to sell mass numbers of products.

Flashing neon signs ultimately foster only distrust; using a lot of hype to promote your business only causes you to need additional hype to bring people back again. On the other hand, genuinely demonstrating greenness and giving the customers the information they want and need will build trust between your business and your customers. Client trust and faith will be the greatest asset for making your endeavors a long-term success.

I encourage you to market genuinely useful products and services. Usefulness always has a market, and you will make sales as long as your goods remain useful to the consumer. This is especially true in times of economic recession. In financially hard times people usually cut out the non-essentials first. They tend to save their money for the useful products and services they really need.

Our country was built by individuals boldly investing in themselves and in their beliefs and abilities to provide useful products and useful services. Have we reached a point today where we have lost our strength and will-power, where we think we can get something from nothing by marketing gimmicks or by mailing our money off to someplace where it is cloned and sent back? I hope not, and I hope that as you seek to increase your personal prosperity you will do so by investing and believing in yourself and in your abilities to make a positive contribution to the world we live in.

"When it is understood that one loses joy and happiness in the attempt to possess them, the essence of natural farming will be realized. The ultimate goal of farming is not the growing of crops, but the cultivation and perfection of human beings."

—Masanobu Fukuoka, *The One Straw Revolution*

5-5
Neighbors & Culture
-Respecting Others Along the Path to Your Dreams-

Here in America we value our personal freedoms—the freedom to dress as we choose, to speak what we believe, to seek our own religion, to choose our own work, and to do what we please with our property to name a few. We like being able to do what we want whenever we want, and we simply do not like other people telling us how to live.

I am reminded of a news report I heard from the Middle East, where a restaurant owner was jailed for merely serving lunch to a group of women who refused to where veils covering their faces. We appreciate our freedom here in the West, but we seldom realize how valuable that freedom is.

Of course, with the freedom to do what we want also comes the responsibility to respect the rights of others. "One man's freedom to swing his fist ends where another man's nose begins," wrote Supreme Court Justice Oliver Wendell Holmes. We are left the burden of being "reasonable and prudent" in our actions toward others.

Property rights are a good case in point. Here in America we can buy land, and for the most part we can do whatever we please with it—at least within reason. But problems develop when we act without considering our neighbors or our culture.

For decades we have been steadily losing the right to choose what we do with our own property, while increasing our control over what others do with their property. This shift in our rights comes as the result of the individuals who have not been reasonable and prudent in their actions.

The shift of property rights naturally started with the extreme cases, such as when individuals turned their land into toxic waste dumps. We describe this as an "environmental problem", but we are by nature an anthropocentric species, and the only real issue at stake is **property rights**[41]. The problem with toxic waste on a piece of land is that it does not stay there. The toxins move through the air and water and violates the freedom of other people to do what they want with their properties. Hence, there are laws prohibiting toxic waste dumps.

As more and more people live ever closer together we are logically continuing to lose more of the freedom to do what we want, while gaining more and more control in what our neighbors can and cannot do. In short, our noses are closer together than they used to be. We cannot operate an unsightly junk yard on just any piece of property we choose, nor could we open a noisy night club in the middle of a subdivision. Freedoms are shortest where people are closest together, so in some places you would be violating the law if you even built a tree-house in the yard or left your lawn uncut.

Unfortunately, there seems to be a growing tension in this country today because we all like laws that limit other people's freedom, but we hate it when those laws apply to ourselves. Like children tattling on each other, we run to the law for support to control our neighbors when they are not using their land in a reasonable and prudent manner. We perceive the law as a "citizens ally", something that we the people created and are in control of. But when others use the law to limit our freedoms, we suddenly perceive the law more as "bureaucracy out of control"— an inhuman entity that must be stopped.

There is no new law that can be written to take away the duality between how we feel when the government is on our side, and how we feel when the government is "out to get us". Nevertheless, there are two solutions to the problem.

The first and obvious solution is be reasonable and prudent in your own actions. The purpose of the *Neighbors & Culture Guideline* is to remind you to consider how your actions will affect other people around you.

Here in Montana the land is being destroyed by individuals who come looking for their piece of the "Big Sky Country". Each person tries to get the best spot with the best view. As a result many areas are littered with towering houses perched on top of every little hill around. One person's quest for the good view ruins the view for everyone else. People get their "piece" of the Big Sky, but nothing more, because the pieces are all that's left. Naturally there are more and more laws entering the books to tell people where and how they can build their houses.

Having good neighbors starts with being a good neighbor. Before you act, you must stop and consider how others around you will react. As long as we give consideration to each other, and we are reasonable and prudent in our actions, then we can obviate the need for yet more of these laws which ultimately limit our own freedoms.

Of course, you already know that you are a reasonable and prudent person, and the real source of the problem is everybody else! It is therefore unrealistic to think that the thoughtfulness of your actions will do much to stop the plethora of new laws that continue to control our lives. That may be true, and that is why the second solution to the problem—consensus building—is so desperately needed.

Consensus building is that process of getting together with the neighbors to discuss common concerns, and to create a common vision for your community. By talking and planning with your neighbors, you will know what each other expects and needs, and you will be more able to respect each other, even as you work towards your unique and individual dreams.

The real value in consensus building is flexibility. Written laws are very inflexible, and we all suffer for that. I remember one story of a family that had to take down a playhouse they built for their children because it was up on stilts, jutting a foot or two above the height allowed by the zoning code. I saw that playhouse, and there was nothing unreasonable about it—it just didn't fit the strict numbers of the law. The value in the consensus-building process is that most of the time people are very reasonable and flexible, especially when they feel that their needs and concerns are being heard. A group of people who listen to each other can find many reasonable and prudent ways to meet the needs and concerns of each individual—without the need to call for more and more government.

Keep in mind that the *Neighbors and Culture Guideline* is not just about property rights, but should influence every decision you make, from the kind of pets you have to the way you wear your hair. How, for instance, would your neighbors react if you cut and dyed your hair to make a green mohawk? How would they react if you kept bats for pets and let them fly around loose in the house? The *Neighbors and Culture Guideline* is a reminder to fit in with those around you.

Certainly there is always a time to challenge the status quo, to try a new fashion, or voice a new ideology, but in each case you have to carefully weigh the potential costs and benefits against your goal. Most of the time it is to your advantage to go along with the crowd.

Teen-agers, for example, often intentionally "rock the boat" among their neighbors and culture, by trying new, ever weirder stunts, like piercing their nose or belly button-for the sole purpose of getting a reaction. Doing something to get a reaction out of people can be fun, and it can get you noticed—these are the benefits of acting this way. There are also costs since the parents and school may disapprove, and getting a job could be more difficult. Teen-agers usually give at least some consideration to the costs and benefits, but they may still decide the costs are worthwhile. The reason is simple, because they have not yet formed a greater Vision or Goal to test the costs and benefits against.

Only when you have established a well-defined goal and a plan for achieving it, can you test the potential costs and benefits of your actions and consider shaking up the neighborhood with radical new ideas. Charles Darwin understood the impact his *Theory of Evolution* would have on society, because he knew how the discovery impacted his own faith.   He knew the idea would shake the very foundations of western culture, but he also understood that the idea had to be published.   He spent forty years collecting the evidence to counter every reasonable argument against the theory before publishing his earth-shattering book, *The Origin of Species*. Darwin finally published the work only because he heard that another biologist had independently arrived at the same conclusion. Darwin published first to get the credit he deserved for the discovery.

Before taking any action yourself you must always consider the effects towards your neighbors and culture. You must consider how you can achieve your goals without compromising the rights or happiness of other people around you.

The only time to stand apart from your neighbors is when you believe a cause is so important that there is no reasonable alternative but to shake up the neighborhood. If that is the case, then you must plan very carefully to achieve your objective without it back-firing in your face. You must have a positive goal for what you hope to accomplish, and a realistic plan for achieving it. You must consider the potential costs and benefits behind every possible approach, and know in advance what you are up against, and how to circumvent every obstacle. Only when you have fully considered your *Neighbors and Culture* in this way, can you take any action, from planting a tree, to starting a revolution.

Part VI
Implementing Your Strategy for Success

"I left the woods for as good a reason as I went there. Perhaps it seemed to me that I had several more lives to live, and could not spare any more time for that one. It is remarkable how easily and insensibly we fall into a particular route, and make a beaten track for ourselves."

—Henry David Thoreau, Walden

6-1

Planning
-Prioritizing Your Action List-

When you have created your personal vision, generated ideas to achieve that vision, and tested your ideas for social, financial, and ecological soundness, then it is time to prioritize your action list. Already you will have begun to prioritize your actions just by using the testing guidelines. The *Weakest Link Guideline* for example, helps identify the single greatest need towards achieving your combined goals—your "A1" priority. When the weakest link has been addressed then you must consider *Marginal Reaction* from that point forward, to achieve the greatest gain for every additional investment of time and resources. In essence, while there may be only one "A1" priority on your agenda, you will no doubt have many other "priorities" as well. The purpose of this chapter is to help you keep your priorities straight, so that you always accomplish the goals that are most important to you—whether that means flying a kite with your child, or flying your own personal jet! In either case, the most important step to getting what you want is knowing what you want. When you know what you want, getting it happens almost automatically.

As human beings we are "cybernetic" organisms, which simply means that as we develop a picture of what we want, our subconscious minds organize our behaviors towards achieving it[23]. Granted a few moments of mental imagery does not make your dreams materialize, but keep your dreams in mind every day from the time you awake until the time you go to bed, and you will soon find the resources you need to realize them.

Thus the most important element to your success is your sustained will power concentrated on your desired dreams. Perhaps the greatest challenge in being successful is not in achieving the goals themselves, but rather, in maintaining a constant attention to them. The rest is relatively easy once you achieve that.

Perhaps the best way to keep your dreams in mind is to extend them beyond your mind. A dream that is in your mind may seem like just that, a dream, but when you express that dream in some fashion then it starts becoming reality. Expressing your dreams or goals through writing, or drawing, or sharing, helps transform them from wishful thinking into real plans. An idea expressed in some physical or tangible form is much easier to "grasp" and hold on to than an idea that is only a floating thought. The more you physically express your dreams the closer you are towards physically attaining them. There are many ways you can do that.

Keep your Dream in mind every day from the time you awake until the time you go to bed and you will soon find the resources you need for success.

When my sister Cherie was a senior in high-school she made a collage of pictures, each of which represented a goal of what she would like to achieve. Expressing her goals in that way helped her to achieve them. She achieved most of them before she turned thirty. She ran in marathons, bicycled across the United

States from coast to coast, worked in the travel industry on airlines, buses, trains and ships, and she toured countries all over the world.

I also tangibly expressed my goals in my senior year of high-school, actually a few months after graduation, but I wrote an eighty-page booklet, rather than doing a collage as my sister had. At the time I did not even realize I was expressing my goals at all. The word "goals" was barely in my vocabulary at the time, and in my mind I was just writing a booklet about how humanity could successfully live in harmony with the earth. In a roundabout way the booklet outlined our plans for a school of primitive and contemporary living skills, and the booklet even included a set of house plans we were working on. I did not realize that I had written an eighty-page goal until five years later!

There are many ways you can express your own goals, including writing, art, or sharing. One method Cherie passed along to me involved writing a letter to a friend. You write a letter dated in the future and expressing what you have been doing, and about the goals you achieved in that time period between the date on the letter and the date you are actually writing it. This is a way of committing yourself by making you accountable to your friends. It helps you to sustain you attention on your goals because you know your friends are paying attention to your goals too. Your friends will be there in the future, with your letter as evidence, to monitor your success.

You should, however, be careful about creating deadlines. The natural world, of which we are part, is not very structured or scheduled. Goals with deadlines seldom work, and you can cause yourself a great deal of unnecessary stress trying to fit our round world into a square grid of events. Deadlines can often be counterproductive, and can actually delay the achievement of the desired goal.

For example, if your goal is to learn to play a particular song well on the piano then you can concentrate fully on achieving that end. But if your goal is to be able to play that song well by a particular date and time, then you may find yourself distracted. You may be checking your progress against the clock, instead of being absorbed fully into the music. Soon your progress can lag behind, as you concentrate less and less on the music, and more and more on the fact that time is quickly passing, and you are not progressing. Shortly afterwards you may be so stressed out that you can no longer play the piano at all.

I tried many times in my life to set deadlines for achieving my goals, but the results never worked out exactly according to plan. The more I focused on the deadlines the less I accomplished. When I concentrated too much, well, I just got sick.

Even so, deadlines are not all bad. Creating a finish date for yourself can be a good way to knock yourself out of your complacency. Many people have learned through high-school and college to put projects off until the night before they are due. Then they are suddenly motivated to stay up all night to get them done. Creating a sense of a deadline can help get you started on a project, as long as you later return your focus to the goal itself, rather than to the time. Many people have wonderful dreams and ambitions, but fall into a rut of complacency and day-to-day routines. A deadline can be used to stress yourself just enough to push out of the rut. Get back on track of your dreams, and you can let go of the deadline and just concentrate on results. Eventually you will find less and less need for deadlines, as you create a new routine in your life-a habit of achieving all your dreams for each and every today to come.

Your personal Vision is like a long-range goal, outlined in very general terms. In order to achieve your long-range goal, you must also establish intermediate and immediate goals to start on. The intermediate goals are the ideas that came out of the brainstorming process, and survived the testing guidelines. The immediate goals are actions that you can take today to incrementally achieve your intermediate goals. If, for example, your Vision is to climb a mountain, then your intermediate goal might be to practice by climbing a hill, and your immediate goal might be to start getting in shape today, with an hour long hike around town.

The prioritizing system outlined here is adapted from Charles R. Hobbs' book, *Time Power*[43]. There is enough information here to get you started, but you may want to consult his book for additional details, especially if are in a potentially high-stress situation where minute-by-minute time management is crucial to staying calm and achieving success.

To prioritize your goals, start by detailing the broad statements from your Vision. For example, let's say you own a health club, and your vision includes statements like: "creating and maintaining a clean, healthful, and pleasant atmosphere for our clients", and "making a profit from the business". You would brainstorm ways to maintain and improve the facilities, then check the ideas against the testing guidelines. Some possible ideas might include:

scrubbing the mildew out of the bathrooms, applying fresh paint, new carpet, a new piece of equipment, adding on a "tea room" for customers to relax and buy health snacks, building a swimming pool, and investing in advertising. All of these ideas might be worth keeping, but some ideas will pass the testing guidelines better than others.

Wiping the mildew out of the bathrooms for example, would almost certainly pass each of the testing guidelines, including the Weakest Link. The mildew would be the "A1" priority, and you would forward the task to your immediate goals list, to complete that day.

Of course, you would probably want to keep the other ideas on the list as well. You determine that the next best action to bring you towards your goals would be a combined investment in fresh paint and carpets, followed by a spree of radio commercials to advertise the new look. These would become the "A2" and "A3" items on the list, and you would make a note to call for bids on painting and carpeting. Later on you might start brainstorming some ideas for the commercials, the "A3" project on the list.

You further determine that the "tea room" would be the next best investment, followed later with a new piece of equipment, and eventually a swimming pool. You might not begin any of these projects until you have recovered the money from the previous investment, so you rank them as lower priorities, like "B1, B2, and C1", as shown in the table. The "B" and "C" items are still considered intermediate goals, and you can continue researching and planning them whenever you have time left over, after attending to each of the "A" goals on the list.

Obviously you will need to update your goals continuously. The mildew project will be done by tomorrow, and you can remove it from the list at that time. By the time the carpets are replaced and painting is done, you may have originated some new ideas that pass the tests even better than the tea room you previously planned on, so you rank the new projects as "A" items, and the "B" and "C" items will have to wait a little longer.

In this example, we have only discussed a very small part of the Vision: "creating and maintaining a clean, healthful, and pleasant atmosphere for our clients" and "making a profit from the business". The vision should also include a statement about self-unifying principles, something about quality of life, and certainly there will be other actions to do as well. Each statement from your vision must be detailed and prioritized, as discussed. Then, you need to prioritize between each category as well.

For instance, you have to decide which is a greater priority, the health club and making a profit, or spending quality time with the family. You can make up any categories you want, and the format of your prioritized list doesn't have to match the exact wording from your Vision-just make sure all your ideals are included one way or another. Also keep in mind that you can reprioritize every day, or as much as you need. My family and my career are both very high priorities for me. I strike a balance by making my family a slightly higher priority in the summer and my career a slightly higher priority during winter.

The example shown here is very simplified. As you prioritize your own goals, you may quickly fill up a couple pages or more with all the things you want to do in life. You may be surprised at how many goals you really have! When you put all your Dreams together in one place you will understand the need to establish the priorities, so you can always achieve the most important goals first. Hobbs recommends spending fifteen minutes to a half an hour every morning to review your goals and prepare a plan for the day.

Upon reading Hobbs' book, I immediately recognized the value in the prioritization system, because it is the same kind of process I have used intuitively for many years. Almost daily, I would mentally evaluate my entire

Prioritized Action List

A1. Family: Spend quality time with my family.
    A1. Eat dinners together.
    A2. Play games.
    B1. Read.
    B2. Travel

A2. Health Club: Create a healthful, pleasant atmosphere.
    A1. Clean mildew out of bathrooms.
    A2. New paint and carpets.
    A3. Advertising.
    B1. Tea room.
    B2. New equipment.
    C1. Swimming Pool.

A3. My Health: Take care of my body and mind.
    A1. Eat high-fiber foods.
    A2. Drink lots of water.
    A3. Think good thoughts.
    A4. Relax.
    B1. Walk regularly.

B1. Intellectual: I want to continuously improve myself.
    A1. Learn to play the piano.
    A2. Read lots of books.
    B1. Attend theater performances.
    C1. Learn Russian

personal Vision and brainstorm ways to achieve it. Then I would prioritize the best ideas and define an immediate course of action.

Occasionally I would spend most of a day reconsidering every aspect of my Dreams, especially when I felt like I was not finding success. I would start out on a walk in a mode of self-doubt and introspection, but would quickly solidify my belief in my Vision, and come back with a whirlwind of new ideas to get back on the path to success. With long-range and intermediate goals in mind, I would define an action list every day. Sometimes I would plan out my day as I lay in bed in the morning, but often I would do that at night before falling asleep. Then I knew exactly what to do when I woke up in the morning.

It has been said that you can tell what your priorities are by noticing whatever thought first comes to mind as you awake in the morning. I know this to be true. When you consider your Dreams and establish your priorities, those priorities will always come to mind with the sunrise. If your priority is to listen to the birds, then you will hear them. If your priority is to give a better speech, then you will awake to an audience in your own mind.

Keep in mind that you do not need to force yourself to work, work, work on your goals. Relaxation and fun should always be included in your Vision. Even when you are focused on an "A1" priority work project, you can still take breaks and attend to other personal goals.

The first thoughts you have when you awake tell you a lot about your priorities.

When I sit down at the computer for instance, I usually plan to write an entire chapter, or an entire article in one day. But I take breaks between almost every idea, to get up and stretch, rest my eyes, wash dishes, water the garden, or feed the chickens. I can attend to any little project, then return refreshed to my "A1" project of the day.

Any project will lead to burnout after awhile. I am able to achieve goals in many areas only because I work on one project for a day or two, then switch to a new project that is fresh and exciting. I might chain myself to the computer for one day, but the next I will be out playing with the kids, cutting firewood, or practicing primitive skills. It is possible to work on important goals every day, while almost never doing the same thing two days in a row. You can be excited about your goals every day of your life!

"To my astonishment I was informed on leaving college that I had studied navigation! —Why, if I had taken one turn down the harbor I should have known more about it."

—Henry David Thoreau, Walden

6-2

Learning & Growth

-Empowering Yourself and Others Around You-

America has always been the symbol of democracy in the world. It is the one place where every person is equal to every other person, regardless of beliefs or race or gender. Each of us has the freedom to pursue our hopes and dreams, and everyone's hopes and dreams together are what makes America great. Most of us have a great deal of pride in that. We can look around at the failing autocratic regimes of the world, their faltering economies and wasted environments, and it is evident that democracy, although not flawless, is still a far more successful way to govern. Most of us are proud to be Americans and most of us believe in the democracy that makes America work. The funny thing is that most of our public and private institutions and businesses never adopted democracy at all. Most of our institutions are relics of an autocratic and distant past.

Children have a sort of boundless fascination for life—they absorb information, ask questions, and are exuberant to experience the world. Children can be totally enraptured with even a single flower. They are stimulated, interested, and motivated to discover life.

Unfortunately something happens when they are told that they cannot experience that flower, that they must come right now; they must sit down, be quiet, and do nothing but listen intently. Day after day, year after year, throughout school these commands take a horrible toll on the human spirit. Our institutions of education do not bend to fit the individual, instead they bend the individual to fit the system. They are not democratic, but autocratic. In time it works, and the individual is bent and broken and loses his or her fascination and motivation to learn. They may listen when told, complete the assignments as given, and turn them in as required, but that is a far cry from an education.

People who learn to do just enough to get by in school often graduate into adult life doing the same thing. It is not their fault; that is simply the way our institutions of education train our youth. In school kids learn to follow orders and to do just what they are told. As adults they often do the same thing. They are, on average, more likely to become employees than employers. They may hang out and work a job and merely do that which is required of them to keep their job. Often, the work place is as autocratic as school, where employees are given direct orders and have no autonomy of their own.

A survey at one eastern university found that only three percent of the graduating class of 1953 had written lifetime goals. Twenty years later those three percent made more income between them, than the rest of the class put together[23]. Money may not be the best measure of success, since one can be equally successful without money, but it is a good measure of self-motivation.

Upon reading these figures many people might conclude that it is normal for most people to not have goals, and that for some reason three out of every one hundred people are anomalies. I disagree. A motivated person is the result of a specific formula of ingredients. Anyone can be motivated by following the recipe. More so, I think that everyone starts with the complete recipe for motivation and it is only through the experiences of our autocratic institutions of education that they lose it. Human beings may enter life with curiosity and creativity, but many become thoroughly stifled by the time they reach adulthood. They may lose much of the inspiration and motivation that they had as children. Life does not have to be that way.

It is possible to use the exuberance of a child as a tool for education. It is possible to let the child lead while still integrating the all important lessons of reading, writing, and arithmetic. When the child and the teacher reach an understanding of what has to be learned, then they can decide together how to meet those requirements in the context of something the child already wants to do. In such an environment, when children own their education, they tend to be stimulated and excited, motivated, about learning. The process of owning one's education is democratic, and it is also, coincidentally, the process of goal setting. If a child goes through school working with a teacher to define and agree on specific outcomes and the means to those outcomes, then she will enter adult life with something very valuable indeed. She gains far more when she sets her own outcomes than when those outcomes are set by someone else. The results of such an approach to teaching have been well documented.

In his book *Freedom to Learn for the 80's*[71], author Carl Rogers wrote about scores of trial cases where teachers and students worked together, and he outlined the specific steps that the teachers were using to be successful. The results of these trials were encouraging in all environments, from grade school to high-school, to even the university level. Exhaustive studies were carried out with hundreds of teachers and thousands of students in several countries, and the results showed that students and teachers both benefited by this novel approach to education. Students were typically more creative, more involved, learned more, and missed fewer days of school. That is the way education should be. Kids today are unchallenged in school, and that would change if they took part in setting their own outcomes. Goals, motivation, and achievement are inevitable when the individual charts her own course. To my way of thinking, it should be natural for 100% of graduating students to have some form of lifetime goals. The fact that there are only 3% of students doing that now is a good measure of the success of our current educational institutions.

Rediscovering our natural curiosity, creativity, and motivation can be challenging as adults, but it is a fulfilling challenge. Most of us have been trained all our lives to take orders from teachers, parents, and employers. We are used to having an exterior framework of sorts around us, where we know what to do, when to do it, and who to do it for. Walking away from that exterior structure leaves us facing ourselves. The structure must then come from inside; we have to begin relying directly on ourselves.

There are many ways to reawaken our inner resources. It is a matter of following and believing in our curiosities and our interests; and after all, motivation is simply pursuing that which we are excited about.

I made the decision to do that while in high-school. I knew I had to step forward and take on some challenges if I were ever to become the whole person I wanted to be. I wanted to learn primitive skills, so I signed up for a 26 day expedition with a school called Boulder Outdoor Survival School. That was between my sophomore and junior years in high-school. I was painfully, agonizingly shy, and signing up for the class was the hardest, scariest thing I ever did. It was also one of the most rewarding moves I have ever made in my life. We hiked 250 miles in those 26 days and ate very little, often about a cup of food a day. It was indeed a challenge, although for me, the biggest challenge was just signing up. The day I gathered my inner strength together and signed up was the day I officially committed myself to owning and directing my own life. I successfully committed myself that one time, and then I had something to build on.

Back in school I stopped working for my teachers or grades and I started working for myself. I did all my assignments as required and stayed within the parameters that were set, but I did those assignments for me. I used my school assignments as opportunities to explore my own interests in primitive living skills and in environmental issues. I listened to my heart, and I followed the interests that excited me. That kept me motivated and interested in the assignments, and motivated to continue trusting in and working for myself, and I have been doing that ever since.

Motivation is simply a matter of being excited about what you are doing. Being excited about what you are doing is simply a matter of

Being motivated to make a big leap in life is simply a matter of being excited about what you are doing.

pursuing that which interests you. Thus, the most important key to your success may be that you make a commitment to yourself and to your interests, and that you allow others around you to have the same freedom.

For example, as an employer, it is important that you allow your employees to "own" the business. Instead of having people work for you; you need to give them the opportunity to work for themselves within your business. Instead of being told what to do they need the opportunity to create what to do. They need the freedom to use their creativity and resourcefulness to help the business, and they need to benefit from their input. The value of such an approach to business is well documented.

For instance, a consultant to a large industrial firm was given the okay to conduct a novel experiment[70]. This person had consulted for the company for sometime with great success, so the company allowed him to test his ideas on a broader scale. The consultant trained the employees and the managers at several factories to work together as equals. They learned to trust each other and to work together towards creating and achieving common goals. Instead of supervising, inspecting, and passing judgment on the employee's work, the managers were able to disperse responsibility and decision making, and everyone grew closer together. They achieved democracy in the work place, and the results were quite remarkable.

The experiment was tested in several factories, while several other factories were left unchanged so the company could compare the effectiveness of this novel, democratic approach. The tests showed that the costs of production fell at the factories with this experimental management. At the experimental plants it cost 22¢ per unit of product, and only three to five managers were required to run the operation. In the control plants however, the same product cost 70¢ per unit to produce, and each plant required seventeen to twenty-three managers to oversee operations and "make sure the job was done right". With this experimental democratic approach the company was able to substantially reduce their costs of production, which offers a tremendous advantage against the competition. That is the value of democracy, and it can be measured in dollars and sense; pun intended.

"The freedom for each person to think for him- or herself has been the hallmark of American greatness." wrote author Carl Rogers[79]. America is prosperous because of democracy. Our shortcomings in government, business, and social stability lay not in our use of democracy, but in that we do not use it enough.

"As for the Pyramids, there is nothing to wonder at in them so much as the fact that so many men could be found degraded enough to spend their lives constructing a tomb for some ambitious booby, whom it would have been wiser and manlier to have drowned in the Nile, and then given his body to the dogs."

—*Henry David Thoreau, Walden*

6-3
Financial Planning
-Managing your Money-

Although this is ultimately a book about personal finance, I have not emphasized any stringent savings plans or accounting, and you may have noticed that I have not mentioned the "B" word, "Budgeting". The reason is simple. You eventually spend every calorie you earn, that is, unless you die before you get a chance to. Being financially successful does not mean that you save all your money; it means you spend it effectively. Money by itself has no value; it is only when you spend it that it becomes valuable. The key to financial success is not to save up a mattress full of money, but to spend it on the investments that give you what you truly want in life.

Knowing what you really want in life is therefore the most vital step on your route to success. If you know what you really want then you may find that you have little need for pencil and paper budgeting. There will be little stopping you once you know what it is you want. You will automatically find the resources to make your dream into reality. Dreams and goals are the most important ingredient of success; the strategies listed here are just icing on the cake to make it easier for you to get there from here. I speak from experience; we never had to write a budget to achieve our own goals.

We never had to create a special savings plan, because we wanted our dream so much that we automatically diverted virtually all of our income towards our dream each year and found ways to live happily on what was left over. Our first year was the only time we actually saved money. We saved our wealth until we got married and bought land. After that we simply invested our incomes directly into building materials; we spent it on our dream before we could spend it anywhere else. You may discover a similar experience, where the only time you need to save money is for a short period to build up the financial capital to launch you towards your dreams. There are a couple ways to do this.

For example, let's say you are a two-soda-pop-per-day person, and you decide you want to gain $365 additional capital this year for something special. Thus you give up pop and replace it with water. At a dollar a day this generates $365 in the coming year. However, if you do not set aside that dollar each

Two Paths to Financial Freedom

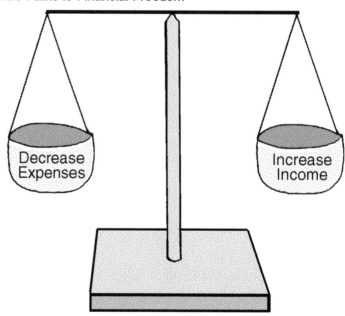

You can increase your wealth by either investing time and money to decrease your expenses, like paying off a mortgage early, or by investing to increase your income, such as by getting a better education to get a better job.

You have to weigh the choices at each moment in time and invest where you feel the greatest return is.

160

day then it will quickly disappear elsewhere and you will not even notice your "profit", nor will you have $365 left over at the end of the year. You can insure that you have your dream fund at the end of the year by putting that dollar in a jar every day. Put your dream on the label, and that jar might fill up faster than you expect. This is a savings strategy that can be useful to gain the financial leverage you need for smaller dreams, such as new toys and so forth.

For bigger dreams, such as a house or a business or a new car then you may want a more aggressive savings strategy to generate a lot of financial capital; you may need to place a finite limit on how much you spend elsewhere. In *Holistic Resource Management*[74] Allan Savory presents an interesting procedure for accounting. It is equally applicable to a home or a business. First of all, determine now much you expect to make this year, that is your **gross income**. Then divide that amount in half. The amount left over is your ceiling, and you plan your budget to meet all your expenses on this amount of money. This discipline insures 50% profitability, so that you actually have something left over at the end of the year. If your income and expenses come on more of a monthly cycle as it does for most people today then it would be wise to plan a general budget in this fashion for the year, then plan some very specific budgets for each month.

Initially the thought of attempting to get by on half of what you are accustomed to may seem entirely impossible. Yet, with pencil and paper, plus a strong desire to achieve your dreams, you may be surprised at how quickly your home or business can become very profitable for you.

For many people and businesses who are heavily in debt, half of their income is not quite enough to cover required expenses, like the mortgage, car payment, and extensive credit card balances, not to mention groceries or anything fun. In this case you may choose to first subtract the required payments from your anticipated income, then divide the remainder in half to cover all other expenses. This will not yield 50% profitability, but in any case, planning for some profitability, even 10%, is better than no profitability.

These strategies can work well for you, especially if you like doing the numbers and paperwork. If you have trouble with that, as we do, then you might try the opposite approach. Instead of making plans to have a certain percentage of your money left over at the end of each month, try putting that percentage away into a special dreams account before you pay any other expenses. The remainder of your budget struggle is no longer pencil and paper work, but day to day resourcefulness through self-imposed necessity. It works.

With the profitability that you do gain, it is always important that this is earmarked for a special purpose, such as by separating it into its own account, or by doubling the amount paid on your mortgage each month. Setting that money aside will insure that your financial capital is really there, and not just a holograph of your imagination and your calculator. Use that money to help you realize all of your dreams.

A traveler met the wise man on the road just outside of town. The traveler said, "I am new in these parts, and I am looking for work. How is the economy here?" The wise man returned, "How was the economy in the town you came from?"

"The economy was in a shambles," the traveler said. "There was no work anywhere, and I had to leave because of it." The wise man said, "Unfortunately, the economy here is in much the same condition." And the traveler passed on his way.

Soon another traveler came along and met the wise man at the edge of town. The traveler said, "I am new in these parts, and I am looking for work. How is the economy here?" The wise man again returned, "How was the economy in the town you came from?"

The traveler replied, "It was in very good shape; there was much work to be found and many opportunities." The wise man then said, "You are fortunate. Our economy is in fine shape and this is certainly the land of golden opportunity."

6-4

The Management Cycle
-Monitoring & Flexibility-

Whether you discover a world of prosperity and abundance or a world of poverty and hardship all depends on you and what you choose to make of your situation.

The path to success begins with an understanding of the ecosystem and the tools for making change. You define a goal for what you want to achieve in the ecosystem then generate ideas to use the tools to accomplish that goal. The ideas are tested for compatibility with all aspects of the goal and for sustainability with the ecosystem. Finally you implement the ideas that pass the testing procedure and monitor to see what happens. It may seem that you have reached the end of the process, but in fact it is just the beginning.

Every action you make causes change in the ecosystem, but even with the best of research it can be difficult to accurately predict the outcome. You have to **monitor** the results of your actions and compare it to what was expected. You have to be **flexible** to adapt to the unexpected. In the end you have a new situation to work with and the cycle begins again.

Some goals have clear ending points, like building a house, when you know you are done and can move on to something else, while other goals are long-term situations, like living in and maintaining the home. The management cycle continues as long as the goal remains in process.

The Holistic Management-Soft Systems

The Holistic Management/Soft Systems Cycle

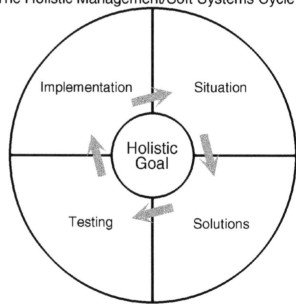

The management cycle revolves around a holistic goal. The existing situation is defined and compared to the goal. Solutions are proposed, then tested against the goal. Any ideas that pass the tests are implemented, creating a new situation to continue the cycle.

-based on Cliff Montagne's *Holistic Thought & Management*

162

Cycle[56] pictured here is a summary of the management cycle, illustrating the four-step process people use to achieve goals. These four steps are 1) defining the situation, 2) generating possible solutions, 3) testing to choose the most practical solutions, and 4) implementing the solutions. Each of us uses this process for minor and major decisions every day throughout our lives, but it helps to be consciously aware of it.

The Holistic Management-Soft Systems Cycle was developed by Cliff Montagne, associate professor of soil science at MSU-Bozeman, by combining principles of holistic management with the circular process first identified in the Myers-Briggs personality inventory for testing how people solve problems. Their model metamorphosed into the "soft systems" process in the book *Systems Approaches for Improvements in Agriculture and Resource Management* by Wilson and Morren, before Montagne added holistic goal at the center. The **situation** is the who and what that are being managed to achieve a goal. You describe the people and the resources that are being managed, plus the community and ecosystem that supports your endeavors. The situation should also include a problem statement indicating the obstacles between you and your goal.

Next you brainstorm possible **solutions** to resolve the problem, by more clearly defining your goals, plus tools, actions, and even paradigms or new ways of thinking. Then you **test** the solutions for compatibility and sustainability with your goals and the ecosystem using the testing guidelines outlined in this book. Ideas that pass these tests are **implemented** in a holistic way, encouraging learning and growth, time management, monitoring and flexibility. Ultimately you reevaluate your situation and run through the cycle again.

This decision making process works whether you are making decisions for a household, a business or an international problem like global climate change. To get a better sense of the whole process in action, lets examine this problem of climate change, which is of serious concern to us all. Please keep in mind that this is a very complex situation and it is possible to come up with right answers that are different than what is shown here.

Situation

Problem Statement: The stability of the climate is threatened by greenhouse gas emissions, especially carbon dioxide released from fossil fuels and deforestation. The ecosystem naturally recycles an estimated 225 billion tons of carbon dioxide each year from processes like respiration, decay, and fires. Most of the carbon is removed from the atmosphere by forests and by microorganisms in the oceans. Human activity has tipped the balance by adding 5.5 billion tons of carbon dioxide to the air each year from fossil fuel use. Deforestation contributes another 2.2 billion tons of carbon a year to the atmosphere while simultaneously reducing the total amount of forests available to remove carbon[22]. Although the amount of carbon dioxide we add to the atmosphere seems small by comparison to the amount recycled by nature every year, we are nevertheless greatly increasing the proportion of carbon dioxide in the atmosphere.

Excluding water vapor, the atmosphere consists of 78% nitrogen, 21% oxygen and 0.9% argon. Other traces gasses, mostly carbon dioxide, make up an additional .039% of the atmosphere, up from 0.028% prior to industrialization[39]. Two-atom molecules like nitrogen and oxygen vibrate at high frequencies, so they do not absorb much of the heat that normally reflects of the earth and bounces back into space. But 3-atom molecules like carbon dioxide, water vapor, nitrous oxide and sulfur dioxide all absorb heat and reflect it back down on the earth, trapping heat in like a window, hence the term "greenhouse effect". Carbon dioxide and other trace gasses may be a very small part of the atmosphere, but they keep the earth's surface about 59° warmer than it would be without these gasses, so even a small increase in the amount of greenhouse gasses can have a big effect on the climate.

While it is virtually certain that altering the atmosphere will alter the earth's climate and weather patterns, it is difficult to predict how it will change. Global warming is the most likely scenario, and already we have melted 4.3 feet of the polar ice caps over the last several decades. Global warming could flood coastal cities, increase the frequency of hurricanes and other weather-related disasters and transform crucial croplands into deserts. Paradoxically, global warming also increases atmospheric humidity, which can increase precipitation and potentially trigger an ice age[27]. Rather than wait to find out what happens, we would likely be wise to alter human behaviors to stop the buildup of greenhouse gasses.

Define the Whole Under Management: The whole under management includes the global ecosystem and the global economic system, including all businesses, all people and all cultures. The management team includes policy makers, professors, scientists and citizens groups.

Solutions

Hypothetical Goal Stated In Positive Terms: The goal of the management team is to help all people in the world attain a satisfying quality of life, including political and religious freedom, free speech, and an equal opportunity for people everywhere to produce an income and attain economic prosperity. Long-term healthy functioning of the natural and economic ecosystems is required to sustain people's quality of life and production activities.

Brainstorm Possible Solutions for the Stated Problem: Each of the following proposals is included in the illustrated chart, "Testing possible solutions for global climate change."

-From graduate students at the Illinois Institute of Technology[22]: 1) Build Chicago-sized solar panels in space from minerals mined on the moon. Beam the energy down in focused microwave beams to receivers on earth to replace fossil fuel use. 2) 3.3 million square miles of the once forested earth is now barren. Massive plastic domes could be used and gradually rotated over 1.9 million square miles to moderate local climates while tree seedlings are established, effectively absorbing 1.1 billion tons of carbon per year. 3) Vast areas of the deep ocean are relatively empty of nutrients or life. Simple floating islands can be built of net like material and strengthened by the interlocking root systems, detritus, and communities of attached oyster clumps or sea kelp to cover 386,000 square miles of open ocean. Propeller pumps would bring up nutrients from the ocean floor. The project would absorb 0.6 billion tons of carbon annually while providing new habitat for fish and shellfish displaced from coastal wetlands.

-From Moshe Alamaro, graduate student at the Massachusetts Institute of Technology[83]: Bomb the planet with tree seedlings grown in aerodynamic, biodegradable cones. The cones would be dropped by the thousands over deforested areas, planted into the ground by the force upon impact .

-From the National Academy of Sciences[18]: 1) Erect a 100 kilometer shade of lightweight material between the sun and earth to reduce the incoming solar radiation. 2) Increase cloud cover to reflect incoming sunlight back into space. Power plants burning sulfur-rich coal cause acid rain on land, but sulfur emissions from decaying algae at sea provide the microscopic nuclei necessary for cloud condensation. Transporting sulfur-rich coal to power plants at sea would provide more sulfur to make more clouds to reflect more light.

-From John Martin of the Moss Landing Marine Laboratory in California[12]: Add iron dust to the polar oceans to stimulate electron transfer so that microorganisms can better use existing nutrients to metabolize and pull carbon dioxide out of the atmosphere.

-From Gregory Benford, science fiction author and Professor of Physics at the University of California at Irvine[12]: 1) Use naval guns to blast dust into the upper atmosphere to reflect sunlight back into space. 2) Adjust the fuel mix in jet airlines to burn rich, so that passing airplanes leave a ribbon of fog as they travel. The fog spreads out and becomes invisible before falling to the ground harmlessly in rainwater after about three months. $10 million in extra jet fuel would theoretically reflect enough incoming sunlight to offset U.S. greenhouse emissions.

-From Rocky Mountain Institute[39] and others (including some of the above): Implement a worldwide system of carbon credits where governments and industry can weigh the cost of emitting carbon dioxide into the atmosphere versus the cost of measures to reduce emissions or sequester their impacts, including energy conservation, reforestation, alternative fuels, and pumping carbon dioxide into gas beds to dispose of it while forcing the natural gas out. Even without carbon credits half of all greenhouse gas emissions could be eliminated at a profit. 2) Implement "green taxes" to penalize fossil fuel use (while reducing other taxes), so that clean alternatives are more attractive.

Testing

Weak Link: Is climate change the weakest link in the overall goal to help all people in the world attain a satisfying quality of life and economic prosperity? Possibly, since climate change threatens worldwide agriculture, coastal cities and may increase natural disasters. Which proposal best addresses the weakest link in attaining the goal? Based on the information available, the carbon credits proposal seems like the best solution because it encourages energy conservation and tree planting which saves money and subsequently addresses the true goal of increasing prosperity and helping to increase quality of life. The second best answer might be the carbon tax, because it also encourages energy conservation , reduces paperwork (see chapter 7-2) and gives people the opportunity to pay less taxes through more efficient resource use. The other answers can still be tested as the next weakest links after these first ideas are implemented.

Testing possible solutions for global climate change.

Proposal	Weak Link	Root Cause	Predicted Effect	Neighbors & Culture	Energy/Wealth Source & Use	Marginal Reaction
carbon tax		cause economic incentive	reduced impact	might not be popular	reduces resource use	
carbon credits	X	cause economic incentive	reduced impact	gaining industry support	reduces resource use	
rich jet fuel		symptom excess heat	similar to volcanos	illogical-hard sell	increases resource use	$0
dust bombs		symptom excess heat	similar to volcanos	illogical-hard sell	increases resource use	$0
iron dust in ocean		symptom carbon removal	unknown	unknown	increases resource use	$0
increase clouds		symptom excess heat	unknown	illogical-hard sell	must transport coal	
solar shade		symptom excess heat	unknown	alters day sky	some resource use	$0
tree bombs		cause deforestation	local climate change	no conflict	moderate resource use	
forest domes		cause deforestation	local climate change	unknown	increases resource use	
floating islands		symptom carbon removal	unknown	unknown	increases resource use	
solar satelites		cause CO2 fuels	reduced impact	alters night sky	mostly off-world resources	new income / new expenses

Marginal Reaction: Which option generates the most additional wealth with the least additional expenses?

76.38 $4 / gal.

CO_2 ? ⟷ $

Root Cause: Does the proposal resolve the cause of the problem or merely treat the symptoms? Some of these proposals only deal with the symptoms of global warming. Several proposals invite continued carbon emissions and hope to compensate for it by reflecting excess heat or by finding new ways to remove the carbon that is generated. The ideas that address the causes of global warming in the ecosystem include various reforestation techniques and solar satellites in space to replace fossil fuel use. But keep in mind that fossil fuel use and deforestation in the natural ecosystem are ultimately the result of incentives in the economic ecosystem to abuse the natural world. Only two proposals truly get to the root cause of climate change in the economic ecosystem, and these are the carbon credits and carbon tax.

Predicted Effects: What other effects might the proposal have throughout the natural and economic ecosystem? The true effects on the natural ecosystem for several of the proposals are unknown, while we can reasonably guess the impacts from other proposals.

Neighbors & Culture: How will this proposal be accepted by the human community? Some of the possible solutions would visibly alter the sky, potentially offending many people. Other ideas might be technically sound, but they defy common sense, like burning more jet fuel to offset the impacts of burning jet fuel, or purposely polluting the ocean sky with sulfur-rich fossil fuel emissions to offset the emissions of burning fossil fuels. It would be difficult to build public support for these kinds of ideas.

Energy/Wealth Source & Use: Does the proposal make optimal use of the earth's natural resources and energy? Most of the proposals actually increase resource use and fossil fuel consumption in the effort to reduce the impacts of fossil fuel use. Only a few of the possible solutions genuinely reduce resource use or restore natural resources in the environment.

Marginal Reaction: Which proposal will generate the most additional income from the least additional expenses? Some of the possible solutions would cost relatively little, but don't bring any return on the investment. Some, like the solar satellites would be very expensive in the present time, but would eventually provide some revenue in return. That option may be more economical in the future. Only the carbon credits and carbon tax would actually increase wealth by encouraging more efficient resource use.

Implementation

Once a plan has been selected then the process of implementation begins, including **planning** to prioritize your action list, **learning & growth** for all who are involved, **financial planning**, careful **monitoring** to see what happens plus **flexibility** to change if needed.

Assuming a worldwide agreement can be reached on carbon credits, then the effectiveness of the program would need to be monitored from day one. If there are unforeseen incentives that harm people or the environment, then those incentives need to be changed. If the carbon credits system is causing economic problems, then those concerns may need to be addressed. If, after a year or so, the carbon credits program doesn't seem to be reducing carbon emissions then the program may need to be modified or possibly replaced or supplemented by some of the other available proposals. In other words, you made a change in the ecosystem and something happened, so now you have a new situation, and the process starts over. The management cycle continues as long as the goal remains in process. By using this kind of process you can make better decisions in everything you do, from managing a household to running a business.

Part VII
Tilting Succession in the Ecosystem

"When the infant lies silently and motionless in his crib upon awakening, mother remains in some other room. The 'tax rate' on mother is zero, yielding zero attentiveness. On the other hand, when baby screams all the time demanding attention, even when fed and dry, he discovers that mother also remains in the other room and perhaps even closes the nursery door. The tax rate is 100 percent, also yielding zero attentiveness. The infant gradually learns that by making some sound instead of remaining motionless he gets a measure of attentiveness and, at the other end of the scale, also gets a measure of attentiveness if he makes less sound. What a complex, perplexing problem confronting the infant. A steady increase in the rate of taxation seems to elicit a steady increase in the amount of revenue, or attentiveness, until a point is reached at which a further increase in the rate of taxation is followed by a decline in revenue."

—*Jude Wanniski, The Way the World Works*[81]

7-1

Economic Stability
-A Game of Musical Chairs-

The bulk of this book has been geared towards individuals, families and businesses for acheiving prosperity and happiness essentially through the process of closing the loop on wasted materials, energy, money, and time. This has been a private sector approach to making change in the world by introducing more efficient resource use to reshuffle economic niches, ultimately forcing wasteful competitors to follow suit. In this final section of the book we switch from the private sector to the public sector and the ways that we can collectively tilt succession by manipulating the rules of economic habitat in favor of cleaner, greener products and services.

Some examples of habitat manipulation were covered in chapter 2-4 Succession, such as implementing a system of pollution credits to create economic incentives for companies to pollute less. Another example was Rocky Mountain Institute's introduction of ultralight high mileage cars into the market place by playing different automakers off of each other until each felt as if they had to invest in the technology to keep up with the competition. Through these next few chapters we will explore additional ways we can use public policy to tilt the economic ecosystem in favor of a better world.

It is important to understand that every single piece of legislation passed has some kind of economic consequences, good or bad, and often very different from what is ultimately desirable. For example, the Rural Electric Administration in the 1950's subsidized power lines to rural parts of the country, creating additional habitat for fossil fuel use, while wiping out habitat for the emerging wind power market. The cost of wind power was falling as farms and ranches invested in the technology, but the market died when the REA subsidized the competition. Eliminating or reversing these kinds of subsidies alters economic niches, tilting the balance in favor of a new mix of products and services. In short, public policy causes changes in the economic ecosystem regardless of whether or not that is the intention. In the past public policy has been implemented essentially unconsciously of the broader implications of cause and effect in the ecosystem. The goal of the REA was to bring power to rural Americans, not specifically to kill research and development into wind power or to make a bigger market for fossil fuels. But what would happen if all our public policies were consciulsy designed like the EPA's new pollution credits with the intent to shift habitat in the marketplace? Before we can answer that we must first take a closer look at the concept of stability in the marketplace and how policy can effect it.

As you will see through this chapter there are several factors already in use that effect the overall stability of the markets, including 1) the availability of credit, 2) tax rates, including barriers to free trade, and 3) technological innovation.

The Availability of Credit

In chapter 3-7 Credit, I described the Grameen Bank, which has successfully offered loans to the poorest of the poor to give them a chance to break the cycle of poverty and build better lives for themselves. Without credit it is almost impossible to start down the path to change. The same is true in an industrial economy as well.

The economy is like a game of musical chairs where the players are the butcher, the baker, and the candlestick maker (plus a few others). In a good economy everyone repeatedly stands up and moves to the next chair, or more accurately, stands up and passes their goods along to the next chair, while receiving other goods that come around the circle. In a stagnant economy the cycle falters and the flow of goods and services slows to a trickle. The baker may want to buy a candlestick, but first he needs to sell his bread to get the money to spend. The candlestick maker may be in the same situation. She wants to buy meat from the butcher, but first she must sell her candles. The butcher may want bread, but first he must sell his meat. All the potential is there, but each person is stuck waiting for every other person to move. Examined in this context, a recession or depression seems sadly comical!

The problem is compounded by the fact that the butcher, the baker, and the candlestick maker may all want to borrow funds to expand the size of their businesses, but there is no way to expand a business when sales are not happening. Economists and politicians wrestle continuously with this game of musical chairs—how do you keep this game flowing so that everyone can get what they want?

In any economy, rich or poor, one of the keys to maintaining economic momentum is the availability of credit. In a very simple economy a loan of $100 or less is all it takes to start a new and sustainable enterprise. A developed economy virtually demands increased production and greater overhead, so $100 probably won't even pay for a telephone hook up.

Banks are the traditional source of credit, where individuals and businesses go to beg to borrow money. Unlike the Grameen Bank, most modern banks require some form of collateral to get a loan, or at least proof that you can already afford to make all the loan payments. It is much more difficult to get a loan on the speculation that your investment idea will succeed and generate the money you do not yet have to make those payments. Banks facilitate trade by making loans, but they also hinder trade by loaning only to those who have proved they don't need it.

Paradoxically, credit card companies (banks) will loan money to absolutely anyone for absolutely anything. The role that credit cards play in keeping goods and services flowing through the economic ecosystem cannot be dismissed. For example, the butcher, the baker, and the candlestick maker can all make their purchases on credit. If they've done good work, then it is just a matter of time before someone walks in the store and makes a purchase, so they can go ahead and spend the profit in advance. Granted, credit cards are badly miss-used by those who make consumer purchases without first doing the work that will eventually pay off those bills, but the stabilizing effect on the economy cannot be dismissed.

Even more crucial is the tens of thousands of small businesses that use credit cards in a positive ways to make investment decisions without the need for approval from a bank. For example, you would not be reading this book without the aid of credit cards, which enable us to print, store, and eventually sell thousands of copies at our discretion. You may hear that consumer credit card debt has risen to record high levels, but much of that "consumer debt" is the investment debt of small businesses like ours who rely on plastic for easy access to credit. Credit cards reduce the barriers to free trade so that anyone with a good idea can run with it, without getting approval from a bank.

Otherwise, the main source of credit to keep the economy flowing is the Federal Reserve. The Fed literally prints money and loans it to banks. Banks loan the money to businesses wanting to expand or to individuals hoping to buy a new house or car. The money is used to purchase calories of labor and materials to cover the investment. The money is not real, but the calories are. By printing new money the Federal Reserve effectively dilutes the money supply, devaluing existing dollars, even as you hold them in your hand.

The danger in printing all this new money is that it can lead to inflation. If we start with an economy of ten loaves of bread and ten dollars, then each loaf of bread is worth a dollar. If we print twice as much money so that there are twenty dollars representing ten loaves of bread, then each loaf is worth two dollars. The key to balance is to invest the money in greater production.

If the economy expands to produce twenty loaves of bread, then each loaf of bread is again worth one dollar. The money supply thus expands without causing inflation. The job of the Federal Reserve is to pick an interest rate that will encourage businesses to borrow money and expand without over-inflating the money supply.

Inflation creates uncertainty over the cost of goods and services, devalues wages, and leads to insecurity in the marketplace. The game of musical chairs grinds to a halt, so that everyone still wants something, but nobody is willing to make the first move. In regulating the prime interest rate, the Federal Reserve walks a very tight line between spectacular success and dismal failure. The stock market and our entire economy rides up or down on every whisper about the potential rise or fall of interest rates. Fortunately there are many other variables besides the prime interest rate that influence the health of the economy.

Tax Rates and Barriers to Free Trade

If the economy were like a machine, then it would be relatively easy to keep it running smoothly, just like fixing a car. There is a mostly linear relationship between the apparent symptoms (i.e.: the engine won't turn over) and the underlying cause (the battery is dead). At worst you may have to trace the linear problem back a little farther (i.e.: the battery is dead because the alternator is not recharging it). But cause and effect are inherently non-linear in an ecosystem, so it is much more difficult to predict the outcome of any given action.

For example, if insects consuming a farm crop are the problem, then pesticides to kill them would seem like the logical and linear answer. But the pesticides can directly or indirectly kill the predators that otherwise attacked the offending insects, further compounding the problem. Use of synthetic pesticides started in the U.S. around 1948, when about 7% of farm crops were lost to insect damage . Today agribusiness pours nearly a billion pounds of pesticides on our farm lands every year, yet the loss to insects has risen to 13%. Meanwhile, the diversity of soil microbes, insects, amphibians, reptiles, birds and small mammals has plummeted and nearly every state in the nation has contaminated aquifers where people can no longer drink the ground water.

For many years the people of Indonesia followed a similar path. The government heavily subsidized pesticide use to stimulate economic growth until the land and people were thoroughly poisoned by DDT and other extremely hazardous pesticides. In 1986 the government changed course and banned the worst pesticides and began a policy of integrated pest management. Integrated pest management uses a mix of tools to prevent or control pest damage, such as planting diverse crops, encouraging healthier plants and soil, releasing predatory insects or birds, plus carefully targeted pesticide applications. The subsidies were completely removed by 1989 and domestic pesticide production plummeted to nearly zero, while pesticide imports dropped by two-thirds. Meanwhile, rice production actually rose by 11% during the period from 1986 to 1990[39].

Tinkering with the economic ecosystem can have similarly unexpected, non-linear consequences , for example, that increasing tax rates can lead to fewer tax revenues, or decreasing tax rates can lead to greater tax revenues. Every single piece of legislation passed has some kind of economic consequences, which can be far different from what is expected.

History books record that the Depression of the 1930's was caused by "over-speculation" in the 1920's. People gambled too much on new businesses until the market "corrected itself" by crashing. President Franklin D. Roosevelt is usually credited with bringing the country out of the Depression with his social programs. His administration initiated the system of transfer payments, with programs like Social Security, Welfare, and Medicaid, that have become the government's number one business today. However, there is strong evidence to indicate that the Depression was not caused by over-speculation, and that Roosevelt did not help get the economy going again, but may have even slowed its natural rate of recovery.

In his book *The Way the World Works*[81] Author Jude Wanniski points out that the tax rates in this country were dropped little-by-little throughout the 1920's, leading to ever greater tax revenues. Tax rates were previously high, due to World War I, but President Warren Harding's Treasury Secretary, Andrew Mellon, convinced Congress to lower tax rates repeatedly in the 20's. Each time taxes were lowered the federal government actually took in more tax revenue. The government was taking a smaller percentage of each person's income, but business was stimulated by the lower tax rates to increase production and hire more employees that the lower tax rates ultimately brought in greater revenues.

The real probable cause of the Crash of '29 and the subsequent Depression was not over-enthusiasm, but a new tax. Author Wanniski argues that the market is never wrong, and never has to "correct itself". He considers the stock market the "collective consciousness" of the business community. Millions of people make economic choices through the stock market every day. No single person may know what specifically it is that makes the market good or bad for them, but every person knows when they are wasting their time. Wanniski points to evidence that the

Depression was caused by the passage of one tax bill.

This bill, called the Smoot-Halley Tariff Act of 1930, was a tax on agricultural and commodity imports into this country, designed with the intent to protect prices for American farmers and industries. But any kind of tariff becomes a barrier to free trade. The bill was passed by Congress and signed into law by President Hoover. Development and passage of the bill took several years. Each time the news reported that the bill was progressing towards passage, the stock market responded with a drop. Every time it seemed that the bill might be abandoned, the stock market responded with gains. When passage of the bill became inevitable, the stock market—and our entire economy—crashed. The tariff was finalized and passed during the following year. Other countries immediately responded with steep tariffs on American products, making American products prohibitively expensive all around the world. No one consciously connected the tariff bill with the Depression at the time, but the day-by-day newspaper coverage of the ups-and-downs of the impending legislation correlate with the downs-and-ups of the stock market. Despite the good intentions, this one simple piece of legislation seems to have triggered the start of the Depression.

The Depression may have been triggered by the Smoot-Halley Tariff Act.

The Depression became permanent when Hoover passed another piece of legislation raising domestic income tax rates. Tax revenues to the federal government crashed when the economy crashed, and the government ran a budget deficit. Hoover raised taxes to make up for the deficit, and thus put forth another serious obstacle to the business world. The Depression was here to stay.

President Roosevelt brought the country out of the Depression through his New Deal policies. He set into motion the multi-multi-billion dollar "entitlements" programs we have today as social security and welfare, etc. Roosevelt's policies created a sort of circulatory pump that keeps the game of musical chairs moving by taking money from those who have it and giving it to those who do not. It is arguable that the economy would have recovered and once again greatly flourished by simply removing Hoover's tax bills.

I am not suggesting that Roosevelt's policies were wrong. In the long run it was probably a good thing to set up the entitlements programs to give greater stability to the economy. As long as the government transfers money from those who have it to those who don't, then the game of musical chairs keeps moving, even if slowly. The need for these kind of transfer payments will only increase in the decades to come, due to automation and the increasing disparity between those that have wealth and those that don't.

But the important point to understand here is that lower taxes and fewer barriers to free trade helps to stimulate the circulation of goods and services through the economic ecosystem. Consider the effects of free trade between the U.S. and Mexico and China.

The North American Free Trade Agreement (NAFTA) gave U.S. companies easy access to cheap labor in Mexico so they could manufacture goods at a lower cost than at home. In the first five years after NAFTA became effective, U.S. companies moved in and hired more than 600,000 employees[54].

The upside to free trade is that all those new employees are able to earn several times as much income as they could in the old economy. Doing business with the U.S. channels massive amounts of money into the economy of northern Mexico, enabling people to take the initial steps to break the cycle of poverty. At first the goods are almost exclusively shipped back across the border to U.S. markets, but the influx of income also creates new markets for goods in Mexico. A similar phenomenon happened in our southern states, starting in the early 1960's.

Big factories moved in from the north to take advantage of cheap labor in that impoverished region of the country. Industry and consumers saved money on the cost of goods, and the new income broke the cycle of poverty in the south, making southerners as well off as the rest of the country in a single generation.

Today small towns in Mexico are quickly being transformed into bustling cities with malls, multiplexes, subdivisions and tract houses. Mexicans who once tried to sneak across the border to find work in the states are instead locating in northern Mexico to find jobs in the new economy.

In China the influx of money has allowed people in that country to start their own industries. Businesses that once contracted to build electronics like VCR's for foreign companies are now producing their own brand names, selling DVD players and other hi-tech goods on the global marketplace, but keeping all of the profits.

The downside to free trade is that there are a lot of abuses along the road to riches. Employees who double, triple, or quadruple their wages may only be making $50 or less a week in the new economy. Part of the reason we live so well in the industrialized world is because there are hundreds of millions of people around the world manufacturing goods for us at virtually slave wages. Slavery is alive and well, sanctioned by governments and the World Trade Organization. In China there are dormitories where employees pay rent for bunkbeds in shared rooms with dozens of other workers. They earn enough money at work to pay for their food and their bed, but little else. At its worst, in places like Pakistan there are still children being forced to sew soccer balls and other products for U.S. markets for just enough food to keep them alive. Their slave masters reap the benefits of their work.

The other downside to free-trade is that impoverished countries usually have few environmental laws, so there is a real cost in poor development plans, toxic waste dumps, polluted waters, and poisoned people. People who object to free trade and the efforts of the World Trade Organization argue that free trade should be coupled with social and environmental rules and ethics, and I agree. It should be possible to have "free trade" without poisoning the people and the places where goods are manufactured.

There is one other effect of free trade, both good and bad, which must be mentioned. Eliminating the barriers to trade tweaks the niches in the economic ecosystem, creating jobs in some places while eliminating them in others. Free trade exports manufacturing jobs to places with cheap labor while typically retaining and increasing the number of high-paying information-related jobs at home. Basically, people in the more advanced economy are paid to think up the designs that are manufactured by cheap labor elsewhere. That translates to higher paying jobs and cheaper goods at the same time. The only trouble with this aspect of free trade is that it requires more specialized knowledge, which some people in our society neither have nor want. It is for this reason that the entitlements and public works programs started by President Roosevelt are so important in the current and future economy.

Author Wanniski is correct that reducing taxes and other barriers to free trade does stimulate business to expand and hire more employees, but it is a different world now than in the 1930's. Most work at that time was manual labor, and just about any person could be brought in off the street and easily trained to do useful work. Now we have information related jobs that require specialized training and creative innovation. When a business expands today they hire people for what they know, not for their muscle mass.

The result is that more and more people are getting left out of the changing economy. There are hundreds of thousands, maybe millions of people in our country who have neither the skills nor the desire to participate in the global economy. Part of my purpose for writing this book was to show those individuals that they can still build a prosperous and fulfilling life, much as we did, without ever getting trapped in the rat race of global economics. I also want to point out that nobody should be forced to participate in the global marketplace. There are many people who have no desire for a Ph.D or a high-tech job. They would find life much more satisfying doing hand labor like trail construction and other public works projects. Our society needs to create meaningful job opportunities to respect the rights of these individuals who would rather earn a living with their hands than with technology. As we progress towards the automated economy these manual jobs will become increasingly important to keep all members of our society involved in this game of musical chairs.

Technological Innovation

The third factor in maintaining the flow of goods and services through the economy is technological innovation. Technological innovation causes restructuring of the available niches within the economic ecosystem.

When you invent a new and useful product or service, you create a new economic niche. For example, by introducing the technology to scan and bill for an entire cart full of groceries without the need for a cashier, you enable grocery stores to reduce the cost of goods to their customers, while also eliminating the customer's inconvenience of waiting in line. The technology creates a new niche manufacturing, selling, and servicing the equipment, while grocery stores are virtually forced to invest in the technology to stay competitive. As long as the technology keeps evolving, then businesses must continue reinvesting to stay competitive. Thus technological innovation helps to drive the game of musical chairs, so the economy doesn't stagnate—even in the face of negative economic factors like high taxes.   I suspect that the booming economy of the 1990's was driven at least as much by technological innovation as it was by free trade agreements like NAFTA.

Continued technological innovation promises to keep the economy booming in the years ahead. With the aid of high-tech equipment it is easier than ever before to innovate and market useful new products and services. Anyone with a good idea can quickly turn it into a million dollars or more, much more. It is so easy to create new wealth that even high taxes have little negative effect on the market.

Further automation promises to multiply individual and corporate wealth far more than now, and it will accelerate the shift in economic niches. It will be a very different world when one person can feed ten thousand or build a house in a day's work, but that time is coming quickly. As with every increase in production capability, it means that fewer people will be employed producing survival essentials and more people will be paid to do something else.

In summary, a booming economy is driven by easy access to credit, reasonable taxes and few barriers to free trade, plus technological innovation. But there is one more point that should be mentioned here, and that is that a complex economic ecosystem is inherently more stable and recession-resistant than a simple one. Of course the same is true of the natural ecosystem.

A healthy ecosystem has many checks and balances for stability. One native field may have hundreds of species of plants, plus hundreds of species of insects, birds, and other animals.   The population of each species will fluctuate from year to year according to the climatic conditions, but overall there is tremendous stability and rarely if ever any serious out-breaks of disease or insect infestation. For example, no single species of insect can get too far out of hand because there are several kinds of birds to prey on it, and more importantly there are complex relationships between the plants, insects, and fungi to minimize the available habitat for any single insect species.

Plowing that field to plant hundreds of acres of a single crop disables the checks and balances, creating a massive open niche for a few species of insects, weeds or disease to invade, subsequently ruining the entire crop if it is not bombed with pesticides to maintain control.

The economic ecosystem is likewise more stable if it is highly complex and diverse. As anyone from a town dependent on a single industry like logging, mining or steel milling can attest, it is really the pits when economic niches shift, instantly collapsing the economy of the entire community. A place with a diverse and complex economy is inherently more stable to the ups and downs of any one industry. This principle of diversity is as true on the national and global level as it is at the local level.

Free trade helps to stabilize the world economy by uniting separate cultures into a global community. The web of links across the globe keeps the game of musical chairs moving for everyone involved. But more importantly, it helps to prevent war.

War is a largely antiquated notion in the emerging global economy. When we all depend on each other for goods and services, then attacking one another would be like attacking ourselves. In fact, one of the motivations behind the Euro, the united European currency, is to help tie the particpating countries together to prevent future wars. The more that we all depend on each other and communicate with each other via e-mail and teleconferencing, the less likely we are to throw bombs at each other. That's pretty important when we have the technology on hand to completely destroy the planet.

"The twelve labors of Hercules were trifling in comparison with those which my neighbors have undertaken; for they were only twelve, and had an end; but I could never see that these men slew or captured any monster or finished any labor."

—*Henry David Thoreau, Walden*

7-2

Taxation
-A Tool For Change-

The concept of taxation is pretty simple in terms of calories. Basically, we all harvest our own calories, then we give a share of those calories over to the individuals who we have hired for public service. I think nearly every person recognizes the need for taxes, they bring us a lot of good, including such things as schools, highways, and vaccination programs. The issue is not if to tax, but how much to tax and how to go about levying the taxes.

It is sometimes erroneously assumed that taxes will stimulate people to work harder. It is thought that if you take a portion of a person's earnings, then they will just work more to make up for the loss. But people are not stupid. A businessman may not realize that up to a third of the money he takes in is his own money that he paid in taxes, but any halfway successful business person knows when they are wasting their time. Like the stone-age cultures where people only worked a few hours per day, there comes a point when any person will choose to have more leisure time, rather than work for more money.

Americans today typically pay out one-third of their annual incomes as taxes. For perspective, just imagine a hunter-gatherer society paying out that much of their harvested calories as a tax. Hunter-gatherer peoples harvested only two or three calories of food energy for each calorie of energy they expended. Initially they may have a choice of hundreds of plants and animals that are edible. Of those plants and animals, all have different caloric values, and all require varying amounts of caloric effort to harvest them. That means that some plants and animals will provide an abundance of calories for the work provided, while others will provide a survivable return, and some will not provide enough calories to cover the cost of harvesting them at all. Levying a one-third tax on all the harvested calories changes that picture significantly. Many of the plants and animals that formerly provided a meager, but survivable income of calories would now be pushed into the category of those that do not recover their costs at all. And many, perhaps all, of the resources that formerly provided an abundance of calories, would now only provide a survivable return. A one-third tax would severely limit the options of a hunter-gatherer society and could potentially cause their extinction.

A one-third tax has a similar effect on modern businesses, but we perceive it differently. Instead of a vegetable plant becoming uneconomical, we have industrial plants that become uneconomical, and people lose their jobs.

Taxes always have a negative effect on the economy, yet we know we still need to levy them. Regardless of the harm taxation itself causes, we still all benefit from at least some of the ways tax dollars are spent. Surely we could do well with fewer taxes, but we certainly cannot completely do away with them. The best tax structure would be one that helped us two ways, instead of just one way. For a tax to work well it should help us both when we pay it and when the government spends it.

There are some simple ways to achieve win-win taxation. Before we touch on that, though, let me first give you an understanding of the shortcomings of conventional methods of taxation, including sales taxes, income taxes, and property taxes.

175

First, consider the **sales tax** in terms of calories. The sales tax, in addition to being incredibly annoying, is also a highly inefficient means of taxation. In a Montana special election, proponents of the sales tax claimed it would net about $40 million in revenues from out-of-state sources, largely through tourism. Opponents counter-claimed that the bureaucracy to levy the sales tax would cost $40 million. Now, $40 million is a lot of money, regardless of the source. That amount of money could hire 1,600 new teachers at a salary of $25,000 a year. Instead that much money would have been lost through the tax collection system. Instead of producing any wealth, that $40 million would have been lost each year in paperwork. The only good aspect of a general sales tax is that it is relatively objective, rather than subjective. A sales tax consistently takes "x" number of cents per dollar of sale, so there is no subjectiveness employed to determine how much to fork over. Fortunately, the proposed sales tax for Montana was voted down in 1993 by an overwhelming 75% to 25%, but it still cost state tax payers several million dollars to fund both a special session of the legislature and a special election to vote on the proposal. The primary focus of the legislature whenever it convenes is taxation. We would be rich if we had all the money back that has been wasted debating tax issues!

An **income tax** is subjective. To pay it you have to first decide how much you earn, which can be a little tricky to figure, especially if your income comes in as a dollar here and a dollar there, from a multiple number of sources. Then you have to deduct your expenses, especially if you are in business, where much of your income is not actually income at all. You have to decide what are truly business expenses and what are not, which can be a matter for speculation. Indeed, I once heard of a study that was done where fifty IRS agents were given an identical tax problem and asked to figure the best return for the hypothetical person filing the taxes. The IRS came up with fifty different answers! The subjectiveness of the income tax system makes it very expensive to administer.

Filing income taxes requires vast inputs of time and natural resources like paper, ink and electricity. Major corporations like H&R Block are dedicated to this project of doing paperwork, yet for all that work, no real wealth is produced. When the tax forms are finally filled out, they are sent to the state and federal agencies who go through each of the forms and try to determine whether or not each return was filled out honestly. That requires a lot of people who consume resources, but produce none. Just imagine what our country might be like if all that human potential went towards constructive work!

Interestingly, when our country was first founded it was supported by taxes on imports and taxes on alcohol and tobacco. We did not have any personal income taxes until 1918 when Congress ratified the 16th Amendment to the Constitution that allowed Washington to levy such taxes. The first taxes affected just the wealthiest Americans, but it didn't take long for Congress to include everyone[72]. Today our income tax laws consist of thousands of pages, and these are rewritten at almost every legislative session, at a cost to us of many millions of dollars.

Like income taxes, property taxes are also subjective. To levy them someone must first go around to decide what each piece of property is worth, give or take a few thousand dollars; then they must reassess the properties every few years. It is a queer system where property owners are penalized for fixing up their property. As a homeowner you can be financially better off by letting the paint peel of the walls of your house, allowing the porch to sag, and otherwise encouraging your property to deteriorate. I have met some people who claim they live that way to avoid and protest paying excessive property taxes.

As with a sales tax or income tax, **property taxes** require an army of employees to administer them, so a large portion of the revenues are spent collecting the taxes. It consumes real resources without producing any real wealth. If we had voted in a sales tax in Montana then we would have been losing tax money on all three tax collection systems, a cost which is not diminished by reducing taxes in each.

Our many tax systems, at the city, state, and federal levels, are highly subjective and costly to administer. Between the private and public sectors, we collectively spend more on bookkeeping, legal, and administrative costs to manage our taxes than we actually pay in federal income taxes[37] (roughly $700 billion in 1996)! Our Congress talks about the space program being expensive when a space shuttle costs a billion dollars or so, but we collectively throw away enough money to buy hundreds of space shuttles every year! By switching to a different tax structure we could cut real costs to US taxpayers at least in half, without reducing government revenues at all.

The administrative costs are so high only because taxes are collected at so many points throughout the economy. Individuals and businesses must keep track of billions of receipts, property assessors must appraise billions of acres of real estate, sales taxes must be collected from hundreds of thousands of businesses. The private sector spends billions finding ways to legally and illegally avoid taxes, and the government hires thousands of auditors at local and federal levels to police the whole process. Is it really any wonder that we have budget deficits?

The money that we spend hiring a tax accountant, or that she spends on rent, power and office equipment, shows up on the Gross National Product as part of our productive output, but it is really consumption. When one person has a job doing paperwork then the rest of us have to do extra work to build their houses, clothe, and feed them. We might be excited when they spend a $100 at our business, but it is actually our money they are spending. The GNP would present a much different picture of the economy if it were adjusted for these kinds of losses.

There are other costs that can be attributed to the tax collection system too. For example, in 1996 the FBI spent a million dollars a day for three months here in Montana in a standoff with the so-called "Freemen" who refused to pay no more than a few thousand dollars in taxes. Situations like this occur because our tax systems are inherently confrontational.

Government agencies are assigned the task of extricating revenue from every citizen and business owner in the country. The individual is pitted against the government, and the carrot of financial incentive encourages people to avoid paying taxes by whatever means necessary, legal and illegal. When the government is perceived as the adversary, is it any wonder that militia groups feel the need to arm themselves against it? The Oklahoma City bombing may not have been an explicit tax issue, but the issue of paying taxes inherently makes the government an adversary rather than an ally. It is this adversarial position that militia groups react to. Switching to a less-confrontational tax collection process would immediately diffuse at least some of the aggression these folks feel. What kind of savings would that give us in both human lives and tax dollars?

Likewise, consider the impacts throughout our culture from the incentive to loophole the system. Our tax laws directly promote cheating, lying, distrust, and dishonesty. What are the true costs we pay for living in a demoralized society? Certainly, the tax collection process is not the source of all evil in our society, but at least it is one of the easier ills to fix. We can save hundreds of billions of dollars and reverse some of the negative energies within the country—without reducing tax revenues and without slashing programs—by simply switching to a simpler tax system.

Taxes do not have to be a negative force on our lives and economy. Taxes can be a tool for achieving positive change in our culture as we work towards our common goals. In considering a taxation plan it is important to remember that any tax, by any name, is ultimately an energy tax. Money is a token we use to represent calories of energy, and energy is the basis of all products and services.

That alone does not explicitly mean we should directly tax energy, but it does suggest that we could realize a considerable savings by taxing energy at its sources. Right now we expend a tremendous amount of energy through the tax collection process because we are collecting the energy only after it has been dissipated through the economy into products and services. The taxation process would be much simpler, and hence less expensive, if we taxed the economy at the sources of energy which sustain it. That way we would be taking the tax at a few hundred or a few thousand locations instead of at millions of places as we do now. A less expensive tax collection system would mean fewer taxes would need to be collected—a savings we could all use.

Of course, an across-the-board energy tax may not be desirable, because taxation is definitely a negative economic force that alters the flow of anything it is applied to. But it is also important to note that an energy tax does not have nearly the negative effect that one might expect. As discussed in Chapter 5-2 *Cause & Effect*, the recessions that accompanied the Arab oil embargo of 1973 and the Iranian revolution of 1979-1980 were caused by not by the increase in oil prices, but by the Federal Reserve tightening the money supply.

The cost of fuel calories actually amounts to only three or four percent of the cost of producing all our goods and services, so a one hundred percent increase in the cost of fuel only increases the cost of goods and services by a couple percent. Thus, a direct tax on energy would not necessarily bring our economy to a standstill. That still does not make it the right thing to do.

Paying taxes should not be a negative burden on our economy, but a positive force in shaping it. By taxing specific types of energy or uses of energy we can tilt market forces in positive ways. For instance, in 1979 we collectively spent $65 billion on foreign oil, and even more since then. That, according to one author, was the equivalent of selling off almost all the farm land in Iowa every year. Of course our losses are dribbled across the entire economy so we do not directly notice it. Nevertheless, the effect is the same. We sell off our assets and become

DIRECT POINTING TO REAL WEALTH

employees of the oil-rich nations. It does not have to be that way. We can halt our financial losses and create an economic boom in the process. By taxing the forms of energy that are hurting our economy we can tilt the market forces in favor of conservation and cleaner forms of energy.

A tax specifically on oil would not explicitly hurt the economy; it would just make other forms of energy that much more favorable. A high tax on oil energy but none on solar energy would make solar energy that much more attractive and financially competitive. The moment that the cost of fossil fuels becomes higher than the cost of solar energies is the moment that our country will almost instantly be transformed into a nonpolluting society.

But perhaps the greatest reason to switch to energy-based taxes is to change the incentives that are created by tax structures. With our current tax structure, there is an incentive to treat the government as our adversary and to cheat on our paperwork so we can pay less in taxes. Energy taxes, on the other hand, would create an incentive for conservation. People would invest in energy efficiency to lower their taxes. They would hire carpenters to insulate their homes, and they would buy new fuel-efficient cars.

Of course, an energy tax would not be a fair tax on the poor, but that is relatively easy to balance out with refunds. Currently we balance out taxation by taxing low income people at lower rates, or by giving them refunds. We could do essentially the same thing by giving low-income families assistance, not with direct refunds, but with grants to help them invest in energy efficiency, especially in the transition years while the income tax system is being phased out. Instead of paying money to accountants to shuffle papers we would be putting our resources towards positive growth for the country, making everyone's homes warmer and putting new energy-efficient cars in every driveway.

"As for the Pyramids, there is nothing to wonder at in them so much as the fact that so many men could be found degraded enough to spend their lives constructing a tomb for some ambitious booby, whom it would have been wiser and manlier to have drowned in the Nile, and then given his body to the dogs."

—Henry David Thoreau, Walden

7-3

Cleaning up Corporacy
Tilting Markets Towards a Better World

Did you ever wonder what happens at the other end of the line when you fill up the car with gasoline, or buy a soccer ball and a new pair of shoes? Few people ever stop to think about the material goods they use to wonder where they were made, by whom, and how. But sometimes filling your car with gasoline ultimately poisons the food supply of a family on the other side of the world. The soccer ball or new shoes you buy may have been made by child slave labor[75]. Through cut-throat competition the major corporations seek out the least-expensive resources around the globe, often exploiting people and the environment in the process.

Shell Oil Company has extracted more than $30 billion worth of oil from Nigeria since the 1960's yet the people there live in utter poverty. They have received essentially nothing for the resource that is being exploited, except for poisoned watersheds from oil spills that have not been cleaned up. In the 1990's Shell was the subject of intense criticism for doing nothing to help the plight of the people. Instead the company funded the autocratic regime in power and subsequently subsidized the death of thousands of civilians. The problem gained international recognition on November 10th, 1995 when Ken Saro-Wiwa and eight other leaders of the democracy movement were tried and executed by the military in what was described as "judicial murder"[8]. Democracy was restored in 1999 and Shell has promised to change its actions in Nigeria, but as is often the case, there is no penalty for Shell's past abuses, and the company's pledges to change are more token than real, offering the least amount of compensation possible to get out of the international spot light while continuing to plunder the country's resource base.

In his book *The Ecology of Commerce*, Paul Hawkin comments that the world's largest corporations are like "separate nations without boundaries" in terms of their economic and political power. Hawkin points out that large corporations have access to the material and labor resources of virtually every country in the world. The five hundred largest companies employ a fraction of one percent of the world's population, yet control 25% of the world gross output. The difference in scale between large and small businesses is so great that 60% of the GNP in the U.S. is produced by only 1,000 of the largest businesses, while the remaining 40% of the GNP is produced by eleven million smaller businesses[38]. It is difficult for small businesses to compete when multi-national corporations contract out to slavemasters in Pakistan who buy and sell children and put them to work as young as three years old, working twelve hours per day for 6¢ per hour to make soccer balls and other goods for American markets[75].

Small business owners are typically involved in their communities and work to make their world a better place, but large corporations are so disassociated from any one place that they often have few goals beyond sheer profit. Many corporations put forth an environmental front with slick commercials detailing special projects, or citing their record about how they comply with all environmental regulations in the U.S., but simultaneously they may be working behind the scenes to weaken that legislation, or they may be simply contaminating the environment of developing countries.

Contributing to the problem of corporate abuse is the fact that it is often profitable to pollute or withhold information about the environmental or health effects of certain products. For example, Waste Management Inc. (now WMX) is the world's largest trash disposal company. The company has disposed of PCBs in ponds and mixed it with heating oil for sale. The company and it's executives have been convicted of bid-rigging, price-fixing and bribing. WMX paid $45 million in fines, settlements and legal fees over a ten year period, yet still achieved a remarkable 20% return on it's investments[38]!

Corporations get away with highly questionable conduct because money speaks loud in politics. Big business spends hundreds of millions of dollars lobbying politicians and voters to get what they want. This "investment" pays off for them, leading to regulatory and tax breaks worth so much more. As a result, the most successful companies are often the most subsidized ones as well—a phenomenon which has been dubbed "corporate welfare". Corporate control over politics is so high in this country that some people have called America a "corporacy" more than a democracy.

Corporations have their roots back as far back as sixteenth century Europe. Debts were considered transgenerational, so the loss of a ship at sea could financially ruin both the family and their descendants. People were sometimes sent to debtor's prison if they could not pay. State-chartered corporations encouraged more risk taking, so that investors were only liable to the extent of their investment and not more. If an enterprise failed then the corporation went belly-up without penalizing the people involved.

The original corporate charters, including those of early America, were carefully drafted to avoid giving too much power to industry. Most were intended for the duration of certain public works projects and were dissolved afterwards. Even the charters for private corporations were usually time-restricted, giving a company the opportunity to take risks and become established. The limited liability wasn't considered necessary after the company was successfully up and running. But it didn't take long for corporations to lobby politicians in favor of more lenient corporate laws[38].

Today corporations can get away with abuses that would put private citizens in prison, such as dumping mass-quantities of toxins into the ecosystem, leading to the subsequent death of an individual, family, or a whole village. At worst the offending corporations are required to pay fines and restitution, but there is no mechanism to dissolve the corporate charter or to hold the individuals responsible for their actions.

There are many potential routes, both private and public, to shift the economic ecosystem away from the corporate abuse of power. Much of this book been dedicated to the idea of shifting markets from the inside by out-competing inefficient, wasteful businesses, but what good does that do when corporations like Shell Oil are taking resources and not giving anything back? It would seem that Shell has optimized its revenues by sucking every penny possible out of Nigeria, without putting anything back. It would only cost money to close the loop on the waste and pollution they've left behind, or so it seems. But Shell Oil has not truly optimized its revenues in Nigeria. The loop of waste is open and in this case the waste is lost opportunity, the opportunity to build and benefit from a whole new economy.

As is often the case with waste in the ecosystem, the problem is a case of focus more than anything else. A factory that builds children's toys focuses on those toys and doesn't pay as much attention to factors like resource use and energy consumption. In the case of Shell Oil, the company has focused on fossil fuels without being aware of other opportunities.

In the 1960's big corporations took advantage of cheap labor in the south and built the southern economy, making both profits and new customers for their products. NAFTA is having the same effect immediately across the border in Mexico. But Shell Oil passed up the opportunity to develop the Nigerian economy, an opportunity that could have been worth far more money to Shell Oil than the money saved by not doing anything for the country at all. The company could have built schools, hospitals and industries, and made billions of dollars more by importing and exporting a variety of goods, instead of just taking the oil and leaving.

The same is true of American companies that have goods made by child slave labor in places like Pakistan. The corporations are not paying the children 6¢ per hour for their work, they are only contracting to the slavemasters who pocket most of the income and give the children just enough to stay alive and continue working. It would not cost anything more for corporations like Nike, Adidas and Reebok to work with communities to establish worker co-ops, schools, and so forth that would genuinely build the local economy. In fact these companies would greatly profit while importing refrigerators, solar panels, and other needed goods and services back to the people that make our shoes and sports equipment.

The driving force that is finally starting to change corporate abuses of people and the environment around the world is consumer consciousness here at home. Companies that directly or indirectly support slavery, bloodshed, or environmental abuse in the pursuit of profit are being publicly criticized by hard-working grassroots organizations. It can take years for this kind of information to catch the attention of the mainstream media, which only reports on these kinds of stories after Americans become out-raged. But once the truth comes out these companies are quick to change to avoid the negative media publicity. Sometimes the change is real, but sometimes the changes are token, just enough to avoid the media, which only focuses on the most outrageous abuses. For example, public outcry over dolphins killed in the nets for tuna fish led to "dolphin safe tuna" on the marketplace, but often it just means that there were no dolphins caught in that particular batch. Some companies continue to catch dolphins in their nets, but send those batches off to separate markets, so they can still sell only "dolphin safe tuna" to U.S. markets. Consumer consciousness has no doubt reduced the number of dolphins killed and made a real difference, but maybe not as much as consumers might realize or expect.

Fortunately consumer consciousness and expectations are continuing to grow, even if slowly. Corporations that used to openly buck all environmental regulations gradually evolved to putting on a slick environmental front, and are now beginning to adopt genuinely green policies. For example, the "Global Climate Coalition", which was originally formed by utilities, oil companies and auto-manufacturers to rebuke scientific studies on global warming, but starting in 1999 and 2000 several individual companies like British Petroleum (BP), Ford, and others defected to publicly declare that climate change is happening, and that something needs to be done about it. The point that is not so clear is if this about-face was driven by consumers or by stockholders, or if these corporations simply realized that they could be the ones selling all this desperately needed clean technology. In any case, clean technology is where the investment dollars are going and change will be fast in coming, at least on this issue.

Grassroots efforts have not always been so successful in making change through public policy. Thousands of volunteers work tirelessly in nonprofit organizations to pass legislation to protect people and the environment, but their voices are too often drowned out by the corporations that spend millions of dollars in advertising to defeat these citizens initiatives. Corporations spend millions of dollars defending the status-quo because they are motivated to do so by profit. Their sales provide a constant source of capital, while lobbying or advertising is an investment that brings in additional profit, or at least minimizes losses. In other words, lobbying makes money for corporations, but costs money to grass-roots organizations. Corporate interests often defeat citizen initiatives on the ballot only by out-spending by grassroots opposition by ten-to-one.

Here in Montana there were citizen initiatives at just about every election to help curb mining abuses. Every initiative was defeated by multi-million dollar campaigns up until November 1998 when the Cyanide Initiative was passed, banning the use of cyanide in gold ore processing at new mines. That initiative would have undoubtedly been defeated by the mining industry too, but the price of gold fell so low that it killed the industry even before the initiative was put on the ballot. Thus the cyanide initiative may be sustainable only as long as the price of gold remains low.

Today there is a nationwide effort to raise awareness of the destruction caused by gold jewelry, which consumes 84% of the precious metal mined from the ecosystem[4]. Whole mountains of habitat are ground up and sprayed with cyanide or sulfuric acid to extract the metal, often leaving the taxpayer stuck with the multi-million dollar cost of reclamation. If people really knew how much damage was caused by gold mining they would stop wearing it, just as furs went out of fashion for ethical reasons years ago. If enough people stop wearing gold jewelry then the price of gold will stay down and the mining industry will not be able to tilt public policy back in its favor.

In other words, it is almost impossible to pass good legislation to control corporations, as long as corporations remain in control of the political process. Legislation that would revoke the rights of corporations for the wrongs they commit would be met by lobbyist dollars in sums that can only be imagined. Campaign finance reform may eventually restrict the amount of lobbying in politics, allowing corporate reform to follow, but for obvious reasons, it will be almost as difficult to achieve the former as the latter.

Ultimately, the best way to reform corporations is still in the marketplace, through the tools of public scrutiny, consumer choice, and by demonstrating that it is more profitable to be a good steward of the planet than to waste it.

Conclusion

This book would have been much easier to write if it was about just one thing, but then it would have been a lot less useful too. All things in the world are interconnected, and everything we do effects everyone and everything else. We are like frogs in a big pond. When we make a splash we cause a disturbance that radiates out in concentric rings across the water. What we do in one place ultimately vibrates in small ways throughout the whole.

I could have written about the frogs, or I could have written about the lily pads, or I could have written about the water, or a thousand other things that might be found in or around the pond. But to write about just one thing or another would be like trying to take a knife and slice a pie-shaped wedge out of the pond. It wouldn't be real.

If you want to achieve your personal Dreams for a quality life and a good lily pad on the pond, then you must understand something about the pond and how it works. Whatever you achieve in life will be the sum of the criteria that you set.

You must consider your desires for quality of life and the actions that interest you, but you must also consider the pond. Keep in mind that the natural ecosystem functions as a closed-loop where the wastes of one organism become useful inputs to another, and all organisms use energy and resources to their fullest potential. You will be able to achieve your Dreams more easily if you work with and mimic the natural ecosystem, to close the loop on wasted resources—including wasted materials, wasted energy, wasted time, money and labor.

When your criteria includes closing the loop on all kinds of waste then you will find that you can achieve bigger Dreams with fewer resources than you might have ever imagined.

Bibliography

1. _____. "*The Big Melt.*" <u>Popular Science</u>. February 2000. Pg. 28.
2. _____. "*Energy record set in magnetic fusion*", <u>Science News</u>, January 1, 1994. Volume 145, Pg. 12.
3. _____. "*The Industrial Symbiosis at Kalundborg, Denmark.*" Indigo Development. Last modified: August 28, 1998. URL: http://www.indigodev.com/Kal.html
4. _____. "*And let's Not Forget What we Get for their Pits...*" <u>Down to Earth</u>. VolumeXXIV, No. 3. August 1998. Pg. 2.
5. _____. "*Ocean Thermal Energy Conversion (OTEC) Fact Sheet.*" State of Hawaii. 1995. Last modified on 8/17/1998. URL: http://www.state.hi.us/dbedt/ert/otec_hi.html
6. _____. "*Plastic from Plants.*" <u>Popular Science</u>. April 2000. Pg. 22.
7. _____. "*Pollution Swap May Halve Utility Emissions.*" Earth Almanac. <u>National Geographic</u>. December 1993.
8. _____. "*Two years on, the Ogoni struggle continues.*" <u>Earthlife Africa</u>. November 10 1997. URL: http://www.earthlife.org.za/campaigns/other/ogoni.htm
9. Avery, William H. and Walter G. Berl. "*Solar Energy from the Tropical Oceans.*" <u>Issues in Science and Technology</u>. Winter 1997-98. Pg. 41.
10. Bass, Thomas. "*Robot Build Thyself.*" <u>Discover</u>. October 1995. Pgs. 64-72.
11. Beard, Jonathon D. "*Test-tube Tomatoes.*" <u>Popular Science</u>.
12. Benford, Gregory. "*Climate Controls*". <u>Reason</u>. November 1997. Pgs. 24-30.
13. Bennett, Steven J.. <u>Ecopreneuring</u>. John Wiley & Sons, Inc.: New York, Chichester, Brisbane, Toronto, Singapore. 1991.
14. Benyus, Janine M. <u>Biomimicry: Innovation Inspired by Nature</u>. William Morrow and Co.: New York. 1997.
15. Burleson, Wayne. "*Our Fences are Shrinking.*" <u>The Whole Approach</u>. Belgrade, MT. Vol. 1: No 1. Pgs. 7-8.
16. Clark, William. "*It takes energy to get energy; the law of diminishing returns is in effect.*" <u>Smithsonian</u>. December 1974. Pg. 87.
17. Dacyczyn, Amy. <u>TheTightwad Gazette</u>. Leeds, ME. No. 31. December 1992. Pg. 8.
18. Dane, Abe. "*Anti-Greenhouse Tech.*" <u>Popular Mechanics</u>. June 1991. Pg. 110.
19. Dasmann, Raymond F. <u>Environmental Conservation</u>. John Wiley & Sons Inc.: New York London, Sydney, Toronto. 1976.
20. Diamond, Jared. "*The Golden Age that Never Was.*" <u>Discover</u>. December 1988. Pgs. 70-79.
21. Diamond, Jared. "*Playing Dice with Megadeath.*" <u>Discover</u>. April 1990. Pgs. 54- 59.
22. DiChristina, Mariette. "*Reversing the Greenhouse.*" <u>Popular Science</u>. August 1991. Pgs. 78-80.
23. Dilts, Robert. Tim Halborn, Suzi Smith. <u>Beliefs: Pathways to Health and Well-Being</u>. Metamorphous Press: Portland, Oregon. 1990.
24. Dominguez, Joe & Vicki Robin. <u>Your Money or Your Life</u>. Viking Penguin: New York, NY. 1992.
25. Drexler, Eric. <u>Engines of Creation</u>. 1986.
26. Durant, Will. <u>The Story of Civilization</u>. 11 vols., Simon & Schuster New York, New York 1935-1975. Pg.1:702
27. Easterbrook, Gregg. "*Return of the Glaciers.*" <u>Newsweek</u>. November 23, 1992. Pg. 62-63.
28. Farb, Peter. <u>Man's Rise to Civilization</u>. Discus Books/Avon Books: New York, NY. 1971, 1969, 1968.
29. Fox, Ripley D. "*Spirulina: The Alga That Can End Malnutrition.*" <u>The Futurist</u>. February 1985. Pgs. 30-35.
30. Fisher, Adelheid. "*Grass is not always Greener*" <u>Utne Reader</u>. September/October 1993. Pgs. 36-38.
31. Fukuoka, Masanobu. <u>The One Straw Revolution</u>. Bantam Books: New York. 1985.
32. Fukuoka, Masanobu. <u>The Natural Way of Farming</u>. Japan Publications, Inc.: Tokyo & New York. 1985.
33. Gable, Wayne & Guy Lushin. <u>Wasting America's Money</u>. Potomac Publishing Company: Falls Church, VA. 1990.
34. Givens, Charles J. <u>Wealth Without Risk</u>, Simon & Schuster: New York, NY. 1988.
35. Grant, Glenn. 1990. "*Memes: Introduction.*", in: F. Heylighen, C. Joslyn and V. Turchin (editors): Principia Cybernetica Web (Principia Cybernetica, Brussels), URL: http://pcp.lanl.gov/REFERPCP.html.
36. Harris, Marvin. <u>The Sacred Cow and the Abominable Pig</u>, Touch Stone Books/Simon & Schuster, Inc.: New York, New York. 1987, 1985.
37. Hawken, Paul. "*A declaration of sustainability*", <u>Utne Reader</u>, September/October 1993. Pgs. 54-60.
38. Hawken, Paul. <u>The Ecology of Commerce</u>. HarperBusiness/HarperCollins: New York. 1993.
39. Hawken, Paul with Amory & Hunter Lovins. <u>Natural Capitalism: Creating the Next Industrial Revolution</u>. Little, Brown & Co.: Boston, New York. 1999.
40. Hawken, Paul. <u>The Next Economy</u>. Holt, Rinehart and Winston: New York, NY. 1983.
41. Heyne, Paul. <u>The Economic Way of Thinking</u>. 4th Edition. Science Research Associates, Inc.: Chicago, Palo Alto. 1973, 1983.
42. Henricks, Mark. Time is Money. <u>Entrepreneur</u>. February 1993. Pg. 44-47.
43. Hobbs, Dr. Charles R. <u>Time Power</u>. Harper & Row Publishers: New York. 1987.

44. Hoffert, Martin I. and Seth D. Potter. "Beam it Down: How the New Satellites Can Power The World." <u>MIT's Technology Review</u>. October 1997. Pgs. 30-36.

45. Hollender, Jeffrey. <u>How to Make the World a Better Place</u>. Quill/William Morrow: New York. 1990.

46. Jackson, Wes. <u>New Roots for Agriculture</u>. University of Nebraska Press: Lincoln, Nebraska. 1985.

47. Jaynes, Julian. <u>The Origin of Consciousness in the Break-Down of the Bicameral Mind</u>. Houghton Mifflin Co.: Boston, MA. 1976, 1990.

48. Lappe, Frances Moore. <u>Diet for a Small Planet</u>. Ballantine Books: New York. 1971, 1982.

49. Lee, Richard B. <u>The Dobe !Kung</u>. Holt-Rinehart-Winston Inc.: New York, NY, 1984.

50. Lerner, Steve. <u>Eco-Pioneers: Practical Visionaries Solving Today's Environmental Problems</u>. The MIT Press: Cambridge: MA. 1997, 1998.

51. Lovelock, James. <u>Healing Gaia: Practical Medicine for the Planet</u>. Harmony Books: New York, NY. 1991.

52. Lovins, Amory B. <u>Soft Energy Paths</u>. Harper & Row, Publishers Inc.: New York, New York. 1977.

53. Mack, Toni. "*The tail doesn't wag the dog.*" <u>Forbes</u>. January 31, 1994. Pg. 66

54. Millman, Joel. "*Mexico: the 'New South'.*" <u>San Francisco Examiner</u>.

55. Mcmenamin, Mark A. and Dianna L. S. <u>Hypersea: Life on Land</u>. Columbia University Press: New York. 1994.

56. Montagne, Cliff. <u>Holistic Thought And Management</u>. 1997 Study Guide PSES 421. MSU-Bozeman.

57. Pennisi, Elizabeth. "*Rubber to the Road.*" <u>Science News</u>. Volume 141. March 7, 1992. Pg. 155.

58. Pospisil, Leopold. <u>Kapauku Papuans and Their Law</u>. Yale University Publications in Anthropology No. 54. 1958. Pg. 145.

59. Ravenswaay, Eileen van. "*The Relationship Between the Economy and the Environment.*" Michigan State University. 1998, 1999. URL: http://www.msu.edu/course/prm/255/textbook.htm

60. Rees, William E. "*Revisiting Carrying Capacity: Area-Based Indicators of Sustainability.*" The University of British Columbia. URL: http://dieoff.org/page110.htm

61. Rifkin, Jeremy. "*Beyond Beef.*" <u>Utne Reader</u>. March/April 1992. Pg. 103.

62. Rocky Mountain Institute, "*The Dragon Stirs: Negawatts in Asia*", <u>RMI Newsletter</u>; Snowmass, CO. Spring 1993, Volume IX, Number I; Pg. 4.

63. Rocky Mountain Institute. "*Photovoltaics—Clean Energy Now & For the Future*", <u>RMI Newsletter</u>; Snowmass, Colorado. Spring 1991. Volume VII, Number 1. Pgs. 5, 7.

64. Rocky Mountain Institute. "*Practical Home Energy Savings*", <u>RMI Newsletter</u>; Snowmass, CO. Spring 1991, Volume VII, Number 1: Pg. 13.

65. Rocky Mountain Institute, "*RMI's Approach to Market Ju-Jitsu*", <u>RMI Newsletter</u>; Snowmass, CO. Fall/Winter 1992, Volume VIII, Number 3; Pg. 1.

66. Rocky Mountain Institute. "*Supercar's Broader Implications*", <u>RMI Newsletter</u>; Snowmass, Colorado. Fall/Winter 1993, Volume IX, Number 3. Pg. 6.

67. Rocky Mountain Institute. "*Water-efficient Showerhead vs. Traditional Investments*", information sheet, Rocky Mountain Institute, Snowmass, CO. 1989.

68. Rocky Mountain Institute. "*Winning the Peace*". <u>RMI Newsletter</u>; Snowmass. Colorado. Spring 1991, Volume VII, Number 1. Pgs. 1,3,4.

69. Rohr, Dixon. "*Too Much, Too Fast.*" <u>Newsweek</u>. June 1, 1992. Pg. 34.

70. Rogers, Carl. <u>Carl Rogers on Personal Power</u>. Delecorte Press: New York, NY.

71. Rogers, Carl. <u>Freedom to Learn for the Eighties</u>. Charles E. Merrill Publishing Co.: Columbus. Toronto, London, Sydney. 1983,1969.

72. Rothschild, Michael. <u>Bionomics: The Inevitability of Capitalism</u>. A John Macrae Book, Henry Holt & Co.: New York. 1990.

73. Sahlins, Marshall. <u>Stone Age Economics</u>. Aldine-Atherton, Inc.: Chicago. IL. 1972.

74. Savory, Allan. <u>Holistic Resource Management</u>. Island Press: Covelo, CA. 1988.

75. Schanberg, Sydney H. "*Six Cents an Hour.*" <u>Life</u>. June 1996, Pages 38-48.

76. Scow, Mary Beth. "*Wheel Deal.*" <u>Buzzworm</u>. Volume III, No. 2. March-April 1991. Pg. 94.

77. Shevchenko, Arkady N. <u>Breaking with Moscow</u>. Alfred A. Knopf: New York, NY. 1985.

78. Bill Shore. <u>Revolution of the Heart: A New Strategy for Creating Wealth and Meaningful Change</u>. Riverhead Books: New York. 1995.

79. Thoreau, Henry David. <u>Walden</u>. Holt-Rinehart-Winston Inc.: New York, NY. Twentieth Printing, December 1966.

80. Tobias, Andrew. <u>Getting By on $100.000 a Year (and Other Sad Tales)</u>. Simon & Schuster: New York: New York. 1980.

81. Wanniski, Jude. <u>The Way The World Works</u>. Basic Books, Inc., Publishers: New York, NY. 1978.

82. White, Peter T. "*The Power of Money*", <u>National Geographic.</u> January 1993. Pg. 84.

83. Wilson, Jim. "*200-mph Trees Bomb Away at Greenhouse Effect.*" <u>Popular Mechanics</u>. January 1997. Pg. 13.

84. Zimmer, Carl. "*Hypersea Invasion.*" <u>Discover</u>. October 1995. Pgs. 76-87.

Index

—Participating in Nature—
Thomas J. Elpel's Field Guide to Primitive Living Skills

Discover nature by using it! Learn to meet your needs for shelter, fire, water and food. Tom's guide gives you a direct, hands-on experience of the world around you. With this book you will discover the thrill of staying warm and comfortable without even a blanket! Experience the magic of starting a fire by friction. Learn about the edible plants of the Rocky Mountain region and the techniques to process them, plus "primitive gourmet" cooking skills.

Braintan the hides from your fall hunting trip and manufacture them into durable clothing. Also covered are: sinews, hide glue, backpacking, felting with wool, fishing by hand, stone knives, wooden containers, willow baskets, twig deer, cordage, stalking skills, trapping, and tire shoes.

Participating in Nature includes dozens of innovative skills and nearly 200 illustrations, plus an encompassing philosophy. Tom does extensive experiential research. He places an emphasis on publishing new information that is not found in any other source.

—Botany in a Day—
Thomas J. Elpel's Herbal Field Guide to Plant Families

Too often people try to learn plants one-at-a-time, without rhyme or reason. Now you can cut years off the process of learning about plants and their uses. Tom's book takes you beyond the details towards a greater understanding of the patterns among plants. Learn how related plants have similar features for identification. Discover how they have similar properties and uses.

Botany in a Day includes more than 100 plant families and over 650 genera—applicable to many thousands of species. By the end of the day you will have a functional knowledge of botany to continue growing your knowledge of plants and plant patterns—in the wild, in your garden, among house plants, even at the florist. Understand the magic of patterns in plants, and the world will never look the same again! *Botany in a Day* is used at herbal and wilderness schools across the country.

—Living Homes—
Thomas J. Elpel's Field Guide to Integrated Design & Construction

Build your Dream Home on a budget! High quality, resource-efficient homes do not have to be expensive, just carefully thought out. *Living Homes* includes the nuts-and-bolts of construction, plus a guide to planning and design with low-cost natural resources.

Living Homes especially focuses on energy-efficiency. In simple terms Tom out-lined the principles involved in building a house with little or no need for a heating system, a matter of finding the right balance between insulation, thermal mass, and solar input. Also covered is how to maintain air-quality in an energy efficient home.

This guide is especially intended for those who want to build their own home from the ground up, with details on slip-form stone masonry, mixing concrete, log construction, and how to make your own terra tiles. Also included in the book is a section on tilt-up stone panels and other ideas to bring high-quality construction to the mass market.

Order on-line at www.hollowtop.com or call HOPS at 406-685-3222.

—"I Transcended and I Didn't Know It"—
Thomas J. Elpel's Audio Field Guide to Consciousness

Consciousness, the ability to think about the past or future or to wonder about our existence, is apparently unique to our species. Until recently it was assumed that consciousness was only biological, the result of our "big brains". However new theories cite evidence that consciousness is also cultural--a skill that is learned, modified and passed down through generations. In other words, the nature of consciousness today is different than it was in the past or will be in the future.

In this audio series Tom outlines the latest ideas on consciousness, providing insights into past and current world events. Parents will find this a useful resource for understanding their own children and the developmental states they are working through.

These tapes are literally a "Field Guide to Consciousness", providing a map of where we've been and where we might be headed. Tom explores the concept of "higher consciousness", speculating how future generations might perceive the world differently than we do today, and what we can do to raise our own consciousness. Please check the website for price and availability.

www.hollowtop.com
gateway to primitive skills on the internet.

the on-line home of:
Hollowtop Outdoor Primitive School
HOPS Contemporary Living Skills Page
The Society of Primitive Technology
Food Insects Newsletter
The HOPS Store
& Tom's Wildflowers and Weeds Page

with numerous on-line articles
plus links to schools and classes across North America

"Primitive & Contemporary Living Skills"

Hollowtop Outdoor Primitive School
www.hollowtop.com

Order on-line at www.hollowtop.com or call HOPS at 406-685-3222.